D1194138

The Laughing Dead

The Laughing Dead

The Horror-Comedy Film from *Bride of Frankenstein* to *Zombieland*

Edited by
Cynthia J. Miller
A. Bowdoin Van Riper

ROWMAN & LITTLEFIELD
Lanham • Boulder • New York • London

Published by Rowman & Littlefield
A wholly owned subsidiary of The Rowman & Littlefield Publishing Group, Inc.
4501 Forbes Boulevard, Suite 200, Lanham, Maryland 20706
www.rowman.com

Unit A, Whitacre Mews, 26-34 Stannary Street, London SE11 4AB

Copyright © 2016 by Rowman & Littlefield

All rights reserved. No part of this book may be reproduced in any form or by any electronic or mechanical means, including information storage and retrieval systems, without written permission from the publisher, except by a reviewer who may quote passages in a review.

British Library Cataloguing in Publication Information Available

Library of Congress Cataloging-in-Publication Data

Names: Miller, Cynthia J., 1958– editor. | Van Riper, A. Bowdoin, editor.
Title: The laughing dead : the horror-comedy film from Bride of Frankenstein to Zombieland / edited by Cynthia J. Miller, A. Bowdoin Van Riper.
Description: Lanham : Rowman & Littlefield, 2016. | Includes bibliographical references and index.
Identifiers: LCCN 2016002166 (print) | LCCN 2016004228 (ebook) | ISBN 9781442268326 (cloth : alk. paper) | ISBN 9781442268333 (electronic)
Subjects: LCSH: Horror films–History and criticism. | Comedy films–History and criticism.
Classification: LCC PN1995.9.H6 L375 2016 (print) | LCC PN1995.9.H6 (ebook) | DDC 791.43/6164–dc23 LC record available at http://lccn.loc.gov/2016002166

♾™ The paper used in this publication meets the minimum requirements of American National Standard for Information Sciences—Permanence of Paper for Printed Library Materials, ANSI/NISO Z39.48-1992.

Printed in the United States of America

PN
1995.9
. H6
L375
2016

To all those whose tales have left us whistling as we walk past graveyards, startling at sudden noises, and laughing in the face of undeath.

Contents

~

Acknowledgments

This volume owes a great debt to so many scholars who have come before and whose work has inspired and informed the essays that appear here. We would like to extend our thanks to all of them, and in particular, to Johnson Cheu and John Dowell, whose own project got us thinking more closely about just how funny the undead can be. Our deepest thanks also go to Stephen Ryan for his ongoing trust in our work and support of this project. Finally, to each of the individuals whose work appears on the pages that follow: You've terrified us, you've made us laugh, and you've met both with good humor and hard work. Thank you, one and all.

~

Introduction

Cynthia J. Miller and A. Bowdoin Van Riper

Let's face it: The undead are unfunny. Or at least, they're supposed to be. Traditional lore surrounding vampires, zombies, ghosts, and other sorts of reanimated entities is brimming over with darkness and dread, and they have long served contemporary popular culture as predatory, putrid vectors of social commentary and cultural critique. Uncanny doppelgängers of the living, the undead have been described in a wide range of colorful and evocative ways: grotesque, horrifying, unsettling, unnerving . . . but comic, amusing, and humorous are not among them. They trouble our understandings of the end of biological life, as well as our spiritual beliefs about the hereafter, suggesting that the grave may not mark the end of our time on earth, but rather, simply serve as a coda—a point of return—from which a distorted version of life is replayed, over and over.

Comedy, however, has the potential to significantly alter—or enhance—the impact of the undead. Intentionally evoked laughter would seem intended to render the most menacing characters impotent. What, then, does it mean when these traditional subjects of horror become feature players in comic tales of mayhem, burlesques of traditional horror tales, or even transform into comic figures themselves? Are we mocking them and their hold on some dark corner of our psyches that houses our superstitions and unrelinquished childhood fears, or are they mocking us instead? Does laughter mitigate our fears of things that go "bump" in the night or simply add a pinch of irony? As the essays in this volume illustrate, the answers are varied, and complex.

Qui Sent, Peure; Qui Pense, Rit

Laughter, as John Morreall, points out, is one of the most basic—and in many ways, difficult to control—physical and emotional experiences.[1] We "contort" with laughter; it "overtakes" us. It is, as Henri Bergson contends, a vital force.[2] Yet, as theorists have observed for centuries, humor (and its functions for both the individual and society) is a very complicated and contentious thing: both an expression of aggression and a means of building rapport; anarchic as well as a symbol of community; a sign of discomfort and a form of release; social medicine and social critique. Humor can be irrational, and it can do significant social work.

As an intentional elicitation of laughter, comedy makes use of all of these. In order to do so, however, it frequently requires a particular set of circumstances, or as Bergson suggests, a "momentary anaesthesia of the heart."[3] As he explains, empathy and emotional involvement—feeling for the world— leads to a magnification of the most inconsequential of actions and states, and "a gloomy hue [that is] spread over everything. Now step aside, look upon life as a disinterested spectator: many a drama will turn into a comedy."[4] Comedy seizes elements of everyday life—from the socially awkward to the politically charged—and uses them, as *New Yorker* columnist Robert Mankoff observes, "as material within the larger context of dramatic form."[5]

For our purposes here, it is that *use* that matters. Parody, satire, burlesque, irony, black humor, absurdity, farce . . . all shine a spotlight on the human condition. While never losing their hold on *play*—pursuits carried out for nothing but "the soul's pleasure"[6]—the narratives explored in this volume are purposefully comedic, using various forms of humor to elicit laughter in the face of undeath. In so doing, they also create a new visual (and in some cases, literal) vocabulary for referencing individuals, groups, actions, and social issues.

While sometimes accomplishing similar goals, horror and comedy appear to occupy opposite ends of the dramatic spectrum, with a vast and unbridgeable gulf between. If comedy is best achieved through detachment, as Bergson claims, horror relies on engagement for its maximum effect, suggesting that the two are not only dramatically opposed, but biologically, psychologically, and philosophically, as well. Reality, however, is more complex. The spectrum bends back on itself, bringing the two genres into unexpected close contact—even overlap. The emotional affects of horror and comedy may be radically different, but the mechanisms by which they operate are strikingly similar.

At their most basic level, both comedy and horror depend on the shock of the unexpected: the subversion of the audience's expectations. The purest and most visceral of cinematic scares—the *thing* that emerges from an unseen hiding place at an unanticipated moment—works by shattering the viewer's assumption that the placid normalcy established at the beginning of the scene will last until the end. The grasping hand that erupts from the ground in the last moments of *Carrie* (1976) or the mutant Nazi behind the curtain in *An American Werewolf in London* (1981) terrify precisely because the moments leading up to them are so banal. The purest of cinematic gags, whether visual or verbal, operate on precisely the same logic. Told to "cut the cards" in *Go West* (1940), Harpo Marx produces a hatchet from his capacious pockets and cleaves the deck in two; the hipster Mephistopheles of *Bedazzled* (Peter Cook) informs a hapless latter-day Faust (Dudley Moore) that the magic phrase that will bring him his heart's desire is "Julie Andrews." Each time, a carefully burnished air of familiarity shapes the audience's expectations of the next moment, and an unexpected eruption from an unanticipated direction shatters them.

A well-crafted horror film is more than just a series of discrete "Boo!" moments, however, just as a well-crafted comedy is more than just a series of discrete gags. Instead, both weave such moments into artfully designed sequences in which later elements escalate the comic or horrific mayhem created by—and subvert the expectations newly established by—earlier ones. The cumulative effect is to dissolve normalcy into chaos, overturn the rhythms of the characters' everyday lives, and undermine their (and the audience's) expectations about the bonds that join causes and effects, creating—at least until the resolution of the plot—a world in which (seemingly) anything, no matter how outlandish, can happen at any moment.

Conventional dramas layer complication after complication onto their protagonists, but do so within the framework of a familiar, essentially realistic world. Science fiction and fantasy do the same, but within the context of imaginary realities that, however fantastic, remain stable for the duration of the story. Comedy and horror stories, by contrast, take their characters' initially stable reality and steadily, relentlessly unravel it around them until—in the moments before the story is resolved—they are left with no safe space in which to rest and catch their breath. Toward the end of *Duck Amuck* (1953), Daffy Duck—whose world is being literally redrawn around him by an unseen animator—responds to the beginnings of some fresh indignity by spluttering "*Now* what?!" The put-upon heroes of countless other comedies could say the same; so could, albeit in desperation rather than exasperation, the terrified protagonists of countless horror films.

Ironically, both comedy and horror can feel "safest" to us when they are at their most extreme, and the chaos besetting their characters is at its most complete. Traditional dramas show us characters who—because they inhabit the same reality we do—have problems that can resonate uncomfortably with our own; mystery stories show us criminals who we can imagine lurking in the dark corners of our own world; even science fiction, when its imagined futures reflect the excesses of our present, can cut uncomfortably close to the bone. Horror and comedy, carefully reined in, can do the same, as films like *Funny Games* (2008) and *The War of the Roses* (1989) make amply clear. Allowed to run unchecked, however, both genres dissolve their characters' everyday realities so thoroughly and so extravagantly—yanking the rug time after time—that they announce themselves as fantasy. Recognizing them as such, we are reassured that the characters' worlds (if not their dignity) will be intact when the credits roll, and that nothing similar could happen to *us*. Freed of such worries, we are free to laugh, and we do.

Laugh, Scream, Repeat

The interweaving of comedy into films about the undead began only a few years into the sound era. James Whale broke the tension created by images of grave robbery, mad science, and violent death in *Frankenstein* (1931) with broadly comic cutaway scenes involving the local villagers. *Bride of Franken-stein* (1935), widely considered Whale's masterpiece, mixed genuine horror and arch comedy in equal measures—a feat of tonal control rarely attempted, let alone successfully, in the decades that followed. *Topper* (1937), a screwball comedy about stuffy banker Cosmo Topper (Roland Young), whose dully conventional life is disrupted by the ghosts of married socialites George and Marion Kerby (Cary Grant, Constance Bennett), pioneered a different approach. The film replicates the comic structure of a Marx Brothers romp or a Bugs Bunny cartoon, with the undead as madcap outsiders and the living as staid straight men (and women). Enormously popular with Depression-era audiences, *Topper* spawned two sequels (1939, 1941), a television series (1953–1956), and a lineage that stretches through *The Addams Family* (TV 1964–1966; films 1991, 1993) and *Beetlejuice* (1988) to *The Littlest Vampire* (2000) and *ParaNorman* (2012).

On the eve of World War II, Bob Hope's performance in *Ghost Breakers* (1940) and Mantan Moreland's in *King of the Zombies* (1941) established a third approach: one that preserved the traditional framing of the undead as horrifying and monstrous and found comedy in living characters' over-the-top reactions to them. The Bowery Boys (*Ghost Chasers*, 1951), Jerry Lewis (*Scared Stiff*, 1953), and Don Knotts (*The Ghost and Mr. Chicken*, 1966) all made films using this formula, but the undisputed masters of it were Bud Abbott and Lou Costello. *Abbott and Costello Meet Frankenstein* (1948) revived the comedy duo's faltering postwar career and enabled Universal Studios to squeeze one last round of films out of the monster-movie franchises that had sustained it through the 1930s and early 1940s. The pair went on to "meet" a malevolent mystic played by Boris Karloff (1949), the Invisible Man (1951), Jekyll and Hyde (1953), and the Mummy (1955)—Abbott, in each case, playing the cynical skeptic, and Costello, the frequently comically terrified innocent.

Abandoned by Universal, the Dracula and Frankenstein sagas were revived in the late 1950s by Hammer Films, based in the United Kingdom, which returned them to their gothic roots while adding vibrant color, copious doses of blood, and discreet sex. The ultra-serious tone taken by Hammer and its imitators left the conventions of the undead-horror genre ripe for deconstruction, with the Rankin/Bass animated feature *Mad Monster Party* (1967) and Roman Polanski's sardonic *The Fearless Vampire Killers* (1967) approaching the task from opposite ends of the comic spectrum. Mel Brooks's *Young Frankenstein* (1974) split the distance between them. A meticulous parody-homage to James Whale's 1930s classics, with Gene Wilder in the title role and Peter Boyle as a monster capable of dancing to Irving Berlin's "Puttin' on the Ritz," it remains among the most critically acclaimed of all undead comedies. The precision with which Brooks re-created the look and feel of the Universal originals—central to *Young Frankenstein*'s success—was absent from subsequent attempts to parody studio-era Hollywood's undead-monster classics. *Maxie* and *Transylvania 6-5000* (both 1985) and *Haunted Honeymoon* (1986) all failed to recapture the magic, as did Brooks's own distant follow-up, *Dracula: Dead and Loving It* (1995).

Love at First Bite (1979) plays, in retrospect, like a sly send-up of John Badham's lavishly budgeted *Dracula* (1979), but it is actually an urban comedy of manners. Evicted from his Transylvanian castle by a communist urban renewal scheme, Dracula (George Hamilton) lands in disco-era New York, where he romances a reincarnation of Mina Harker (Susan St. James) and fends off the grandson of his old nemesis Van Helsing—a psychiatrist (Richard Benjamin) with a sketchy grasp of vampire lore. The box office success of *Love*, like that of *Young Frankenstein* five years earlier, produced a string of largely unsuccessful imitations. The most promising of them, *Buffy the Vampire Slayer* (1992), found success on television—but only after subordinating comedy to action and teen-relationship drama.

More significant for the intertwining of humor and undead horror were new makeup and special-effects techniques that, in the last decades of the twentieth century, enabled filmmakers to push the frontiers of the comic

grotesque. John Landis's *An American Werewolf in London* (1981), for example, featured scenes in which the title character receives sardonic advice
from the rotting corpse of his best friend, who grows more decomposed with
each appearance. Subsequent productions such as *Ghostbusters* (1984) and
Beetlejuice offered audiences more elaborate (though, in keeping with their
PG ratings, bloodless) visual spectacles: translucent specters with grinning,
skull-like visages, and a character whose face (seen from behind) transforms
into a writhing nest of snakes. The *Reanimator* series (1985, 1990, 2003)
and *Evil Dead II* (1987), freed by the flexibility offered by their "R" ratings,
embellished the briefly glimpsed gore of *Werewolf* to Grand-Guignol levels.
Both sets of films, however, adopted Landis's most lasting innovation: weaving caustic dialogue and black humor so thoroughly into the horror that the
two became inseparable.

The approach pioneered by Landis, evolved and embellished over two
decades, is evident in many of the most successful horror-comedies of the
twenty-first century. The slacker-heroes of *Shaun of the Dead* (2004), press-
ing a box of vintage records into service as weapons to use against zombies,
argue over which albums to fling and which to preserve. *Zombieland* (2009)
evokes the zombie apocalypse with scenes of, among other things, a terrified
suburban mother fleeing a horde of zombified little girls in princess costumes.
The Nazi-zombie film *Dead Snow* (2010), like *American Werewolf* before it,
takes refuge in comedic audacity, with grotesque sight gags involving out-
houses, hand grenades, and intestines used as rappelling ropes. Low-budget
productions for which such bravura visual and makeup effects were out of
reach made a virtue of their own cheapness, featuring threats that—as in
Gingerdead Man (2005), *Poultrygeist* (2006), and *Zombeavers* (2014)—were
not only undead, but unhuman.

The mixture of comically grotesque mayhem, visual absurdity, and
mordant dialogue embodied by these films is the most visible manifestation of comedy-horror films in the new millennium, but not the only
one. Undead comedy aimed at children, seemingly the least promising
of subgenres, has flourished in productions like *Monster House* (2006),
Frankenweenie (2012), and the *Hotel Transylvania* series (2014). Director
Andrew Currie's *Fido* (2006), on the other hand, combined comedy with
George Romero's use of zombies as vessels for social commentary in a
satire of suburban life (and 1950s mores) aimed squarely at adults. Combined with new stories about subjects long deemed tacitly off-limits—like
zombie romantic comedy in *Warm Bodies* (2014)—this outpouring of new
stories for the new millennium suggests that the golden age of the undead
horror-comedy is now.

The Laughing Dead

Each of this volume's three segments explores the collision of horror and comedy in a wide range of cinematic tales of the undead. We see that while the vampires, zombies, ghosts, and other reanimated beings brought to "life" in these narratives invoke the traditional symbols, motifs, and moral messages of the horror genre, the varying degrees and configurations of humor present can altogether alter their impact. Sometimes, as in the case of family entertainment, humor renders the monstrous familiar and fears are eased; at other times, dark comedy reshapes traditional horror into a surreal nightmare; and in both cases, as laughter dulls the supernatural threat of undead predators, the social commentary the characters deliver becomes correspondingly sharper.

The essays in the opening section, "Playing with Genre," begin this discussion by exploring some of the many ways that comedy shifts, transforms, or entirely up-ends traditional undead horror narratives. In his essay "'Oy, Have You Got the Wrong Vampire,'" Thomas Prasch looks at Roman Polanski's *The Fearless Vampire Killers*, a comic remapping of Bram Stoker's Dracula tale which, despite a troubled post-production history, remained one of the filmmaker's favorite projects. As Prasch explains, Polanski's use of comedy, from sight gags to burlesque-inflected comedy routines—in a style reminiscent of the visual humor of silent films—allows the filmmaker to take on subjects like the deep histories of oppression that beset Central Europe and reflect on his own personal history as a survivor of both the Holocaust and Stalinism. The section turns from past history to history in the process of unfolding with "Zany Zombies, Grinning Ghosts, Silly Scientists, and Nasty Nazis: Comedy-Horror at the Threshold of World War II." Christina M. Knopf examines the role of supernatural hijinks in World War II–era films ranging from *King of the Zombies* to *The Canterville Ghost* (1944). Knopf pays particular attention to the uses of doors in these films, as symbols, thresholds, and of course, as fans of *Rowan & Martin's Laugh-In* will recall, comic tropes. Doors, similarly, are tropes of undead horror, and as such, Knopf points out, serve as an apt passage between the two genres.

George A. Romero all but created the modern image of the zombie with *Night of the Living Dead* and its sequels. In "'The Limeys Are Coming, Barbara, and They're Laughing!'" Steven Webley shines a spotlight on a specific aspect of Romero's influence—the zombie as a tool for cultural critique—as it was appropriated in two British zombie comedies, or zom-coms: the now-cult feature film *Shaun of the Dead* and the television miniseries *Dead Set* (2008). Webley examines the debt owed to Romero by these two divergent

zombie narratives—one lighthearted, the other a dark satire—and the ways
in which their respective flawed, comic anti-heroes use the undead to come
to terms with their own Britishness, and in so doing, stand for the struggles
of a post-ideological world. The next essay in this section, Gary D. Rhodes's
"Undead in the City: *The Vampire's Kiss* (1988) and Its Kin," takes on the
urban vampire, exploring the legacy of Dracula's fascination with the pace,
glamour, and anonymity of London. Rhodes illustrates that in a field of urban
vampire films—such as *Love at First Bite*, *Dracula: Dead and Loving It*, and
Vampire in Brooklyn (1995)—*The Vampire's Kiss* takes an original and darkly
humorous approach to the subgenre, casting the city itself as the antagonist
that both creates and destroys the vampire.

The section's final essay, "Beyond Fear in *The Book of Life*: Discussions
on Children, Death, and Latinidad" by Eric César Morales, offers a look at a
unique entry in the undead horror-comedy canon—a film that directly addresses multiple forms of life after death, specifically designed for young children. Drawing its inspiration from the Mexican Day of the Dead, *The Book
of Life* (2014) uses Latino traditions, often inflected with everyday humor, to
weave a tale around death and the afterlife for juvenile audiences generally
considered by Americans to be too young for such topics. Morales illustrates
how, through its casual, direct, and frequently humorous treatment of the
porous borders between life and death, the film naturalizes the subject and
neutralizes the horror that, for children, is often associated with it.

The second section of this volume, "Horror, in Theory," includes essays
that explore the construction of undead horror and its elements and the ways
in which these are both enhanced and challenged by the addition of comedy.
It opens with "The Humor of William Castle's Gimmick Films," Murray
Leeder's exploration of how Castle's experiments with devices like vibrators
wired to theater seats and plastic skeletons that "flew" over the audience on
wires turned low-budget horror films like *The Tingler* (1959) and *House on
Haunted Hill* (1959) into exercises in audience participation. Far from being
the failures they are often presented as, Leeder argues, Castle's gimmick films
took shrewd advantage of filmgoers' desire to be part of the action, and of
the uncanny similarities between our reactions to the frightening and the
comically absurd, using the gimmicks to knowingly provoke laughter amid
the horror. The theme of unexpected humor continues in "We're Not All
Dead Yet," by Martin F. Norden, a study of the unexpected merging of humor and horror in James Whale's *Bride of Frankenstein*. Norden analyzes the
film itself, deleted scenes, and scripted but unfilmed scenes to illustrate how,
though constrained by the Motion Picture Production Code, Whale and his
associates used comedy—from instances of comic relief to thinly veiled (and

not-so-veiled) commentary—to cloak their humorously subversive views on sexuality, gender, and religion, and invite audiences to read between the lines of the film's narrative for the rich cultural critique that lay just beneath the surface.

The section continues with two essays built around unexpected perspectives. Few are accustomed to thinking of *Abbott and Costello Meet Frankenstein* as a classic of comedy *or* horror, but Deborah Carmichael's in-depth history of the film makes the case that it is both. Universal Studios' 1948 pairing of "masters of mirth" Bud Abbott and Lou Costello with "monsters of menace" like Dracula, the Wolf Man, and Frankenstein's Monster began, she argues, as a calculated attempt to wring a few more dollars from two fading (but once lucrative) franchises. Yet, it became a vehicle that showcased both the comic duo and the monsters without diminishing either. We are, conversely, accustomed to thinking of vampires as many things—malevolent, hypnotic, soulful, seductive—but not as comic. In her essay, "Humor in Vampire Films: The Vampire as Joker," however, Mary Y. Hallab argues that even the most serious of vampire films, from *Nosferatu* (1922) and *Dracula* (1931) through the Hammer films of the 1950s and 1960s to *From Dusk till Dawn* (1996), are laced with humor, and that the horror they traffic in could not exist without it. The classical vampire, Hallab contends, is an inherently ridiculous figure: one whose assault on our sense of what is "normal" can induce involuntary laughter, but also prepares us to accept as real the deeper, more profound violations of the natural order that vampirism offers—superhuman powers and everlasting life.

The final two essays in this section examine the divergent ways in which the intersection of horror and comedy becomes a vantage point from which to unearth, and critique, the conventions of the horror genre. Lisa Cunningham's "Queerness and the Undead Female Monster" examines a trio of low-budget horror films—*Bordello of Blood* (1996), *Jennifer's Body* (2009), and *All Cheerleaders Die* (2013)—featuring queer female characters who die, then return as undead "monsters" to wreak vengeance on the living. All three films, Cunningham contends, are as much about the characters' queerness as about their newly undead nature or their violent acts. The complex, layered portrayals of the central characters render their designation as "monstrous," and thus the larger culture's equation of queerness and monstrosity, deliberately problematic. The monsters in *Zombieland*, in contrast, lack any semblance of complexity; they are exactly what they appear to be—ravenous, cannibalistic zombies that behave in perfectly predictable ways—and that, Chris Yogerst argues in "Rules for Surviving a Horror Comedy," is the point. Yogerst's essay explores how *Zombieland*, building on the genre-savvy humor of *Scream*, constructs a post-apocalyptic world in which every character has internalized the conventions of the zombie-apocalypse subgenre, reframing them as "rules for survival." The film, Yogerst argues, moves beyond *Scream* by taking for granted that the audience understands the elaborate comic game being played on-screen.

Incongruous juxtapositions abound in comedy, and the final section of the volume, "There Goes the Neighborhood," examines films whose comedy depends on introducing the undead into unexpected settings. Michael C. Reiff leads off the section with "Better Living through Zombies," a close reading of director Andrew Currie's *Fido*. Set in an idealized post-(zombie) war suburb, Currie's film imagines a world where the omnipresent corporation Zomcon has made "tamed" zombie servants into a middle-class status symbol. Reiff's essay examines the dark heart that lies beneath the film's candy-colored suburban surfaces, exploring its use of zombies to satirize consumerism, gender roles, and middle-class angst.

Turning from the suburbs to the city, A. Bowdoin Van Riper argues, in "'Who You Gonna Call?' The Supernatural and the Service Economy in the *Ghostbusters* Films," that the humor and horror of *Ghostbusters* (1984) and *Ghostbusters II* (1989) are both inextricably linked to their New York City setting. Horrific specters, shape-shifting Sumerian gods, and the spirits of dead Romanian tyrants are, in the *Ghostbusters* universe, just one more hazard of urban life, and the title characters just one more set of service providers. Throughout both films, New Yorkers—famously difficult to impress—meet the undead with their trademark mixture of practicality, seen-it-all calm, and wisecracking humor.

Whereas New York is popular culture's ultimate symbol of diversity, suburbia is its ultimate example of enforced uniformity. The personal growth experienced by the eponymous hero of *Shaun of the Dead* is profound, as Shelley S. Rees argues in her essay "The Queer and the Dead: Transgressive Sexuality in *Shaun of the Dead*." A dazed, disaffected young man living on the outskirts of London, Shaun finds an unexpected opportunity when the outbreak of a zombie apocalypse disrupts his life of modest ambitions and limited prospects. Rees's essay shows how Shaun's journey through the zombie-ridden streets facilitates a more significant inner journey, during which Shaun rebuilds (or frees himself from) his dysfunctional relationships with those closest to him—particularly his best friend, Ed. In their essay, "Undead in Suburbia: Teaching Children to Love Thy Neighbor, Fangs and All," Leila Estes and Katherine Kelp-Stebbins consider what happens when suburban conformity is challenged by the intrusion of the undead: the ultimate Other. Examining a quarter-century's worth of films, Estes and Kelp-Stebbins show that in horror-comedies the suburban undead frequently serve as a vehicle for messages of tolerance and shared humanity. Child-friendly comedies like *The Littlest Vampire* and darker, more adult works like *Beetlejuice* follow a shared narrative arc, in which distrust of difference softens into acceptance, and the "threat" posed by the arrival of the undead comes to be seen (by the newly enlightened living) as an opportunity for growth and new friendships.

In the volume's closing essay, "Some Assembly Required: The Do-It-Yourself Undead," Cynthia J. Miller explores a cluster of films that trace their roots to the story of Frankenstein's monster, but illustrate the comic "democratization" of reanimation, as their characters wrest the creation of life from the hands of scientists and physicians, claiming a power for the masses that is ordinarily reserved for a mere few. As Miller discusses, films such as *Frankenweenie* (1984/2012), *Weird Science* (1985), *Frankenhooker* (1990), and *Rock 'n' Roll Frankenstein* (1999) all suggest that the creation of life is more dependent on creativity than on technical expertise and offer an anarchic look at the outcomes of scientific power in the hands of everyday individuals.

Notes

1. Morreall, *Comic Relief*, 2.
2. Bergson, *Laughter*, 124.
3. Ibid., 118.
4. Ibid.
5. Robert Mankoff, "Untitled," *The New Yorker*, January 27, 2014. http://www.newyorker.com/cartoons/bob-mankoff/untitled.
6. Aquinas, *Summa Theologiae*, 217.

Bibliography

Aquinas, Thomas. *Summa Theologiae*, volume 44. Translated by Thomas Gilby. New York: McGraw-Hill, 1972.

Bergson, Henri. *Laughter: An Essay on the Meaning of the Comic*. Translated by Cloudesley Brereton and Fred Rothwell. London: Macmillan, 1913.

Morreall, John. *Comic Relief: A Comprehensive Philosophy of Humor*. West Sussex, UK: Wiley-Blackwell, 2009.

PART I

~

PLAYING WITH GENRE

CHAPTER ONE

~

"Oy, Have You Got the Wrong Vampire"

Dislocation, Comic Distancing, and Political Critique in Roman Polanski's The Fearless Vampire Killers (1967)

Thomas Prasch

Ruthless suppression of . . . those bloodsuckers, vampires, plunderers of the people and profiteers, who batten on famine. That is the policy of the working class.

—V. I. Lenin[1]

At the close of Roman Polanski's *The Fearless Vampire Killers* (a.k.a. *Dance of the Vampires*,[2] 1967), all seems well: the damsel, the innkeeper's daughter Sarah (Sharon Tate[3]), rescued; the pursuer Koukol (Terry Downes), the hunchbacked, snaggle-toothed servant of Count von Krolock (Ferdy Mayne), skiing after them down the Alpine slopes in a handy coffin, evaded; Professor Abronsius (Jack MacGowran) at the sleigh's reins and his not-especially-competent assistant Alfred (played by Polanski himself) sappily mumbling sweet nothings into Sarah's indifferent ear;[4] the frozen road to their future (and the West) apparently clear. But a sudden reversal changes everything. Sarah rouses and sinks her teeth into Alfred's neck as Abronsius, oblivious to Alfred's death throes behind him, drives on. The narrator's voice resonantly declares: "That night, fleeing from Transylvania, Professor Abronsius never guessed he was carrying away with him the very evil he sought to destroy. Thanks to him, this evil would at last be able to spread across the world."

3

Commentators have made much of the fact that this ending defies the conventions of closure that typify the traditional horror film. Polanski himself was quite aware of the fact: "In every vampire film the vampires are always killed at the end and the Professor saves the world from their terrible plague. Here, it's the menace that wins out."[5] Will Rocket points to the distinctive "practice of narrative open-endedness coupled with the triumph of evil" in this and other Polanski films.[6] S. S. Prawer argues that the film's last lines "point not only onwards in time but also outwards into our own world," suggesting "that the events we have seen on the screen may be linked . . . with more 'real' horrors."[7] Michael Elm personalizes that real-world horror, reading "this narrative structure—avoiding closure of the narrative, revealing the world to be an unsafe place and insertion of the spectator into the narrative" as a mark of "cultural trauma."[8] For William Paul, the moment anchors his argument for the film as forerunner to a type of horror comedy that would fully emerge in a couple of decades: "In *The Fearless Vampire Killers*, the final laugh is quite specifically conflated with the final scream."[9] Comedy and horror become one precisely at the point where the narrative refuses closure.

But consider what the casting does to that final laugh/scream: Polanski has placed himself in the critical position of final victim and source of new contagion. At the time, Polanski was a recent exile from the Warsaw Pact, having left Poland on the promising success of his first feature-length film, *Knife in the Water* (1962), a transition made possible by the brief de-Stalinizing thaw of the late 1950s and early 1960s.[10] So he, like the Professor and Alfred at movie's end, fled the frozen East (with all the analogies that go with it; we call those periods of relatively relaxed state censorship "thaws") for the safety and freedom of the West. But, in that ironic twist, they bring "the very evil they sought to destroy" along with them. In a sense, the movie we have been watching—an Eastern European filmmaker's embrace of that horror identified, from Bram Stoker's time forward, with his home territory—is that contagion, an ironic reclaiming of the vampire that, originally constructed out of Central European folklore, had since become an archetype of Western horror.

Polanski makes the vampire Central European again. Indeed, the Transylvanian spaces of the film feature landscapes (especially Alpine ones) and cultural formations (most notably a strong Jewish subculture) that locate the work far more firmly than is typical of the horror film, in either its Hollywood or Hammer incarnations. He simultaneously remakes the vampire film to comment wryly on Cold War politics and the communist regimes of the Eastern bloc, amplifying a subtheme of the Hammer Dracula series; he also anticipates a striking cultural feature of the breakdown of communist regimes, when vampires would rise from their graves throughout the ex-Soviet bloc.

But Polanski also remaps it as comedy. The move was not utterly un-precedented—Dracula had been one of the main monsters in *Abbott and Costello Meet Frankenstein* (1948)[11]—but the shift in tone breaks from the film's most important precedents. *Nosferatu* (1922), the Universal *Dracula* (1931), and the Hammer Dracula films (beginning with *Horror of Dracula*, 1958) were never funny, save occasionally unintentionally (who can help but giggle, say, at an obviously rubber hand dissolving in the sunlight?). Precisely because of the distancing effects of laughter, the film can take on subjects like the deep histories of oppression that beset Central Europe; because of the laughter, Polanski can employ the horror genre to reflect on his personal past, as a survivor of both the Holocaust and Stalinism.

The form of comedy offered in *Fearless Vampire Killers* is varied: one-liners; character-based comic routines (above all else focused on Alfred—as incom-petent lover, in his pursuit of Sarah, and as reluctant love object, in his eva-sion of the homosexual flirtations of the Count's extremely effeminate son Herbert [Iain Quarrier][12]); comedy rooted, as in good Marx Brothers movies, in over-the-top stereotyping (the very Yiddish-theater innkeeper Shagal [Alfie Bass], Herbert's limp-wristed homosexual, Koukol's more-deformed-than-Igor servant,[13] even the hypersexualized, very bosomy Sarah and Magda [Fiona Lewis], the inn servant after whom Shagal lusts), producing the effect, Polanski later stated, of a "cartoon with people"[14]; heavy double entendre and innuendo, enhancing all the sexual situations (anytime we find Sarah, as we oddly often do, in a bath, for example); and situational comedy, mostly playing upon the incompetence of the vampire chasers (Alfred's inability to drive a stake through a vampire's heart, for instance).

But above all else, the film pulls its humor from sight gags: the confused business of the inn's denizens, the recurrent hilarity of people frozen stiff, the choreographed comedy of the dance scene at the vampire ball, and the film's assorted screwball chase sequences.[15] Indeed, as some critics have noted, *Fearless Vampire Killers* almost plays as silent film. To accomplish this end, Bruce Hallenbeck observes, Polanski returns to the tactics of old silents:

> Long stretches are dialogue-free, allowing Polanski plenty of opportunity to give the movie the feeling of a silent, from under-cranking some footage—a style often used in older films for comic effect, and rarely for eerie effect, as in F. W. Murnau's 1922 *Nosferatu*—and with his liberal use of sight gags. . . . If you can imagine Murnau combined with Charlie Chaplin, you'll have a very good idea what Polanski achieves.[16]

Shagal is pushed down the stairs in a coffin.

Under-cranking, which gives characters' motion a choppy, sped-up effect, thus doubly alludes to silent film and to one of the classics of the vampire genre, while at the same time giving an extra giggle to the frenzied action (in the inn or in the chase scenes especially). The tactic doubles the distancing effect of comedy as well: We are not only, unexpectedly, laughing at horror, but seeing horror done in a long-defunct, now laughable style. While such distancing might well have served Polanski's purposes, however, critics and audiences appreciated it less.

That mix of unexpected comedy and Central European spirit played a part in the problems the film faced once Polanski completed shooting.[17] American producer Martin Ransohoff, to whom Polanski had signed over final cut, hated Polanski's version and proceeded to "fix" it: retitling (ineptly, since the film's protagonists are neither "fearless" nor "killers"), chopping some dozen minutes, redubbing, and fiddling with the credits and the score.[18] Polanski, furious but helpless because of the terms of his contract, complained: "What I made was a funny, spooky fairy tale, and this is a sort of Transylvanian *Beverly Hillbillies*."[19] Polanski requested his name be removed from the credits, and Gene Gutowski, his Polish producer, telegraphed the *New York Times* that the film "has been so radically changed by reasons of recutting, redubbing, revoicing, altered dialogue, altered sound track and altered sound effects that it no longer represents the motion picture created, written and directed by Roman Polanski."[20] Polanski would later recall: "Watching this,

I felt the way a mother must feel when she finds out she's given birth to a deformed child."[21] In interviews—for instance, when calling Ransohoff a "hypocrite in disguise," a "philistine who dresses himself up as an artist," and a "brute," with "genuinely malicious intentions"[22]—Polanski makes Ransohoff himself something of a vampire.

Overseas, where Ransohoff's rights did not hold, Polanski's cut (with Polanski's title) was released, with, Christopher Sandford reports, dramatically different results: "The film appeared in two distinct versions: Polanski's in Europe, where it was a huge hit, and Ransohoff's in America, where it bombed."[23] While the evidence is not quite clear for European success, the signs of its bombing in the United States are abundantly evident. From Roger Ebert: "The night I went to see 'The Fearless Vampire Killers' . . . nobody laughed."[24] The film was dismissed in *Time*: "Neither spooky nor spoofy; it never manages to get out of the coffin."[25] In the *New York Times*, Bosley Crowther groused: "This beautifully produced, superbly scenic and excitingly photographed spoof of old-fashioned horror movies is as dismal and dead as a blood-drained corpse."[26] A few weeks later, Crowther returned with a final stake, using the film as an example of the way Hollywood ruined foreign directors: "And most depressing is Roman Polanski's 'The Fearless Vampire Killers' . . . an ultimate example of what can happen when a good regionally trained director is lured out of his métier by money and an invitation to pitch to a vulgar taste."[27] With such reviews, the dismal box office returns can be no surprise.

The film does have defenders. Ivan Butler insists: "To dismiss *Dance of the Vampires* as no more than a parody of the horror film is to underrate it to an absurd degree," and he calls the film "a reflection of, and a parable for, our time."[28] Donald Glut calls it "one of the finest vampire films ever made,"[29] stressing its atmospheric Transylvanian settings and humorous borrowings from the vampire film canon. James Craig Holte asserts it is "perhaps the perfect vampire film for the end of the 1960s: it recognizes that vampire films have become a subgenre of their own and as such deserve both homage and parody."[30] Julia Ain-Krupa underlines the way the film works with one of Polanski's most familiar themes, a fatalism refracted through a sort of existentialist-infused absurdity: "In *The Fearless Vampire Killers*, it is through absurdist comedy that Polanski explores the subject of destiny."[31] Hallenbeck concludes his account: "If *Abbott and Costello Meet Frankenstein* is the Cadillac of comedy-horror films, then *The Fearless Vampire Killers* is the Rolls Royce."[32] A number of critics have noted themes in the film that recur regularly in the Polanski film canon. Sandford, for example, points out: "*The Fearless Vampire Killers* is, in its director's cut, something close to a greatest-hits collection of Polanski themes. There's violence, nudity, a touch of both homosexuality and sadomasochism, among other, darker corners of the human psyche, and of course voyeurism."[33] Such catalogs serve to make the film seem far less an outlier among Polanski's works.

Other critics go even further, positioning *Fearless Vampire Killers* as a significant contribution to film. Both Prawer and Paul, as noted above, see the film as a key precursor to later trends in horror cinema. And for James Morrison, *Fearless Vampire Killers* is one of a trilogy of Polanski films—along with its two immediate predecessors, *Repulsion* and *Cul-de-Sac*—that, with its cross of Eastern European film traditions and Western capital, its international mix of actors and crew, its genre hybridizing, and its mix of high art and low sources, redefined the international art film. Polanski himself partially anticipates Morrison's argument: "The film has central European sensibilities but was filmed from an American perspective with a lot of confusion and laughter. There's also something profoundly English about it. For me, exile is about this need to travel."[34] In Morrison's reading of the late 1960s, "a time at which the cultural hybridity of the art film, especially in its capacity to traverse cultural levels with great tractability, had never been more apparent,"[35] Polanski played a pivotal role:

> Of the key figures in the 1960s European art film, Roman Polanski traded most brazenly in comedy and horror . . . most often where these forms intersect with melodrama. Perhaps the most eclectic art-film auteur of the decade he was— maybe for that reason—most instrumental in opening up the art-film canon and disturbing its established hierarchies.[36]

To these varied assertions of a path-breaking role for *Fearless Vampire Killers*, we can add one more: It pioneered the vampire as emblematic monster of the communist bloc, reclaiming the East European folk tradition from its Western high-modernist deployment and turning it into a symbol of Soviet rule (while arguing the equivalence between that particular form of tyranny and the medieval/feudalistic dominions that gave the monster its birth, via Vlad the Impaler).

The film has one other significant defender: Polanski himself. When asked in 1984 to name his "favorite film" he answered: "*The Fearless Vampire Killers*. It is an amusing and unpretentious film, and I really enjoy watching it."[37] Given the troubled post-production history and the dismal critical response, such fondness for the work might seem surprising.

At least part of Polanski's continued fondness for the film stems from the way it captures a particular Central European sensibility, with historical echoes of both a traditional feudal past (its vampire folklore roots) and a more recent history of Nazi, then Soviet, occupation. Indeed, Polanski initially thought he might film in Poland, and then tried to arrange to shoot in Romania, before financial (and doubtless political) exigencies forced him to use the Italian Alps for his location work.[38] Douglas Slocombe, cinematographer for the film, captures both this sensibility and the difficulties it created for Western audiences in his recollections of the project:

> I think he put more of himself into *Dance of the Vampires* than into another [*sic*; doubtless "any other" is meant] film. It brought to light the fairy-tale interest that he has. One was conscious all along when making the picture of a Central European background to the story. Very few of the crew could see anything in it—they thought it old-fashioned nonsense. . . . The figure of Alfred is very much like Roman himself—a slight figure, young and a little defenceless—a touch of Kafka. It is very much a personal statement. He used to chuckle all the way through.[39]

Even critics less inclined to chuckle all the way through have noted the importance of the Central European background. Adrian Martin has called the film Polanski's "personal, playful nod to the lore of East European superstition."[40] Hallenbeck argues that "Polanski's intention was to inject his unique brand of Central European humor into a classic Gothic horror story,"[41] and Ain-Krupa similarly notes the film is "suffused with a brand of Polish absurdist humor particular to this part of the world."[42] Morrison writes:

> The beautifully designed sets of *Dance of the Vampires* mimic a kaleidoscopic fantasia of an Eastern Europe of the mind, but they are so eccentrically stylized as to suggest that the weird, moonstruck geographies they represent are lost to history—if they ever existed—and can be accessed only through myth and imagination.[43]

This captures the sense of engagement and distancing that figures in Polanski's fantasized Eastern Europe, as well as its anchoring, at least in part, in what has been lost to the depredations of the twentieth century. The results can be seen most clearly in the film's most distinctive figures: the Jew and the vampire.

The case of the Jew has particular resonance for Polanski, given his personal history: both his parents were caught up in the mechanics of the Holocaust, his mother dying in the extermination camps, and Polanski was left effectively orphaned at the age of eight.[44] How closely this bears on *Fearless*

Vampire Killers can be gauged by Polanski's answer when asked how "familiar" he was with the film's "Jewish humor." Polanski answered:

> In the film there's an Eastern European culture which was desolated by the Germans and that's been killed off for good thanks to Polish Stalinism. It's the kind of thing that you see in the works of figures like Marc Chagall and Isaac Babel, and also in certain Polish paintings. This culture, which never reappeared after the war, is part of my childhood memories. There just aren't any traditional Jews in Poland any more.[45]

Comedy it may be, but it also reflects on a culture and a people that had been exterminated in successive moments of Eastern European history.

Three features of this answer are worth highlighting. First, the weight of a vanished culture exterminated by Nazism and Stalinism provides an awfully weighty backdrop for a light comedy. Second, the emphasis on the "traditional" Jew figures into the choices Polanski makes in shaping the film's most central Jewish figure, the innkeeper Shagal (the close resemblance of his name to the artist Polanski cites has been noted by critics). This also informs Polanski's initial resistance to casting Tate in the role: "She didn't look Jewish enough."[46] Third, Polanski's answer emphasizes that the devastation of East European Jewry was not just the work of the Nazis' Final Solution, but was completed by Soviet-sourced Stalinism in its wake. This trope of successive and largely indistinguishable occupations, at the expense both of Polish and Jewish culture, constitutes a routine gesture in Polish cinema: Think of Agnieszka Holland's *Europa, Europa* (1990) or Andrzej Wajda's films, perhaps most explicitly in the recent *Katyń* (2007), but more subtle variations of the theme can be traced in his great trilogy of postwar Poland, *A Generation* (1955, in which a young Polanski played a bit role), *Kanal* (1957), and *Ashes and Diamonds* (1958).[47]

Fearless Vampire Killers can, at one level, be read as an excavation of this vanished Jewish past, but distanced through comedy. Polanski gives Shagal the best (and most quoted) one-liner in the film. Once turned into a vampire by the Count, he continues preying on the inn's voluptuous servant girl Magda. When she tries to ward him off with the film-tested device of raising a crucifix, he responds: "Oy, have you got the wrong vampire." Although Shagal's story figures as no more than an amusing side plot throughout the film, he persistently pops into the action: Initially, as innkeeper, stomping on sauerkraut and lusting after Magda, he sets the comic tone; the finding of his frozen body after he sets out to chase Count von Krolock after his daughter's kidnapping provides a good sight gag; seeking to claim a place in the vampires' crypt, he is refused entrance (in a clearly anti-Semitic action) and unceremoniously exiled to the animal stalls, but by the time Alfred is open-ing coffins he has found his way in and is curled up at the Herbert's feet;[48] and he continues to prey upon Magda, setting up a bit in which Abronsius seeks to dissuade him by speaking from the rooftop, Shagal taking his dis-embodied voice as that of his (very Jewish) God. "Don't you touch her," the voice orders; "I'm not touching, who's touching?" Shagal responds (but he bites the girl anyway).

By pushing Shagal's character so far toward stage stereotype, however, Polanski risked being misunderstood. Ewa Mazierska, for instance, takes the stereotyping as a different form of distancing, arguing:

> It feels as if Polanski has no personal experience or memory of the respective traditions, but in order to depict them he must rely on someone else's testimo-nies. Furthermore, in his films the director reveals no yearning for his Jewish or Polish past or cultural roots. On the contrary, he underscores the lack of per-sonal involvement in these cultures by using very stylised acting and mise-en-scène which often produces a comical effect. For example, Alfie Bass's Chagal [sic] in *Dance of the Vampires*, with his "goatie" beard, long kapota, exaggerated gestures and poor hygiene (he disapproves of his daughter's frequent baths), looks and behaves like an archetypal Jew or even a caricature of a Jew from Eastern European folklore (which was largely anti-Semitic).[49]

This seems fundamentally to misunderstand Polanski's deep engagement with Central Europe and the Jewish character (and gets wrong as well why Shagal worries about those baths; just look where they lead, after all, since the Count kidnaps Sarah from her tub while Alfred spies on her through a keyhole, two reasons beyond "poor hygiene" to have concerns).

Brenda Gardenour, however, gets it even more wrong, accusing Polanski of anti-Semitism and classic blood libel: in the end, Magda

> is dead, her body completely drained of Christian blood by the Jewish vam-pire's insatiable hunger. In Shagal, the audience is laughing at an image of historical imagination that is colder, blacker, and more toxic than the vampire itself. For over a thousand years, the toxic blood-sucking Jew and the vampire have shared the same imaginary body.[50]

But such a reading rather misses the effect of laughter on stereotype. Much as with the comic effect of other forms of Polanski's exaggeration—the over-heavy cobwebs, the over-deformed servant, the ultra-incompetent vampire hunters—the tactical deployment of Jewish stereotypes, and the inclusion of anti-Semitic responses (like Shagal's exclusion from the crypt), undermine the archetypal forms.

Polanski's vampire presents a more complicated figure. On the one hand, he is the familiar vampire of the film canon, from *Nosferatu* through Bela Lugosi to the Hammer series. But the temporality, and thus the historical resonance, is disturbed, broadened to include not just the early-modern/feudal past but the postwar contemporary as well. The traditional vampire tale, at least insofar as Bram Stoker's canonical *Dracula* inscribes folkloric tales of Vlad the Impaler, has essentially not just Central European but feudal foundations. He is a Count, after all. Even if, in Stoker and most adaptations that follow from him, the real action is set in motion with the coming of this exotic Other to the modern metropole—and thus modernity itself is woven into the texture of the encounter—back in Transylvania, Dracula remains firmly rooted in the feudal past. Polanski's time frame is more complex: simultaneously alluding to that early-modern setting (in the castle, the aristocratic tradition of portraits lining its halls, the Baroque ball) and to the pall cast by communist domination over Eastern Europe (especially in the Count's self-accounting).

In taking the vampire as emblematic representative of communist dominion, Polanski pioneered an approach strikingly often followed by filmmakers working in his wake, especially after the collapse of the Soviet system. Indeed, even the weakening of the state apparatus of Soviet rule, in periods of thaw, prompts the revival of the vampire. Prague Spring in Czechoslovakia—Alexander Dubček's "socialism with a human face"—produced (although it was not released until after Russian tanks crushed the movement) Jaromil Jireš's wild surrealist vampire tale, *Valerie and Her Week of Wonders* (1970), which combined coming-of-age tale, heightened sexuality, surrealist storytelling, and vampire theme.[51] Andrew Horton sees in the film a thinly disguised account of a "nation being defiled and abused by foreign aggressors."[52] David Melville points out the Stalinist shadow in the film's account: "The vampire curse that haunts Valerie's family life is the legacy of the older generation that is irredeemably compromised by the traffic with dark powers."[53] A few years later, the relaxation of censorship in Yugoslavia led to a surge of antitraditional, oppositional filmmaking known as the Black Wave, including the first Yugoslav exploration of the vampire film: the television movie *Leptirica* (*She-Butterfly*, 1973).[54] The film features some striking parallels to Polanski's: lurid sexuality and bloodshed combined with comic bits. And in Russia, as Tomas Jesús Garza has noted, the rise of the vampire begins with Gorbachev's relaxation of Soviet controls on expression: "As *glasnost* took hold in practice toward the end of the 1980s, subject matter that was virtually unheard of or unseen in the Soviet period suddenly became germane for public consumption . . . the vampire quickly emerged as both a theme and symbol of New Russia's new constituents."[55] But the handful of vampires in periods of Soviet thaw are dwarfed by the explosion of vampire culture after the fall of the Berlin Wall in 1989.

Among these new territories witnessing the re-rise of the vampire, two stand out: Russia, the Soviet heartland, and Romania, traditional haunt of Vlad and Dracula. In Russia, Garza tracks the theme, in particular in popular music that he describes as ranging from "post-punk to gothic": "Once again the *upyr'* [Russian vampire], who had lain relatively quiet through more than seventy years of Soviet rule, returned from the dead in a quite different guise . . . to signify new 'Others' in post-Soviet society and once again be employed to vilify the unwelcome visitor."[56] But the vampire has also emerged as a strong figure in post-Soviet Russian literature, serving, Alexander Etkind argues, as a suitable monster to discuss both memories of the Soviet state and more recent developments.[57] Asked about his choice of vampires as a symbol for post-Soviet Russia, novelist Victor Pelevin answered, only partly disingenuously, "I simply wrote a book about vampires. They've interested me for a long time. I knew intuitively that vampires in Russia would be more than just vampires. And so I tried to explore just how much more."[58]

In film, too, the vampire has been resurgent in Russia. Guy Dolgopolov points out: "There is a complex relationship played out in post-Soviet Russia between the undead horror, memory, exhumations of the dead, and recuperating national trauma that is allegorized in the figure of the vampire."[59] The Putin regime, Garza notes, has further amplified the trend: "With the election of Vladimir Putin in the spring of 2000, vampire imagery . . . increased significantly in Russian cultural production."[60] Current Russian politics suggest we are likely to see more.

And in Romania, which experienced the bloodiest, most confused, and least complete post-Soviet transition (no "Velvet Revolution" here), the vampire has above all else emerged as an allegorical symbol for the last Soviet leader of the state, Nicolae Ceauşescu (and often his wife Elena as well). As Pia Brînzeu puts it: "Due to Ceauşescu, the two themes—that of the political tyrant, desirous to rule through terror, and that of the vampire, sucking the blood and energy of his victims—have merged into the common topos of the vampire-dictator."[61] Much of this was the work of Western commentators, in political commentary during the transition and later in film (like *Bloodline* and the *Subspecies* series), theater (Caryl Churchill, after an extended workshop visit to Romania immediately after the revolution, constructed the Ceauşescus as vampires in her play, *Mad Forest* [1990]),[62] and literature (like Dan Simmons's *Children of the Night*).[63] But the vampire symbolism had currency within Romania as well. Peter Siani-Davies notes that "it was not just the outside world that embraced the image. Inside Romania an anti-Ceauşescu montage mounted on the side of a tank in Timişoara pictured the Romanian leader [as] 'the most renowned among vampires' with fangs and horns."[64] Andrei Codrescu recalls: "I could see that Ceauşescu had already become a creature of legend. . . . In Bucharest and other cities the demonstrators shouted 'Down with the vampire!'"[65] Dracula had come home.

It is not so much that all these post-Soviet vampires draw on Polanski for their inspiration, but rather that Polanski discovered sooner, because of his privileged status as exile from the Soviet bloc, the resonance of the vampire as symbol for the Soviet state. The combination of bloodsucking (to cover basic oppression) and work in the night (paralleling the secrecy of the Soviet security apparatus) makes the vampire an irresistible emblem of communist states. The temporal hedging—making a feudal symbol stand in for modern power—underlines the argument routinely made by Soviet-bloc dissidents: that the new power created elites difficult to differentiate from older forms.

Nor was this, quite, pure invention on Polanski's part. The politics of Polanski's vampire draws heavily on his most immediate model, the Hammer Dracula films, commencing with Terence Fisher's *Horror of Dracula* (just plain *Dracula* outside the United States, 1958). The extent of the Hammer films' promotion of Cold War anxieties about the Soviets, constellated as a discourse on totalitarianism, has largely been missed by critics, perhaps because the films' most visible attributes—the amped-up gore and sexuality—have distracted from their political content. Thus, for example, Cynthia Hendershot misreads the Hammer series as offering "the erotic as antidote to cold war historical specificity."[66] Brian Wilson misses the mark even more widely in arguing that the Hammer films "worked to engender progressive forms of ideological awareness through the utilization of traditional generic structures as a method through which to reflect and subvert a conservative value system."[67] But the sex and gore distract Wilson, too; it is almost entirely the Hammer films' challenges to censorship that he reads as "subversive."

The Hammer films, however, firmly reinscribe the fear of the Other so central to the vampire myth onto the Cold War constellation of "totalitarian" systems. Consider, for example, *Horror of Dracula*: The focus on the stone eagle in the film's credit sequence deliberately calls to mind the Nazi eagle, while the remarks Van Helsing tape-records about the vampire threat— metaphors of contagion and addiction, concern about secret groups (read Leninist cells) penetrating Western society, and a central message about the need for vigilance and awareness of Western weaknesses—instantiates classic Cold War takes on the Soviet menace.[68] This stance gets picked up by Polanski and infused with his own Eastern European, Soviet-survivor consciousness, while given the protective glaze of comedy.

In this context, the most striking feature of Polanski's Count von Krolock is his difference: In a movie full of wildly exaggerated characters—stereotypes, comic foils, and assorted clowns—the Count is the only one who plays it straight. He takes his vampirism seriously, and the film takes it seriously as well: none of the comic business centers on him. Further, in a film with remarkably few set speeches and little sustained dialogue—a movie full of sight gags that takes silent film as a model, after all—it is only von Krolock who delivers extended monologues. This reverses the general tendency in vampire films, where it is the vampire hunter who gets to make the long speeches.

The first of these speeches, a long discourse to the Professor just before the ball, begins with a disquisition on life once Abronsius and Alfred, too, are made vampires: "It will be my pleasure to fill in the gaps in your learning when you have reached my 'spiritual level.' We shall then have long winter evenings before us for our discussions. The long evenings of many winters." (Note the equation of vampirism with winter, a main visual trope in the film.) He continues with a prophecy of world conquest: "As brooks go into streams, streams into rivers, and rivers into the sea, so shall our adepts flow back to us and swell our ranks. Soon we shall be victorious and triumphant. We shall then hold sway over the earth as autumn awaits winter." Looking down in the courtyard, seeing Shagal bringing Magda to the ball, the Count grows meditative, in a way that suggests the "radiant future"[69] propaganda of Soviet states: "Look at him. Almost an old man. With his flabby stomach and skinny legs bringing with doglike devotion a fresh adept who only a few nights ago was under his protection. . . . But tonight he's happy. See how he frisks and capers." Both the vision of world conquest, the equation with winter, and the myth of the happy subject reflect a critical perspective on Soviet-style state systems.

Count von Krolock's final speech, at the start of the vampire ball, twists the metaphor by framing his welcome as sermon: "A year ago. A year ago, exactly, on this same night, we were assembled here in this very room. I your pastor, and you my beloved flock. With hope in my heart I told you then that with Lucifer's aid we might look forward to a more succulent occasion. Cast back your minds. There we were, gathered together, gloomy and despondent around that single meager woodcutter." The religious bent of von Krolock's welcome plays on another familiar trope of Cold War anticommunism: communism as alternative (and failed) religious faith, perhaps most familiar in

The vampire ball.

the widely circulated collection *The God That Failed* (1949).[70] There is no failure in the Count's vision, however: his flock continues to expand. And, at the end, as Sarah bites Alfred's neck, "this evil would at last be able to spread across the world." The Cold War vibe still chills in Polanski's vision.

What relieves this dire prophecy, as it provides Polanski distance from the darknesses of his own past, is the film's resolutely comic tone. Comedy also separates Polanski's vampiric vision from the broad array of post-Soviet vampire films. At the same time, Polanski's adherence to a Cold War anti-communism, built up from Hammer roots but drawing on his own experience—not much noticed at the time, perhaps because of the same distractions (sex and gore) that keep critics from noticing the politics of Hammer films—separates his work and his political consciousness from many of the new filmmakers in Western Europe at the time. Only a year after *Fearless Vampire Killers*, that political distance would become evident in the split between Polanski and French *nouvelle vague* directors Jean-Luc Godard and François Truffaut, when Polanski refused to endorse their New Left–inspired May Day effort to close down the Cannes Film Festival.[71]

The Fearless Vampire Killers stands as a testament to Polanski's complex negotiation of his exile status and his dissident (but not New Left) political positioning in the late 1960s, as he tried to come to terms with the Western cinematic apparatus. It remains perhaps the most successful comic twist on the vampire genre, even if that achievement went largely unappreciated at the time. Finding a place for it in the canon of classic horror is, perhaps, what midnight screenings have always been for.

Notes

1. Lenin, "Comrade Workers, Forward," 58. And yes, it is cheating a bit, since the elided words—"the kulaks"—changes the meaning significantly. But it seems much funnier to make him seem to be talking about actual vampires, rather than the rich Russian peasant class Lenin targeted for reprisals and public hangings during the mid–civil war grain seizures of 1918 and who were ruthlessly suppressed, indeed almost entirely exterminated, during Stalin's agricultural collectivization. See? That isn't funny at all.

2. *Dance of the Vampires* was Polanski's original title; his American producer Martin Ransohoff—the man Polanski eventually came to call "a compulsive butcher of other people's work" (Polanski, *Roman by Polanski*, 250)—was responsible for the American title (and often neglected subtitle: *Or, Pardon Me but Your Teeth Are in My Neck*).

3. Yes, this is the film during which Polanski's romance with Tate was kindled, although back in London they had already dropped acid together and had sex as dawn broke (insert your preferred vampire reference here). See Polanski, *Roman by Polanski*, 252. (And for the French-born multilingual Polanski, we might wonder what it means that he titles his autobiography with his first name, which means "novel" in French.)

4. Ivan Butler notes that, in talking about warming Sarah's cold hands, Alfred quotes from Puccini's *La Boheme*, Sarah's vampire-bit malady made analogue to Mimi's consumption. See *Cinema of Roman Polanski*, 137.

5. Ciment, Perez, and Tailleur, "Interview with Roman Polanski," 46. Butler puts the case in very similar terms in *Cinema of Roman Polanski*, 134.

6. Rocket, *Devouring Whirlwind*, 153.

7. Prawer, *Caligari's Children*, 61. Ewa Mazierska, drawing on Prawer, reads into a number of Polanski's film narratives the intent to make the world "unsafe"; see *Roman Polanski*, 170. This figures into Mazierska's problematic intent to read his films as shadow autobiography: "It could be argued that in Polanski's biography we could also detect a vampiric trajectory: from an abused child to a paedophilic abuser" (14).

8. Elm, "Screening Trauma," 53.

9. Paul, *Laughing Screaming*, 418.

10. On the thaw and Polish cinema, see Haltof, *Polish National Cinema*, 77–79.

11. On this and subsequent vampire comedies, see Handler, et al., "The Cold Hard Stats of Vampire Comedies."

12. The parallel pairs of Professor/Alfred and Count/Herbert are central in Anna M. Lawton's reading of *Fearless Vampire Killers* in terms of the doppelgänger theme she finds in Polanski's films ("The Double," 122–25), although the doubling is only occasionally what makes it funny.

13. Ewa Mazierska takes Koukol's character as evidence that, in Polanski, "laughter is never jovial and it usually contains a dark side because the director, in a Rabelaisian fashion, invites us to laugh at human inadequacies, such as physical disabilities and clumsiness" (*Roman Polanski*, 183), but it is less than clear that Polanski (or Rabelais) intends such comedy as "dark."

14. Quoted in Butler, *Cinema of Roman Polanski*, 127.

15. For a catalog of other sight gags in the film, see Butler, *Cinema of Roman Polanski*, 132–33; see also, on the "certain amount of *schtick* in the film" (the term is revealing about the roots of Polanski's humor), Sandford, *Polanski*, 102.

16. Hallenbeck, *Comedy-Horror Films*, 84. Butler notes the allusion to another early vampire classic, Carl Dreyer's *Vampyr* (1932), especially in the opening scenes in the inn; see Butler, *Cinema of Roman Polanski*, 139.

17. Indeed, troubles were already evident during the shooting. Polanski shares a niggling producer's memo calling for a variety of fixes to the script, ranging from worries about nudity to censoring of suggestive lines; see Polanski, *Roman by Polanski*, 259–60. Doubtless it did not help that Polanski was, by that time, behind schedule and over budget.

18. The story is a familiar one in Polanski lore. See, for example, Ain-Krupa, *Roman Polanski*, 58, 61–62; Parker, *Polanski*, 110; Sandford, *Polanski*, 105; Leaming, *Polanski*, 81.

19. Quoted in Sandford, *Polanski*, 105.

20. "Polanski Disavows 'Vampire' Film Cuts," *New York Times*, November 14, 1967.

21. Polanski, *Roman by Polanski*, 275. Robert Horton uses this quotation to explicate Polanski's next work, *Rosemary's Baby* (1968); see https://roberthorton.wordpress.com/2008/10/26/halloween-countdown-rosemarys-baby/.

22. "Hypocrite in disguise," in Delahaye and Narboni, "Interview with Roman Polanski"; "philistine" and "brute" (plus "hypocrite" again), in Ciment, Perez, and Tailleur, "Interview with Roman Polanski"; "malicious" and "jealous," in Maillet, "Roman Polanski"; all in Cronin, *Roman Polanski: Interviews*, 22, 39, and 89, respectively.

23. Sandford, *Polanski*, 105.

24. Ebert, "*The Fearless Vampire Killers*."

25. Quoted in Sandford, *Polanski*, 105.

26. Crowther, "Screen: 'Fearless Vampire Killers.'"

27. Crowther, "The Melting Pot Boils Over."

28. Butler, *Cinema of Roman Polanski*, 128, 129.

29. Glut, *The Dracula Book*, 275.

30. Holte, *Dracula in the Dark*, 66.

31. Ain-Krupa, *Roman Polanski*, 59. Butler similarly notes: "Once more we are obsessed by the realization of human solitude and helplessness. No one, in the last resort, is able to assist or make contact with anyone else" (*Cinema of Roman Polanski*, 131).

32. Hallenbeck, *Comedy-Horror Films*, 85–86. Hallenbeck also quotes Phillip Hardy, who wrote in *The Encyclopedia of Horror Films* that "the film is an astounding tour de force that is funny, chilling, and intensely lyrical at the same time" (85).

33. Sandford, *Polanski*, 103. For similar lists of parallel themes, see Parker, *Polanski*, 107; Butler, *Cinema of Roman Polanski*, 129–31; Leaming, *Polanski*, 78–79; Mazierska, *Roman Polanski*, 37–38, 71; and Lawton, "The Double," 122–25.

34. de Baecque and Jousse, "Interview with Roman Polanski," 150. Parker makes a similar point in *Polanski*, 265–66.

35. Morrison, *Roman Polanski*, 40.

36. Ibid., 40–41.

37. Giesbert, "Roman's Novel" (the title loses its pun when translated from French), 107. Polanski repeated this preference in 1986 and 1990; see Boutang, "Polanski on Polanski" and Midding, "Being Merciless," both in Cronin, *Roman Polanski: Interviews*, 112 and 139, respectively.

38. On Poland: see Haudiquet, "I Made This Film for Myself," 12. On Romania: see Hallenback, *Comedy-Horror Films*, 82.

39. Quoted (from a personal interview) in Butler, *Cinema of Roman Polanski*, 82.

40. Martin (2001), quoted in Hondrila, "Persistence of the Imago-Myth," 97.

41. Hallenbeck, *Comedy-Horror Films*, 85.

42. Ain-Krupa, *Roman Polanski*, 59.

43. Morrison, *Roman Polanski*, 82.

44. Probably the fullest accounts of Polanski's wartime experience are Polanski's own, in *Roman by Polanski*, 17–59, and in Sandford, *Polanski*, chapter 2. This personal history informs Polanski's engagement with the Holocaust story he tells in *The Pianist* (2002).

45. Ciment, Perez, and Tailleur, "Interview with Roman Polanski," 44. Polanski also tells Michel Delahaye and Jean Narboni ("Interview with Roman Polanski," 14) that the film draws on "childhood memories."

46. Polanski, *Roman by Polanski*, 253; see also Ain-Krupa, *Roman Polanski*, 59; Sandford, *Polanski*, 102. Polanski solved that problem with a red wig (and/or by falling in love with her).

47. The Western variation on this discourse, the Cold War–era "totalitarian" model that equates Nazism and Soviet-style communism as parallel efforts at globalizing, systematizing domination, can be traced from Arnold Toynbee's *A Study of History* (1934–1961) forward to, most notably, Karl Popper's *Open Society and Its Enemies* (1945) and Hannah Arendt's *Origins of Totalitarianism* (1955). But the totalitarian model has more to do with the vampire than the Jew.

48. This scene is the focus of Lester D. Friedman's account of the film in *Hollywood's Image of the Jew*, 206–7.

49. Mazierska, *Roman Polanski*, 16. Mazierska also oddly insists on reading Polanski's *The Pianist* as "impersonal" (90).

50. Gardenour, "Biology of Blood-Lust," 63; see also 51. Gardenour shows no evidence that she is aware that she is writing about a man with Jewish roots who lost his mother in the Holocaust.

51. See Krzywinska, "Transgression, Transformation and Titillation"; Owen, *Avant-Garde to New Wave*, chapter 6; Rush, "*Valerie and Her Week of Wonders*," 132–34.

52. Quoted in Owen, *Avant-Garde to New Wave*, 175.

53. Melville, "The Eccentric Carnival."

54. See Miller, "Serbian Movies"; Mondozilla, "Leptirica"; Lynch, "Halloween Edition: An Incomplete Guide to Yugoslav and Post-Yugoslav Horror." The film also merits a brief discussion in Obreht, "Twilight of the Vampires," 165–66. For background on the Black Wave in Yugoslav film history, see De Cuir, "The Yugoslav Black Wave."

55. Garza, "From Russia with Blood," 197.

56. Ibid., 197.

57. Lipovetsky and Etkind, "Salamander's Return," 18. (The piece is a dialogue between Lipovetsky and Etkind, with each speaker's contributions identified by name.) See, more generally, Etkind, Warped Mourning, especially chapter 10.

58. Quoted in Khapaeva, Nightmare, 235. Pelevin also suggests that Soviet vampires are much scarier than Western sorts: "We watch Bram Stoker's Dracula just to relax and unwind" (235).

59. Dolgopolov, "High Stakes," 50. See also Stojanova, "Mise-en-Scènes of the Impossible," 99–100.

60. Garza, "From Russia with Blood," 201.

61. Brînzeu, Corridors of Mirrors, 99.

62. Churchill, Mad Forest, in Plays.

63. See Ken Gelder's discussion of "post-Ceausescu vampire narratives" in Reading the Vampire, 6–8. Gelder, however, neglects Subspecies, so for that see Melton, The Vampire Gallery, 331 (although it is not, as Melton contends, the first of Romanian vampire film; Bloodlines [1989] beats the first of the Subspecies series by a couple of years).

64. Siani-Davies, The Romanian Revolution of 1989, 283.

65. Quoted in ibid., 283.

66. Hendershot, I Was a Cold War Monster, 44, and generally 44–50. For general background and plot summaries (but not much critical analysis) of the Hammer series, see Glut, Dracula Book, chapter 8.

67. Wilson, "Notes on a Radical Tradition," 53, 55.

68. Richard S. Primuth, although primarily interested in representations of homosexuality in the period's popular culture, catches some of this in noticing how the Hammer film agenda "is reminiscent of McCarthyism and the quest to force dissidents—along with homosexuals—out into the obliterating light of public exposure" ("Vampires Are Us," n.p.). Note too, in Horror of Dracula, that the vampire's crypt is located on Marx Strasse.

69. I borrow the term from Aleksandr Zinoviev's exquisite dystopian critique of the Soviet system, the novel Radiant Future (1978).

70. Crossman, The God That Failed, with contributions by well-known lapsed communists including Richard Wright, Andre Gidé, Stephen Spender, Ignazio Silone, Louis Fischer, and Arthur Koestler.

71. Polanski's own account of the dustup can be found in Roman by Polanski, 294–97. John Parker provides perhaps the bluntest summary of the outcome: "Godard told Polanski to fuck off back to Hollywood" (Polanski, 132).

Bibliography

Ain-Krupa, Julia. *Roman Polanski: A Life in Exile*. Santa Barbara, CA: Praeger, 2010.

Arendt, Hannah. *The Origins of Totalitarianism*. New York: Meridian Books, 1955.

Boutang, Pierre-André. "Polanski on Polanski." In Cronin, *Roman Polanski: Interviews*, 112–14.

Brînzeu, Pia. *Corridors of Mirrors: The Spirit of Europe in Contemporary British and Romanian Fiction*. Lanham, MD: University Press of America, 2000.

Butler, Ivan. *The Cinema of Roman Polanski*. London: A. Zwimmer, 1970.

Churchill, Caryl. *Mad Forest* (1990). In *Plays: 3*. London: Nick Hern, 1998.

Ciment, Michel, Michel Perez, and Roger Tailleur. "Interview with Roman Polanski" (1969). In *Roman Polanski: Interviews*, edited by Paul Cronin, 31–46. Jackson: University of Mississippi Press, 2005.

Cronin, Paul, ed. *Roman Polanski: Interviews*. Jackson: University of Mississippi Press, 2005.

Crossman, Richard, ed. *The God That Failed: A Confession*. New York: Harper, 1949.

Crowther, Bosley. "The Melting Pot Boils Over." *New York Times*, December 3, 1967.

———. "Screen: 'Fearless Vampire Killers': Baronet Shows Picture Its Author Disowned." *New York Times*, November 14, 1967.

Day, William Patrick. *Vampire Legends in Contemporary Culture: What Becomes a Legend Most*. Lexington: University of Kentucky Press, 2002.

de Baecque, Antoine, and Thierry Jousse. "Interview with Roman Polanski" (1992). In *Roman Polanski: Interviews*, edited by Paul Cronin, 146–53. Jackson: University of Mississippi Press, 2005.

De Cuir, Greg, Jr. "The Yugoslav Black Wave: The History and Politics of Polemical Cinema in the 1960s and 1970s in Yugoslavia." In *A Companion to Eastern European Cinemas*, edited by Aniko Imre, 403–24. New York: Wiley-Blackwell, 2012.

Delahaye, Michel, and Jean Narboni. "Interview with Roman Polanski" (1969). In *Roman Polanski: Interviews*, edited by Paul Cronin, 13–30. Jackson: University of Mississippi Press, 2005.

Dolgopolov, Guy. "High Stakes: The Vampire and the Double in Russian Cinema." In *Transnational Horror across Visual Media: Fragmented Bodies*, edited by Dian Och and Kirsten Strayer, 44–66. London: Routledge, 2014.

Ebert, Roger. "*The Fearless Vampire Killers, or Pardon Me but Your Teeth Are in My Neck/Dance of the Vampires*." *Chicago Sun-Times*, January 22, 1968.

Elm, Michael. "Screening Trauma: Reflections on Cultural Trauma and Cinematic Horror in Polanski's Film Oeuvre." In *The Horrors of Trauma in Cinema: Violence Void Visualization*, edited by Michael Elm, Kobi Kabalek, and Julia B. Köhne, 46–67. Newcastle-on-Tyne, UK: Cambridge Scholars, 2014.

Etkind, Alexander. *Warped Mourning: Stories of the Undead in the Land of the Unburied*. Stanford, CA: Stanford University Press, 2013.

The Fearless Vampire Killers (full title: *The Fearless Vampire Killers, or Pardon Me but Your Teeth Are in My Neck*; a.k.a. *Dance of the Vampires*). Directed by Roman Polanski. 1967.

Friedman, Lester D. *Hollywood's Image of the Jew*. New York: Frederick Ungar, 1982.

Gardenour, Brenda. "The Biology of Blood-Lust: Medieval Medicine, Theology, and the Vampire Jew." *Film & History* 41, no. 2 (2011): 51–63.

Garza, Tomas Jesús. "From Russia with Blood: Imagining the Vampire in Contemporary Russian Popular Culture." In *The Universal Vampire: Origins and Evolution of a Legend*, edited by Barbara Broadman and James E. Doan, 195–208. Lanham, MD: Fairleigh Dickenson Press/Rowman & Littlefield, 2013.

Gelder, Ken. *Reading the Vampire*. London: Routledge, 1994.

Giesbert, Franz-Olivier. "Roman's Novel" (1984). In *Roman Polanski: Interviews*, edited by Paul Cronin, 102–111. Jackson: University of Mississippi Press, 2005.

Glut, Donald F. *The Dracula Book*. Metuchen, NJ: Scarecrow Press, 1975.

Hallenbeck, Bruce G. *Comedy-Horror Films: A Chronological History, 1914–2008*. Jefferson, NC: McFarland, 2009.

Haltof, Marek. *Polish National Cinema*. Oxford: Berghahn Books, 2002.

Handler, Rachel, Keith Phipps, Genevieve Koski, Nathan Rabin, Tasha Robinson, and Scott Tobias. "The Cold Hard Stats of Vampire Comedies." *The Dissolve*, February 18, 2015. https://thedissolve.com/features/by-the-numbers/929-the-cold-hard-stats-of-vampire-comedies-1948-2012/.

Haudiquet, Philippe. "I Made This Film for Myself" (1966). In *Roman Polanski: Interviews*, edited by Paul Cronin, 8–12. Jackson: University of Mississippi Press, 2005.

Hawkins, John. *Cutting Edge: Art-Horror and the Horrific Avant-Garde*. St. Paul: University of Minnesota Press, 2000.

Hendershot, Cynthia. *I Was a Cold War Monster: Horror Film, Eroticism, and the Cold War Imagination*. Bowling Green, KY: Bowling Green State University Popular Press, 2001.

Holte, James Craig. *Dracula in the Dark: The Dracula Film Adaptations*. Westport, CT: Greenwood, 1997.

Hondrila, Iulius. "The Persistence of the Imago-Myth: Bram Stoker's *Dracula*." In *The Essence and the Margin: National Identities and Collective Memories in Contemporary European Culture*, edited by Lauren Rorato and Anna Saunders, 87–104. Amsterdam: Edelstein Rodopi, 2009.

Khapaeva, Dina. *Nightmare: From Literary Experiments to Cultural Project*. Leiden: Brill, 2013.

Krzywinska, Tanya. "Transgression, Transformation and Titillation: Jaromil Jireš's *Valerie a tý den divů* (*Valerie and Her Week of Wonders*, 1970)." *Kinoeye* 3, no. 9 (September 15, 2003). http://www.kinoeye.org/03/09/krzywinska09.php.

Lawton, Anna M. "The Double: A Dostoevskian Theme in Polanski." *Literature Film Quarterly* 9, no. 2 (1981): 122–25.

Leaming, Barbara. *Polanski: The Filmmaker as Voyeur: A Biography*. New York: Simon & Schuster, 1981.

Lenin, V. I. "Comrade Workers, Forward to the Last, Decisive Fight!" (written August 1918; published January 1925). In *Collected Works*, vol. 28, July 1918–March 1919, 54–58. Moscow: Progress Publishers, 1965.

Lipovetsky, Mark, and Alexander Etkind. "The Salamander's Return: The Soviet Catastrophe and the Post-Soviet Novel." *Russian Studies in Literature* 46, no. 4 (Fall 2010): 6–48.

Lynch, Lily. "Halloween Edition: An Incomplete Guide to Yugoslav and Post-Yugoslav Horror." *Bturn: Music, Culture and Style of the New Balkans*, October 31, 2012. http://bturn.com/9516/halloween-edition-serbian-horror.

Maillet, Dominique. "Roman Polanski" (1981). In *Roman Polanski: Interviews*, edited by Paul Cronin, 86–92. Jackson: University of Mississippi Press, 2005.

Mazierska, Ewa. *Roman Polanski: The Cinema of a Cultural Traveller*. London: I. B. Tauris, 2007.

Melton, J. Gordon. *The Vampire Gallery: A Who's Who of the Undead*. New York: Visible Ink, 1998.

Melville, David. "The Eccentric Carnival: *Valerie and Her Week of Wonders*." *kagablog*, January 12, 2012. http://kaganof.com/kagablog/?s=valerie+and+her+week+of+wonders.

Midding, Gerhard. "Being Merciless" (1990). In *Roman Polanski: Interviews*, edited by Paul Cronin, 139–45. Jackson: University of Mississippi Press, 2005.

Miller, Margaret. "Serbian Movies: Leptirica." *Blooming Twig*, March 6, 2015. http://www.bloomingtwig.com/leptirica/.

Mondozilla. "Leptirica (Yugoslavia 1973)." *Horrorpedia*, October 9, 2013. http://horrorpedia.com/2013/10/09/leptirica-the-butterfly/.

Morrison, James. *Roman Polanski*. Champaign: University of Illinois Press, 2007.

Muir, John Kenneth. *Horror Films of the 1970s*. 2 vols. Jefferson, NC: McFarland, 2002.

Obreht, Téa. "Twilight of the Vampires." In *Best American Travel Writing*, edited by Sloane Crosley, 159–77. New York: Houghton Mifflin, 2011.

Owen, Jonathan L. *Avant-Garde to New Wave: Czech Cinema, Surrealism and the Sixties*. Oxford: Berghahn Books, 2001.

Parker, John. *Polanski*. London: Victor Gollancz, 1993.

Paul, William. *Laughing Screaming: Modern Hollywood Horror and Comedy*. New York: Columbia University Press, 1994.

Polanski, Roman. *Roman by Polanski*. New York: William Morrow, 1984.

Popper, Karl. *Open Society and Its Enemies*. 2 vols. London: Routledge, 1945.

Prawer, S. S. *Caligari's Children: The Film as Tale of Terrors*. New York: Da Capo Press, 1990.

Primuth, Richard S. "Vampires Are Us." *Gay and Lesbian Review Worldwide*, February 11, 2014. http://www.glreview.org/article/vampires-are-us/.

Punter, David. "Bram Stoker's *Dracula*: Tradition, Technology, Modernity." In *Post/modern Dracula: From Victorian Themes to Postmodern Praxis*, edited by John S. Bak, 31–43. Newcastle on Tyne, UK: Cambridge Scholars, 2007.

Rocket, Will H. *Devouring Whirlwind: Terror and Transcendence in the Cinema of Cruelty*. Westport, CT: Greenwood Press, 1988.

Rush, Zachariah. "*Valerie and Her Week of Wonders*." In *Directory of World Cinema: East Europe*, edited by Adam Bingham, 132–34. Bristol, UK: Intellect, 2011.

Sandford, Christopher. *Polanski*. London: Palgrave Macmillan, 2008.

Siani-Davies, Peter. *The Romanian Revolution of 1989*. Ithaca, NY: Cornell University Press, 2005.

Stojanova, Christina. "Mise-en-Scènes of the Impossible: Soviet and Russian Horror Films." In *Alternative Europe: Eurotrash and Exploitation Cinema since 1945*, edited by Ernest Mathijs and Xavier Mendik, 90–105. London: Wallflower Press, 2004.

Stoker, Bram. *Dracula*. London: Constable & Robinson, 1897.

Toynbee, Arnold. *A Study of History*. 12 vols. Oxford: Oxford University Press, 1934–1961.

Wilson, Brian. "Notes on a Radical Tradition: Subversive Ideological Applications in the Hammer Horror Films." *CineAction* 72 (2007): 53–57.

CHAPTER TWO

⁓

Zany Zombies, Grinning Ghosts, Silly Scientists, and Nasty Nazis

Comedy-Horror at the Threshold of World War II

Christina M. Knopf

Every door may be shut but death's door.

—Chinese proverb

And every door might be Death's Door.

—Charles Dickens, *Bleak House*

Oh, I hate this part with the doors!

—Velma, *The Scooby-Doo Project*

The horror movies of the 1940s rarely made explicit reference to the war raging around the globe, lest the fantastic bloodletting, rotting corpses, body fragments, insanity, and grisly experimentation on screen come too close for comfort to their counterparts in reality. Nonetheless, wartime horror films inspired by the grim realities of Hitler's reign reflected the public's war-related angst, paranoia, and guilt, at the same time their forays into the supernatural offered audiences consolation in the possibility of life after death.[1] The addition of comic elements to these films did even more, giving form to audiences' fears and faith and providing contrast to crisis,[2] while allowing for both an emotional catharsis and an escape from tedium.[3] Despite government concerns about casting the war into the realm of fantasy,[4] the war repeatedly served as an off-screen MacGuffin that provided motivation for such supernatural features as the lycanthropy experiments of *The Mad Monster* (1942), the presence of a ghost in *Happy Land* (1943), and monsters in *The Return of the Vampire* (1943). The same was true of comedy-horror-war films, which often featured mad scientists working for the war effort, foreign spy rings "haunting" houses to discourage visitors, and the returned dead or undead as supernatural agents in the eternal war of good versus evil. A good point of entry for examining the particular strain of morale-boosting entertainment encouraged by these comedy-horror-war films, is, perhaps unexpectedly, through a door.

At first glance, the cinematic door serves a number of mundane purposes. In film, as in reality, doors coordinate movements, allowing actors and spectators to move from one scene to another.[5] They are also often used as comedic props. For example, the "Freleng Door Gag," also known as the "Scooby-Doo Doors" trope, is a standardized visual comedy sequence that involves a static shot down a hallway lined with doors through which characters randomly enter and exit in physically impossible sequences during a chase scene.[6] This opening and closing of doors through which individuals appear and disappear similarly provides comedic effect in the Joke Wall featured on *Rowan & Martin's Laugh-In* and the Gag Wall of *The Banana Splits*.[7] Doors are also key props in generating fear: the creaking door, the door that opens or closes by itself, and the door behind which danger lurks,[8] all heighten the tension felt by the films' characters and the viewing audience. The door, standing for house and home,[9] is also a symbol of the haunted house—a stock narrative figurative and major subtype of ghost stories because of the centrality of setting to the horror genre.[10]

When considering the more complex cultural work occurring at the intersections of doors/thresholds, comedy/humor, and horror/death, Mikhail Bakhtin's ideas are of particular relevance. Thomas Elsaesser and Malte Hagener explore the metaphor of the door in film theories premised upon the work of Bakhtin and others. They emphasize that, through movies, spectators enter a familiar, yet unfamiliar, world—crossing from one physical space to another and from one ontological or temporal realm to another, finding themselves at the threshold between this world and the world of the film, between reality and myth.[11]

Bakhtin's work was concerned with pivotal thresholds: "those between being and nonbeing, deathlessness and deathliness,"[12] falsehood and truth, sanity and insanity, present and future. His conception of the Carnival represents a threshold situation, or state of becoming, in which regular conventions are suspended or overturned creating a transitional space[13]—in much the same way that hauntings make the familiar unfamiliar in order to alter the perspective of past, present, and/or future.[14]

The Carnival is characterized by laughter and the temporary dismissal of a serious reality, and Bakhtin's conception of carnivalesque humor is not unlike subversive or gallows humor. The carnivalesque is a mockery of the serious, which often features bodily functions and the grotesque, just as gallows humor is a mockery of death, often highlighting bodily failures and death, disease, and disfigurement. Laughter is a social phenomenon and laughter in the context of gallows humor—the intentional and purposeful mockery of death that arises in relation to a dangerous situation—is a marker of strong morale and a spirit of resistance. Writing about humor in the literature of World War II, Joseph J. Waldmeir notes "the peculiar relationship between humor and pain."[15] It is a self-effacing laugh at one's own vulnerability, whether with lighthearted bravado, bitter irony, or poignant invectives—both a defiance of, and an escape from, grim realities—a way of distancing oneself from the weight of reality. Making fun of death and of the dying reassures us that we are alive, that we are in essence better, or at least better off, than the dead.[16]

The ability to laugh at such experiences requires distance from them.[17] Horror plots often provide that distance, giving substance to fears, and allowing audiences to face them. When combined with slapstick antics, puns, and zippy one-liners, those fears are diminished and audiences can literally laugh in the face of (un)death.

Knock, Knock. Who's There?

During war, society stands on a threshold between the past and future, freedom and tyranny, life and death. During World War II, the cinema played a prominent role in projecting and negotiating this liminal position.[18] Comedy-horror films such as those considered here—*King of the Zombies* (1941), *The Invisible Agent* (1942), *The Boogie Man Will Get You* (1942), *Ghosts on the Loose* (1943), *Revenge of the Zombies* (1943), and *The Canterville Ghost* (1944)—brought audiences to Death's door, opened it, and encouraged them to laugh in the face of death—and undeath. Characters are shown passing through or purposely standing at doors an average 78 times per movie, ranging from 52 times in *The Canterville Ghost* to 127 times in *Ghosts on the Loose*. Movement through doors is even more frequent if the count is extended to include implied exits and entrances through doors known to be just off-screen. More than simply a means for characters' movement or a rationale for their presence, the doors in these wartime films are pivotal to the realization of the films' comedic horrors. Taking spectators through the cinematic door and all the diegetic doors within, these films turn the horror genre on its head in order to make death less frightening and buoy up courage in the face of not only imagined horrors in the movie theater, but real ones in the overseas theaters of war.

King of the Zombies was the first comedy-horror film to acknowledge the war. The story begins when a plane crash-lands on an island somewhere in the Caribbean, following a mysterious radio broadcast. The American passenger, his black manservant, and the pilot take refuge in a doctor's mansion. After being convinced that zombies haunt the island, the marooned Americans discover a voodoo ritual being conducted in the cellar, where the doctor—a foreign spy—is trying to acquire naval intelligence from a captured U.S. admiral. Doors are central to much of the film's action, with characters moving through them at an average of once every two minutes. Moreover, the opening and closing of doors helps to create a tension-filled atmosphere. Scenes feature locked doors mysteriously opening, hidden doors that create the illusion of people walking through walls, and doorknobs that seem to rattle by themselves. Doors also provide a means of escape from such scary moments and are used to humorous advantage by the manservant, Jeff (Mantan Moreland), as he runs from one fright to another, back and forth through a series of doors.

The most deliberate and focused inclusion of the war in a comedy-horror film is in Universal's *The Invisible Agent*, part of the studio's Invisible Man franchise. After being threatened by German and Japanese agents (Cedric Hardwicke and Peter Lorre, respectively) who are looking for Dr. Jack Griffin's "invisible man" formula, Griffin's grandson, Frank (Jon Hall), uses the secret formula himself to spy on the Nazis with the help of an old carpenter and a beautiful double agent named Maria (Ilona Massey). Because Frank is invisible for most of the movie, the opening and closing of doors is a crucial means of following his activity. Suspense builds when his unseen hand rattles a locked door when he is trapped by the Nazis, and comedy ensues as he prevents the usually poised Maria from closing doors until he has passed through behind her. Door-related movement takes place, therefore, at a rate of just under once per minute.

Lorre appeared in another war-tinged horror-comedy later the same year: *The Boogie Man Will Get You*, a madcap, comic book–inspired twist on *Arsenic and Old Lace*. In this film, divorcee Winnie Layden ([Miss] Jeff Donnell) gets more than she bargains for when she purchases an old New England house to turn into a colonial inn. She agrees to let the previous owner,

Professor Billings (Boris Karloff), continue his scientific experiments in the basement. Unbeknownst to her, the professor is working on a process that he believes will turn an ordinary man into "the super Superman himself" and thus win the war—if only the test subjects, recruited from among travelling salesmen who call at the house, would just live through the procedure.

Further complicating these endeavors are Layden's drafted ex-husband, hired hands fixated on raising livestock, the ghost of Uncas from *The Last of the Mohicans*, snooping guests, vanishing corpses, and an Italian-fascist saboteur who has escaped from a prison in Canada with plans to blow up the nearby munitions dump. Door-related movements occur at an average of once every 45 seconds in the movie and include secret doors and hidden passages, corpses hidden behind doors, and the ever-creaking door to the professor's basement laboratory, but it is the unlucky "door-to-door peddlers" who agree to serve as Professor Billings's experimental subjects that give the door its greatest significance to the plot.

Ghosts on the Loose, featuring horror legend Bela Lugosi, was part of Monogram Pictures' East Side Kids franchise, about a gang of well-meaning juvenile delinquents trying to make it on their own—an early precursor for the teenage-sleuth genre of *Scooby-Doo*.[19] The Kids try to fix up a house for newlywed friends, but when they accidentally enter the "haunted" house next door, they encounter a ring of Nazi spies trying to frighten everyone away from a secret printing press being used to produce leaflets for the New Order. Movement and action involving doors happens at an average of once every 30 seconds in this movie, not surprising given that it is set between two houses, one of which has a number of secret rooms, hidden passages, and concealed panels. The villains of the story initially use these passageways as a means of frightening the Kids away from the house—which leads to sight gags and slapstick antics when the Kids encounter living paintings, moving pictures, doors that appear and disappear, and disembodied sounds. In a frantic chase scene through these same passageways the Kids prevail. One by one they knock out the enemy agents, who fall in a pile at the base of the house's front door.

The door takes on added meaning in this film. The comparative size of the two houses is repeatedly emphasized: The house being used for nefarious purposes is large and the front door is locked, whereas the house purchased by the new groom is small and the front door is open. This distinction suggests an evil of excess—a corruption of national identity and the American Dream—particularly during the leanness of the war years, which is emphasized by dialogue about Victory Gardens and coffee rationing. In a related scene, the war's influence on the American worldview is made pointedly, if

From the climactic chase scene of *Ghosts on the Loose,* demonstrating doors as a humor device. Characters repeatedly nearly miss one another while circling a revolving door disguised as a bookcase.

comically, at the film's end when a door with a "quarantine" sign closes on the heroes, because one of them has contracted German measles—manifested as tiny swastikas speckling his face.

Revenge of the Zombies, a quasi-sequel to *King of the Zombies*, was released the same year, becoming the first such film to assume that audiences already knew about zombies.[20] Scott Warrington, accompanied by his black manservant Jeff (Mantan Moreland) and a detective, visits Louisiana upon the mysterious death of his sister, Lila. After several strange encounters with moving corpses, they discover that her widower, Dr. von Altermann (John Carradine), has been perfecting a way to turn the dead, including Lila, into an unstoppable army of the living dead who will serve Hitler. Much of the film's action takes place through and near doors, which are used an average of more than once per minute. The most prominent are two adjacent doors in the basement—the one on the right leading to the pantry, and the one on the left to Dr. von Altermann's laboratory. The layout sets up a comedic interlude in which Jeff, searching for strawberry preserves, attempts to decipher which door is which. One of them—the laboratory door—figures prominently in the film's climax, first when the protagonists line up outside it and then break through it with an axe, and later when the doctor's zombie minions enter against his wishes, under the leadership of his dead wife, at the stroke of midnight. For a final touch, as the film ends, the camera pans over to the open door of the estate's crypt, slowly shutting by itself to reveal the words, "The End."

As the war approached its conclusion, *The Canterville Ghost* was released by MGM as a war-era retelling of an Oscar Wilde story. When, during the seventeenth century, Sir Simon de Canterville (Charles Laughton) flees a joust in fear and retreats to the family castle, his father traps him and curses Simon to haunt the estate until a descendant restores the family honor with an act of bravery. Hundreds of years later, his descendant Cuffy Williams (Robert Young), an American soldier stationed at the castle, hopes to free Simon from his curse by displaying courage against the Nazis. Doors are not as prominent in the action as they are in the other films, being used an average of only every one and three-quarters minutes, but one particular door is especially significant to the plot. When Simon hides from the joust, he does so in a curtained alcove until his father, goaded by Sir Simon's opponent, seals the door with stone and mortar, essentially burying Simon alive in "a tomb of thy own choosing." The heir to the castle, six-year-old Lady Jessica (Margaret O'Brien), is dreadfully afraid of the ghost and goes to great lengths to avoid the door to Sir Simon's quarters until Cuffy takes her inside to meet the less-than-fearsome, indeed rather pathetic, spirit. Doors are also important to Simon's appearances, initially

From the first haunting of *The Canterville Ghost*, demonstrating doors as a horror device. Simon's ghost enters the sleeping chamber of the American soldiers as mist through a keyhole.

occurring at midnight. He is able to pass through keyholes as mist and to walk through doors without opening them, an ability that leads Cuffy to inadvertently walk into a closed door, simultaneously establishing an eerie atmosphere and providing an amusing gag.

Death. Death Who?

If all these entrances and exits indicate characters' passages between physical spaces, they also bring audiences to the threshold of metaphorical spaces. Crypt doors, tomb doors, laboratory doors, and doors that move of their own volition all serve as gateways to some kind of other world or afterlife. The ominous creak, or uncanny movement, of a door represents the fear and uncertainty of facing death and ushers in the films' use of gallows humor. *King of the Zombies*, which was actually released seven months before the United States entered World War II, practically opens with death-related humor. After the plane crash, Jeff awakens beneath a headstone that reads, "Rest in Peace," and his boss tells the pilot they've landed in a "marble orchard." Using race-related humor that the Office of War Information (OWI) worked to avoid in later years,[21] Jeff remarks that he is "off color to be a ghost"—the first of several witty observations to reassure himself that he is still alive. Irreverence continues as zombies, which in this film are traditional hypnosis/voodoo victims, are described as "dead folks what's too lazy to lay down" and as "fugitives from the undertaker." In the sequel, *Revenge of the Zombies*, cheeky remarks about the (un)dead are replaced with more thoughtful observations about how the "dead can't hurt you," nor can they be hurt. Death humor, instead, stems from folkloric traditions and the war itself. The "corpse handed around" folklore motif[22] takes various forms in the movie, from Lila's post-death wanderings, to Jeff repeatedly encountering, and then losing, an unknown corpse—giving both the characters and the audience opportunities for amusing double-takes. A skeleton stored in the doctor's lab also gets moved from place to place and handled by three different people, prompting jokes about the "Meatless Tuesday" initiative of war rationing, the Neolithic skeleton "Charlie" excavated in the 1920s, and skeletons in the closet.

Death humor is more infrequent in the other films. It is particularly sparse in *The Invisible Agent*, though slapstick antics fill much of the movie, particularly at the expense of the Nazis—much to the chagrin of the OWI, which did not think a very real menace should be reduced to the equivalent of the Keystone Cops.[23] In fact, death is almost absent from the film—with the exception of enemy agents killing each other (or themselves) and coffin building by Griffin's contact in Germany. When

From the final shot of *Revenge of the Zombies*. The crypt door closes by itself, suggesting there may be more to the story beyond the movie's end.

Griffin gets to Berlin, he is directed to a carpenter of whom he is to ask for "a coffin, Empire style," signaling that he is a friendly agent. Later, the Japanese capture Frank and Maria and sneak them to the Japanese embassy in two of the coffins. *Ghosts on the Loose* takes a similar approach of staining life with death, when the bride's brother borrows a tuxedo from a mortuary to wear as best man at the wedding, and the Kids pick up a funeral arrangement, which had tumbled from the back of a delivery truck, to use as flowers for the wedding.

The Boogie Man Will Get You and *The Canterville Ghost* are perhaps the most philosophical on the subject of facing death with good humor. In *Boogie Man*, when asked about the ghost of Uncas haunting the house, Professor Billings replies, "The pros and cons of survival after death are so confusing I prefer not to think about it." Indeed, regarding the door-to-door peddlers who have apparently died in his experiments, he prefers the term "martyrized" to "murdered" and explains, "I killed no one. They're heroes—immortal martyrs of my grand experiment." While Karloff's naïvely adamant delivery makes these lines charming and amusing, the distinction is an important one during a time of war, when killing may be justified or sanctioned. Fortunately for Professor Billings, and even more fortunately for the salesmen, no one actually dies in the experiments; they prove to simply be in a state of suspended animation, from which they recover, heralding the discovery of "a method to preserve life." With the exception of a line about the ghost of Sir Simon "playing possum," and some melodramatic hauntings by Laughton, whose performance has been described as both funny and winsome,[24] death is not a laughing matter in *The Canterville Ghost*. Sir Simon's ghost is not happy for his prolonged presence in life and wishes, "If only I could rest, if only I could die. To be buried in the soft, brown earth in the garden beyond the pine woods, to have no yesterday and no tomorrow, to forget time, to be at peace." The spiritual undertones of this desire are reinforced at the film's end when, believing the curse upon him to be broken, Sir Simon calls out, "Father! Father!" so beseechingly that one expects him to inquire about being forsaken.

Death . . . Defying Courage

The underlying message of standing at Death's door and laughing is the value of courage in the face of fear. In wartime, fear is acceptable, but cowardice is not.[25] These movies each emphasize the importance of bravery in conquering adversity, effectively echoing Franklin Roosevelt's 1933 sentiment that "the only thing we have to fear is fear itself—nameless, unreasoning, unjustified terror which paralyzes needed efforts to convert retreat into advance."[26] In *King of the Zombies* and *Revenge of the Zombies*, it is the superstitious Jeff who first recognizes that things are not what they seem and who, despite his fear, perseveres to help defeat the Nazi agents both times. The East Side Kids exhibit both faintheartedness and false bravado throughout *Ghosts on the Loose*, but it is clear that even they have limited tolerance for cowardice. When one is too scared to investigate the strange house, Mugs, the group's leader, tells him: "Remind me when we get back to town to give you the Iron Cross for bravery—right over your skull." The Iron Cross was a Prussian decoration from the Napoleonic Wars, reinstituted by the Germans during World War I, making the reference an insult twice over. And, when they discover that the house is haunted not by ghosts but by spies, the term "spooks" continues to be used to refer to the villains.

Frank Griffin, as *The Invisible Agent*, insists on using his grandfather's invisibility formula himself to help the war effort, not wanting to put other soldiers or spies at risk of its insanity-inducing side effects. Professor Billings, alongside his compatriot Dr. Lorentz (Lorre), in *The Boogie Man Will Get You*, shows little fear of the armed Italian saboteur who breaks into the laboratory and continues his experiments on behalf of the war effort. But it is the reflective *Canterville Ghost* that most clearly demonstrates the value of courage. Cuffy tells Lady Jessica of the ghost, "You don't have to be afraid of him, you only think you do." Lady Jessica later repeats this sentiment back to him, when a parachute bomb threatens his platoon and he is paralyzed with fear, in a vernacular restatement of Roosevelt's first inaugural address.

Added to this is the revelation of these films that there would be no shortcuts to ending the war. As Lady Jessica tells Cuffy in *The Canterville Ghost*, "You nearly always have to wait for anything you want very much." The characters in the other movies gain this insight through failure: failure to create a superman to win the war, the enemy's failure to use voodoo to extract war secrets, failure to acquire and use an invisibility formula, failure to destroy a munitions dump, failure to spread Nazi propaganda in the United States, and failure to create an army of the undead. In the midst of war, failure is always possible; the message here is that, though it is preferable for one's enemy, it does not necessarily mean defeat.

Conclusion

The audience is placed in a liminal position throughout these films; pivotal moments happen between night and day, and at the stroke of midnight—the Witching Hour, when zombies rise and ghosts appear. Characters hover somewhere between life and death: trapped in suspended animation (*The Boogie Man Will Get You*) or the living death of hypnosis (*King of the Zombies*), or existing as reanimated corpses (*Revenge of the Zombies*), restless ghosts (*The Canterville Ghost*), the ghostlike living created by invisibility serums (*The Invisible Agent*), or those "scared to death" when their senses are questioned (*Ghosts on the Loose*). The movement of these characters, and therefore the directed movement of the audience's attention, happens between spaces—through doors that uncannily open and close, unlock and lock, appear and disappear, causing characters to not only be frightened but also to look silly in their fright. The in-between-ness is what gives the movies their spooky humor and what may have given audiences an acceptable outlet to laugh at death, the most disturbing reality of war. Comedy-horror films of the war era provided audiences with a doorway into a world that was simultaneously the same as and different from everyday reality—one filled with war and death, but also with fantastic possibilities. Thresholds allow for the familiar to be made unfamiliar—they provide distance from situations that permit fears to be faced and humor to be discovered. Though any door may be Death's door, doors go both ways, so what appears to be the end might be only the beginning.

Notes

1. Doherty, *Projections of War*; Corupe, "Hypodermic Needles and Evil Twins"; DeGiglio-Bellemare, "Val Lewton, Mr. Gross, and the Grand Guignol"; Ellbé, "Making Visible the Sonic Threat"; Skal, *Monster Show*.
2. Doherty, *Projections of War*.
3. Schneider, "Monsters as (Uncanny) Metaphors."
4. Worland, "OWI Meets the Monsters."
5. Cole, "Wavering between Two Worlds"; Stephens, "Why Are There So Many Doors in the Movies?"
6. Costello, "F"; "Scooby-Dooby Doors."
7. Bianculli, *Dangerously Funny*, 235.
8. For example, see discussion in Toop, "Chair Creaks but No One Sits There."
9. Haight, *The Symbolism of the House Door*.
10. Bailey, *American Nightmares*; Pilar Blanco, *Ghost-Watching American Modernity*; Ruffles, *Ghost Images*; Wolfreys, *Victorian Hauntings*.
11. Elsaesser and Hagener, *Film Theory*.
12. Beasley-Murray, "Reticence and the Fuzziness of Thresholds," 426.
13. Bakhtin, *Problems of Dostoevsky's Poetics*; Collington, "The Chronotope."
14. Gordon, *Ghostly Matters*.
15. Waldmeir, "What's Funny about That?" 15.
16. Obrdlik, "Gallows Humor"; Thorson, "Did You Ever See a Hearse Go By?"; Morreall, *Taking Laughter Seriously*; Sanders, *Sudden Glory*.
17. Gordon, *Ghostly Matters*.
18. Doherty, *Projections of War*.
19. Janisse, "The Child Witness."
20. Dendle, *The Zombie Movie Encyclopedia*.
21. Worland, "OWI Meets the Monsters."
22. For more, see Koven, "Traditional Narrative, Popular Aesthetics."
23. Worland, "OWI Meets the Monsters."
24. Hallenbeck, *Comedy-Horror Films*.
25. Collins, *Violence*; Dixon, *On the Psychology of Military Incompetence*.
26. Roosevelt, "Inaugural Address."

Bibliography

Bailey, Dale. *American Nightmares: The Haunted House Formula in American Popular Fiction*. Madison: University of Wisconsin Press, 1999. Kindle edition.

Bakhtin, Mikhail. *Problems of Dostoevsky's Poetics*. Edited and translated by Caryl Emerson. Minneapolis: University of Minnesota Press, 1984.

———. *Rabelais and His World*. 1968. Translated by Helene Iswolsky. Bloomington: Indiana University Press, 1984.

Beasley-Murray, Tim. "Reticence and the Fuzziness of Thresholds." *Common Knowledge* 19, no. 3 (2013): 424–45.

Bianculli, David. *Dangerously Funny: The Uncensored Story of "The Smothers Brothers Comedy Hour."* New York: Touchstone, 2009.

Cole, Georgina. "'Wavering between Two Worlds': The Doorway in Seventeenth-Century Dutch Genre Painting." *Philament* 9 (2006): 18–37.

Collington, Tara. "The Chronotope and the Study of Literary Adaptation: The Case of *Robinson Crusoe*." In *Bakhtin's Theory of the Literary Chronotope: Reflections, Applications, Perspectives*, edited by Nele Bemong, Pieter Borghart, Michel De Dobbeleer, Kirstoffel Demoen, Koen De Temmerman, and Bart Keunen, 179–94. Gent: Academic Press, 2010.

Collins, Randall. *Violence: A Micro-sociological Theory*. Princeton, NJ: Princeton University Press, 2009. Kindle edition.

Corupe, Paul. "Hypodermic Needles and Evil Twins: The Poverty Row Wartime Horrors of Sam Newfield." In *Recovering 1940s Horror Cinema: Traces of a Lost Decade*, edited by Mario DeGiglio-Bellemare, Charlie Ellbé, and Kristopher Woofter, 261–74. Lanham, MD: Lexington Books, 2015.

Costello, E. O. "F." *Warner Brothers Cartoon Companion*, 1996–1998. http://www.warnercompanion.com/eowbcc-f.html.

DeGiglio-Bellemare, Mario. "Val Lewton, Mr. Gross, and the Grand Guignol: Re-Staging the Corpse in *The Body Snatcher*." In *Recovering 1940s Horror Cinema: Traces of a Lost Decade*, edited by Mario DeGiglio-Bellemare, Charlie Ellbé, and Kristopher Woofter, 67–86. Lanham, MD: Lexington Books, 2015.

Dendle, Peter. *The Zombie Movie Encyclopedia*. Jefferson, NC: McFarland, 2001.

Dixon, Norman F. *On the Psychology of Military Incompetence*. Sydney: Random House, 2011. Kindle edition.

Doherty, Thomas. *Projections of War: Hollywood, American Culture, and World War II*. New York: Columbia University Press, 1993.

Ellbé, Charlie. "Making Visible the Sonic Threat: *The Inner Sanctum Mysteries* Radio Series and Its Universal Studios Film Adaptations." In *Recovering 1940s Horror Cinema: Traces of a Lost Decade*, edited by Mario DeGiglio-Bellemare, Charlie Ellbé, and Kristopher Woofter, 129–46. Lanham, MD: Lexington Books, 2015.

Elsaesser, Thomas, and Malte Hagener. *Film Theory: An Introduction through the Senses*. New York: Routledge, 2010. Kindle edition.

Gordon, Avery F. *Ghostly Matters: Haunting and the Sociological Imagination*. Minneapolis: University of Minnesota Press, 2008. Kindle edition.

Haight, Elizabeth Hazelton. *The Symbolism of the House Door in Classical Poetry*. New York: Longmans, 1950.

Hallenbeck, Bruce G. *Comedy-Horror Films: A Chronological History, 1914–2008*. Jefferson, NC: McFarland, 2009.

Janisse, Kier-La. "The Child Witness: Peril and Empowerment in 1940s Horror from The East Side Kids to *The Window*." In *Recovering 1940s Horror Cinema: Traces of* a Lost Decade, edited by Mario DeGiglio-Bellemare, Charlie Ellbé, and Kristopher Woofter, 109–28. Lanham, MD: Lexington Books, 2015.

Koven, Mikel J. "Traditional Narrative, Popular Aesthetics, Weekend at Bernie's, and Vernacular Cinema." In Of Corpse: Death and Humor in Folklore and Popular Culture, edited by Peter Narváez, 294–310. Logan: Utah State University Press, 2003.

Morreall, John. Taking Laughter Seriously. Albany: State University of New York Press, 1983.

Obrdlik, Antonin J. "'Gallows Humor': A Sociological Phenomenon." American Journal of Sociology 47, no. 5 (1942): 709–16.

Pilar Blanco, María del. Ghost-Watching American Modernity: Haunting, Landscape, and the Hemispheric Imagination. New York: Fordham University Press, 2012.

Roosevelt, Franklin D. "Inaugural Address, March 4, 1933." In The Public Papers of Franklin D. Roosevelt, Volume Two: The Year of Crisis, 1933, edited by Samuel Rosenman, 11–16. New York: Random House, 1938.

Ruffles, Tom. Ghost Images: Cinema of the Afterlife. Jefferson, NC: McFarland, 2004.

Sanders, Barry. Sudden Glory: Laughter as Subversive History. Boston: Beacon Press, 1995.

Schneider, Steven. "Monsters as (Uncanny) Metaphors: Freud, Lakoff, and the Representation of Monstrosity in Cinematic Horror." Other Voices 1, no. 3 (1999): n.p. http://www.othervoices.org/1.3/sschneider/monsters.php.

"Scooby-Dooby Doors." TV Tropes, June 14, 2007. http://tvtropes.org/pmwiki/pm wiki.php/Main/ScoobyDoobyDoors.

Skal, David J. The Monster Show: A Cultural History of Horror. New York: Faber & Faber, 1993.

Stephens, Mitchell. "Why Are There So Many Doors in the Movies?" Columbia Journalism Review, March/April (2000): 58–59.

Thorson, James A. "Did You Ever See a Hearse Go By? Some Thoughts on Gallows Humor." Journal of American Culture 16, no. 2 (1993): 17–24.

Toop, David. "Chair Creaks, but No One Sits There." In The Spectralities Reader: Ghosts and Haunting in Contemporary Cultural Theory, edited by María del Pilar Blanco and Esther Peeren, chapter 17. London: Bloomsbury, 2013. Kindle edition.

Waldmeir, Joseph J. "What's Funny about That? Humor in the Literature of the Second World War." Journal of American Culture 12, no. 3 (1989): 11–18.

Wolfreys, Julian. Victorian Hauntings: Spectrality, Gothic, the Uncanny and Literature. New York: Palgrave, 2002.

Worland, Rick. "OWI Meets the Monsters: Hollywood Horror Films and War Propaganda, 1942 to 1945." Cinema Journal 37, no. 1 (1997): 47–65.

CHAPTER THREE

~

"The Limeys Are Coming, Barbara, and They're Laughing!"

The Art of the Romeroesque in Shaun of the Dead *and* Dead Set

Steven Webley

You can't make cult films intentionally, it doesn't work.

—Ben Barenholtz, *Midnight Movies*

In 1967, a 27-year-old college dropout named George A. Romero, together with a small group of friends, decided to make *Night of the Living Dead* (1968). The result was a film with a style that parodied *cinéma vérité*—one that would go on to become a cult classic and the most influential of a small cabal of low-budget 1970s cult movies that penetrated the dark underside of the American Dream.[1] Romero's genius was not just to reinvent the zombie by bringing the classic Haitian zombie *drone* together with the taboo of cannibalism, but also to politicize it, reinvigorating horror as social critique.[2]

Prior to Romero's re-visioning, horror movies were considered adolescent entertainment, portraying conscious fears of science run amok, alien invasion, nuclear holocaust, and communism. Many of the films, however, relied on a consistent motif—monstrous Otherness that was so huge and so terrifying it was unable to occupy the same conceptual and physical space on screen as its human victims.[3] Romero's zombie brought monster and human together in a singular cadaverous cannibalistic subject, evoking the duality of human nature and mobilizing audiences' repressed anxieties about late-twentieth-century society.[4] The new zombies were perfect uncanny doppelgängers,[5] mirroring modernity's repressed anxiety regarding human mortality.[6] Contextualized by the failed libertarian goals of Romero's countercultural generation, his uncanny undead also began cannibalizing narrative and thematic conventions.[7]

Night of the Living Dead was shockingly original, destabilizing both filmmaking and film audiences. The new "Romeroesque" style of horror it launched—fully consolidated in *Dawn of the Dead* (1978) and *Day of the Dead* (1985)—exhibited postmodern ironic sensibilities and established a new constellation of tropes: literary naturalism, grotesque realism, and a new-age American gothic. It fluctuated between the cold, rigid pessimism of myth and tragedy on one hand, and the adventurous and animistic optimism of folklore and fairy tales on the other.[8] The interplay between these two extremes dissolved any notion of the narrative closure to which audiences had become accustomed. The human characters struggling to survive in *Night* are pitiable victims whose fates are defined by the collapse of life's expected norms. The film ends, for the characters, either in the rigid finitude of death or in the infinitude of undeath—the latter darkly mirroring the lack of narrative closure felt by audiences. Normality disappears in a downward spiral symptomatic of an inability to work through trauma, into a "nonredemptive" narrative of "gluey bottomless horror."[9]

The second film of Romero's Cold War "Dead Trilogy," *Dawn of the Dead*, mixed comic-book fantasy, violence, and parody with horror, pathos, fable, and ridicule.[10] *Dawn*, like *Night*, became a cult classic, and remains the most fondly remembered of Romero's oeuvre. Set in a shopping mall, where zombies and humans are lured by the promise of a paradise that is both temple and fortress,[11] it is narratively and thematically different from *Night*. *Dawn*'s slapstick custard-pie-throwing bikers and bumbling consumer zombies, along with the final escape of two remaining protagonists, brought a subtle hint of redemptive closure to the fledgling genre. *Day of the Dead* parodied the Cold War's revitalized paranoia, ideological investment in Mutual Assured Destruction, and dysfunctional state institutions in a narrative that vacillated between the ridiculous, the abject, and the sublime.[12] By 1985 Romero's zombies had evolved, appropriating a constellation of affects: sympathy, plaintiveness, regret, avarice, anxiety, desire, and most significantly, humor. Like their human opponents, they flock to occupy the remaining vestiges of a defunct civilization. But, while hubris and desire lead the human survivors to implode in conflict, the zombies are apparently able to live quite peacefully in the absence of human contact.[13]

Romero's passion for horror comics led him to infuse self-parody, ridicule, and comedy into *Dawn* and *Day*, creating the basis for future social

A mall zombie takes a pie in the face in *Dawn of the Dead.*

satires.[14] The Romeroesque inscribed itself into cinematic mainstream as a type of postmodern traumatic narrative that, construed from a post-traumatic perspective, resists any form of closure and harmonization. Within the Romeroesque we are compelled to gleefully repeat the collective trauma that haunts us. Audiences are caught in an endless cycle of narrative irresolution—the "end" either entails the complete destruction of the survivors' humanity or the false hope of redemption that is created as survivors escape into a twilight we know cannot last.[15]

After a two-decade hiatus that saw the collapse of communism, the end of the Cold War, and the beginning of the War on Terror, Romero returned, in 2004, to the massively popular genre of post-apocalyptic satire that he had single-handedly crafted decades before.[16] It was a genre landscape populated by innumerable Romero aficionados, all paying homage to his visual style, thematic content, and parodic approach. During Romero's two-decade absence, the inherently self-referential essence of Romeroesque horror fostered a distinct zombie-comedy subgenre. Today, zom-coms mirthfully question the motives, efficacy, and durability of state, corporate, media, and social institutions. From shopping malls to social media, Romero's zombies, mobilized by an occult and emblematic revolutionary ethic, continue to captivate and amuse on a global scale.[17] No cultural product seems safe from cannibalism by the Romeroesque, including zom-coms made for British TV and cinema. Edgar Wright's *Shaun of the Dead* (2004) uses Romero's trademark blend of mythic tragedy and fantasy adventure to trace the title character's journey—by way of a zombie outbreak—from an unsatisfying present to the false dawn of a (seemingly) better future. Charlie Brooker's TV miniseries *Dead Set* (2008), on the other hand, mixes the downward narrative spiral of Romero's *Night* with the politicized zombies of *Dawn* and *Day* in a savage dissection of reality-TV conventions and media-age consumerism. The gulf between Wright's lighthearted gruesomeness and Brooker's pitch-black satire suggests the flexibility of Romeroesque zombies as a tool for comic social commentary.[18]

> Shaun of the Dead *was possibly my favorite zombie film that wasn't made by me!*
>
> —George A. Romero, in *Doc of the Dead*

Set in Finsbury Park, London, *Shaun* follows the daily travails of a 29-year-old TV salesman and electronics shop employee as he tries to exert some control over his life and relationships. Questioning his lot in life, Shaun is encouraged by his housemate and sidekick Ed not to ruminate over things, but to spend his time playing video games, smoking, and drinking in their local pub, the Winchester Tavern. While this state of affairs suits Ed, Shaun is aware that to everyone else in his life he appears as a "nobody," in a nobody job, earning nobody money. Troubled by his awareness of his own under-

They're British, they're all messed up—Saturday morning in Finsbury Park, London. The opening credits of *Shaun of the Dead.*

achievement and societal displacement, he is made to feel insecure by junior staff at work and hopelessly inadequate by his mother, stepfather, and second housemate, the relentlessly sober Pete. Shaun is also all too aware that he has to change if he is to keep his girlfriend, Liz, who is eager for a more secure and rewarding relationship.

The opening sequence introduces Shaun and his gang of friends (minus Pete) who at "last orders" are drinking at the Winchester (again), questioning Shaun's unhealthy attachment to Ed, and analyzing Shaun's relationship with his mother and Liz. Liz's friend Dave, a university lecturer, asks, "Are you ashamed by your mom, Shaun?" This comes seconds after Liz remarks that she sounds like Shaun's mother, nagging him to change and to do more exciting things than drinking with Ed.

Shaun and Ed seem inseparable, to the point that Shaun refers to himself and Ed collectively.[19] Ed never seems to leave the downstairs couch, smoking pot and playing video games—something Shaun would very much like to do. We see him moan and lurch, zombie-like, into Ed's domain and begin to play, only to be reminded by Ed that he has work that morning.[20] Shaun exists in limbo within his own home, spending his life in diplomatic negotiations between Ed and the sober-but-volatile Pete. Pete is either upstairs or at work and only appears downstairs to angrily remonstrate with Shaun, and threaten Ed. He is eager to blame Shaun for Ed's behavior: "The front door is open *again* . . . I can't live like this . . . you want to live like an animal go and live in the shed you thick fuck . . . *sort your fucking life out.*" Shaun unsuccessfully pleads with Ed to humor Pete and pull his weight around the house, to which Ed responds, "I ain't doing nuffin' for that prick."

Shaun's world soon goes even further awry, however, and after a long night at the Winchester he finds himself single, hung over, and surrounded by the shambling hordes of the zombie apocalypse that has just begun. Freed from the disapproval of Pete—who was bitten the night before and is now zombified—he seizes the moment, steals Pete's car, and embarks with Ed on a fantasy adventure across London. Taking cricket bat in hand, he resolves to collect his mother, round up Liz and her friends, and go to the Winchester for a nice cold pint until everything blows over.

Ed remains true to himself throughout the adventure, remonstrating with Shaun to let Liz go—"Fuck her . . . you got your pint, you got your pig-snacks, what more do you want?"—and directing vulgar sexual innuendos toward Shaun's mother. Ed's *pièce de résistance* is to impersonate film star Clyde the Orangutan and suggest that tomorrow they keep on drinking. Despite his boorishness, however, Ed demonstrates a social savvy that has a direct influence on both Shaun and the world they live in. His superficial, vulgar readings of people and situations are so often correct that he seems to be surreptitiously directing the events of the film. By the climax, however, Shaun has not only survived the zombie apocalypse but gained the confidence to be (modestly) independent of his friend. Having killed the zombified versions of both his mother and Pete, and made peace with his now-zombified stepfather (before leaving him locked in his prized Jaguar), he has resolved his neuroses and freed himself of those who fueled them. Having learned to regulate his relationship with the zombified (and thus more pliant) Ed, he is now free to have a successful romance with Liz—the only one who, in the end, he was able to save.

> *You would fuck a fisherman's dog if there was a Heat cover in it.*
>
> —Patrick the producer, *Dead Set*

The comic possibilities of a zombie apocalypse were also apparent to British satirist Charlie Brooker, whose television shows have become known for their acerbic wit and surreal and profane pessimism. His *Weekly Wipe* series is well known for its homages to Romero,[21] and Brooker's fans welcomed his decision to make a satirical zombie miniseries based on and filmed on the set of the *Big Brother* reality TV show. *Big Brother*, in which a group of contestants are confined to a house under 24-hour surveillance and vote to evict one of their number at the end of each episode, was ready-made for a Romeroesque satire. Brooker took full advantage, imagining the show unfolding as a zombie apocalypse raged outside the house. He put his trademark cynicism into overdrive in order to comment on a format he had already pilloried as uncouth. The result, titled *Dead Set*, was a behind-the-scenes comedic *vérité* that portrayed reality TV as a shockingly obscene form of entertainment.[22]

Along with the actors playing the *Big Brother* houseguests and production crew, *Dead Set* features stars from past seasons of *Big Brother* in cameo roles, along with TV personalities such as Davina McCall, host of the British edition of *Big Brother*. The (fictional) *Big Brother* housemates represent a cross-section of young British society, all of whom are filmed constantly while subjected to humiliation and the threat of possible death-by-eviction, in the hope they will behave in a suitably indecorous way. The production crew is a collection of runners and gofers—sycophantic, browbeaten, and neurotic—under the dominion of producer Patrick Goad, who berates contestants, crew, and audience alike and treats them all like contemptible idiots. Goad spouts a continual diatribe of obscenities and vulgar commands. He has pet names for each contestant, such as "fucking-spastic" or "sour-flaps," and refers to his staff as "minions." It soon becomes clear that Goad recognizes the show's unacknowledged, grotesque appeal to viewers and does everything in his power to cater to it.

Dead Set begins on a Big Brother eviction night as the zombie apocalypse is breaking out. As waves of zombies swamp Britain, the screams from outside the house are interpreted by crew and cast alike as screams of adulation and excitement from the live audience. Brooker's undead are not Romero's shambling, comedic type, but the snarling sprinting variety popularized by post-9/11 films like 28 Days Later. Civil disorder spreads across Britain, threatening Big Brother's live prime-time broadcast and prompting the producer, Patrick, to remark: "One fucking estate on fire in Newcastle and a couple policemen killed in Liverpool . . . Stockwell, Cardiff, Portsmouth all bolloxed. If this gets much worse we are going to get bumped in favor of a news update! Why do people riot anyway? It's not the '80s, they've got distractions. They should stay in and watch telly."

The opening conversation between two of the housemates, Pippa and Joplin, sets the tone and establishes Brooker's own anxiety as an independent journalist and satirist who has become a mainstream TV personality. Joplin—the oldest and most insightful of the housemates, who is castigated by fellow housemates and crew as "boring Gollum"—ruminates on the nature and purpose of reality TV as being a "big fat arrow that points away from the problem." He then informs Pippa, a fellow housemate who is painting her toenails, that he decided to participate in the show to engage with reality TV to change it from within. Pippa replies to this self-revelation by asking, "Do toes have bones in them?"

As the apocalypse unfolds, crew runner Kelly Povell emerges as the hero. Determined to save herself and as many housemates as she can, she embarks on a mission to locate Riq Rahman, her boyfriend and fellow runner. Viewers, meanwhile, watch the darkly comic spectacle that ensues as the zombie threat worsens. The housemates express disbelief at their situation, convinced that the apocalypse is a publicity stunt, while Patrick sacrifices those around him in order to stay alive—even pushing a wheelchair-bound staff member into an oncoming zombie so he can hide in the disabled toilet stall. Viewers are left with the horrifying realization that, if Britain survives, it will be repopulated by offspring of the cast and remaining crew of Big Brother.

Dead Set ends in a self-referential feedback loop as Kelly, in a futile attempt to rescue the last remaining unbitten housemate, bursts forth from the safety of the Diary Room into a mass of undead. The viewer is left with the closing shots of a zombified Kelly staring into the live-feed cameras of

"Break with the group and the group breaks you!" Patrick is tied up in the toilet, awaiting execution by the contestants he berates.

Big Brother, her image televised and projected onto the multiple screens in an electronics shop in a shopping mall, where it is stared at myopically by a now-docile and victorious throng of the undead.

> *I think, that the feeling of something uncanny is directly attached to the figure of the Sand-Man, that is, to the idea of being robbed of one's eyes. . . . Uncertainty whether an object is living or inanimate is quite irrelevant in connection with this other, more striking instance of uncanniness.*
>
> —Sigmund Freud, *The Uncanny*

Cinema and psychoanalysis were born of the same era, and by the early half of the twentieth century psychoanalysis had a symbiotic relationship with films and filmmaking in the United States. Freud's mapping of the self—superego, ego, id—along with psychoanalysis's focus on jokes, dreams, slips of the tongue, humor, vulgarity, and the uncanny in popular and folkloric narratives was readily embraced by bohemians and intellectuals as a progressive way of understanding the world.[23] In the genre of horror, the concept of the uncanny was readily utilized; however for Freud, the uncanny was a problematic concept that coalesced with three other psychic phenomena—dreams, slips of the tongue, and humor—into what he considered to be a road into the unconscious. Freud's term for the concept, *unheimlich*, is a negation of the German word *heimlich* (meaning homely, cozy, intimate, secure) and thus suggests its opposite. *Heimlich* also, however, encompasses the concepts of being hidden away, secretive, and concealed from the outside world—by extension then, what is hidden may be threatening, fearful, occult, dismal, or ghastly—that is, uncanny.[24] This is the point at which the *unheimlich* creates anxiety—the point of negation.[25] What is homely and restful can, in a sublime instant, reveal itself to be uncanny, creating a moment of disjuncture that separates comedy and horror, laughter and nightmare, and what is ridiculously funny from what is abjectly terrifying.[26] Freud obsessed over the uncanny, as it signified a central "knot" of universal human experience, a dimension that haunts humanity in close unity with societal change and insecurity.[27]

By the 1960s, mainstream U.S. filmmaking was turning its back on psychoanalysis and losing sight of a powerful dimension of Freudian theory: its intimate relationship with the down-to-earth, comical worldview of Yiddish humor.[28] Brimming over with burlesque, irony, satire, and farce, Yiddish humor has, in more contemporary times, been understood as deriving its characteristics from a complex constellation of ethnic identity, socioeconomics, and cultural history, but when Freud first formulated his theories of humor, prevailing cultural perceptions of Jewish self-deprecation had a strong influence on his notions. For Freud, Yiddish humor embodied self-disparagement—a comic strategy frequently documented in many culturally subordinate minority groups—deploying humor against members of their own group rather than risk the consequences of focusing humor on the group in power. In *Jokes and Their Relation to the Unconscious* (1905), Freud interpreted Yiddish humor as a playful subversion of the pretentions of the powerful, the wealthy, and the elite,[29] and symptomatic of the lure of prohibition, which drives desire for what is censured. Laughter, in this view, is an explosive *yarp* of bodily pleasure in nonsensical defiance of the economics of repression.[30] Informed by popular perceptions that linked Jewish humor to "dirty jokes," Freud posited that such humor creates a surge of psychological energy that would ordinarily be expended in censoring childish associations between words and meanings.[31] Freud located Jewish jokes and humor within the realm of folk wisdom, arguing that they communicate a shared pleasure in instinctual life's ingenuity in defending itself from stifling self-reproach.[32] Jewish humor, he argued, drew on generations of cultural experience as a subordinate people, demonstrating a comic insight into human vanity and social inequity.[33] "Incidentally, I do not know," Freud wrote, "whether there are many other instances of a people making fun to such a degree of its own character."[34]

Freud's observations on the functioning of Jewish humor underpinned his reading of folkloric fables as an instinctive and unconscious form of wish fulfillment that had the ability to lift the mask of social relations, exposing hypocrisy and the exercise of power and discipline. Wealth, abundance, and gratitude were, for the underclass, worthy of laughter when they massaged the vanity of the elites.[35] Freud's writings on humor abound with popular Jewish caricatures—opportunistic matchmakers, eager to attest to the problems in others' relationships; stubborn bachelors; intellectual down-and-outs; lucky-but-egotistical millionaires; and the faithful gullible underclass—whose conscious actions lead to unintended discoveries about unconscious everyday social relations.[36]

> *Can I get any of you cunts a drink?*
>
> —Ed's opening line, *Shaun of the Dead*

Freud's theories of psychoanalysis highlight the power of humor to communicate critical perspectives on cultural mechanics, while expressing solidarity with the underclass.[37] Jewish witticisms commonly begin with a thinly veiled statement of aggression. This aggression is often sudden and shocking, but can be quickly turned inward toward the subject himself in such a way that the identities of aggressor and victim, and the boundaries between them, are subverted and confused.[38] The result is a playful, if not wholly authentic, subversion of agitator/victim roles. The real aim of this display of aggression turned self-criticism is an unconscious desire to win the approval of the interlocutor—a wish to fully regain one's dignity.[39]

Writing during the social upheavals of the 1950s and 1960s, British anthropologist Geoffrey Gorer expressed concern that as British social rituals were progressively displaced by modernity, the traditional British fear of expressing emotions and the mechanics of class consciousness would become the dominant psychic motif of Britishness.[40] Today, the notion that we exist in a post-ideological era in which our major redemptive ideological fantasies have ceased to function is built on the idea that those fantasies have been replaced by a crippling cynicism. That cynicism, we tell ourselves, is the elementary gesture of a new form of ideology: one that we call "post-ideological," on the strength of a false belief that we can separate ourselves from, exist outside of, and objectively comment on, ideology itself.[41] Both *Shaun* and *Dead Set* offer a redoubling of Romero's self-parodying style and ethic, and both utilize the Romeroesque to focus on the social, financial, and familial conditions and mores of a new generation of British "twenty-somethings," who are apparently ideologically unaware.

It is fitting that British contemporary filmmakers redoubled the parody of the Romeroesque to produce new-age comic anti-heroes for a post-ideological zombie apocalypse. In a new age, where cynicism has become the standard riposte of hegemony as it appropriates for itself the very satirical and sarcastic elements traditionally used to undermine its narratives of power, laughter may indeed be the safest, if not only, respite for a new generation of the disillusioned. For Wright and Brooker, the end of the Cold War and the victory of capitalism seem to have changed nothing—even if we follow Romero's lead in keeping an ironic distance from incessant injunctions to consume, we still keep doing so. For us the uncanny doppelgänger is not the zombie (returned from the grave to trouble our ideas about the boundaries of life and death), but repressed ideology (returned from the past to trouble our belief that we exist in a post-ideological age). Post-ideology is a new zombie for a new age, a fetishistic ideology that excels in its denial of itself.

The traditional agents of Jewish humor, the focal points of our laughter, are now well-accepted archetypes. The *nebbish schlemiel*—the self-critical loser, the awkward innocent—carries within a sense of failure and reflects an ambivalent unity of pride and cynicism.[42] These qualities ultimately shape the character's sense of identity as the subject of a larger imposing Otherness, the power of which is so compelling that our only recourse is to laugh.[43]

Freudian influences are evident in both the characters and the spaces of *Shaun*. Shaun is ego, trying to rationalize and balance the injunctions of Pete, the superego, and the vulgar desires of the id, Ed. Pete is either at work, asleep, or in the shower preparing for work; Ed resides downstairs in perpetual relaxation and enjoyment; and Shaun hovers anxiously betwixt them. Before the zombie apocalypse, many of the scenes are shaped, and the thematic underpinnings of the narrative are established, by the dialectical relationship of these three characters. Things are gradually made more dynamic with the introduction of Shaun's dysfunctional parental relationships and his love for Liz, who comes with attached baggage in the form of the jealous David and well-meaning Dianne. The actual zombies, who enter the story via the zombification of Pete, only serve to highlight the ridiculousness of Shaun's self-imposed predicament.

Like the Romeroesque closure in *Day of the Dead*, there is a happy, if mordant, ending, as Shaun revitalizes his sense of self and regains a degree of agency in the world. The status quo is restored as society appropriates the zombie for itself in the very naming of the event as Z-Day. The new Shaun is pretty much the old Shaun, but by passing through Z-Day he has experienced a Romeroesque apocalypse in miniature, taming his instinctual fantasies while retaining an [un]healthy dose of post-ideological cynicism. Having found a new, stable balance in his life, Shaun splits his time between playing with his zombified id, Ed (who now is, indeed, living in the shed like a fuck-ing animal), and playing at his relationship with Liz, whose desires he has learned to acknowledge and indulge. Like the tragic hero Oedipus, Shaun is cast out of society and becomes the "uncanniest" of characters, destined to return via the making of his own history.[44]

> I've seen this hundreds of times. Break with the group and the group breaks you! . . .
> See ya losers!
>
> —Patrick, episode 5, Dead Set

While not as overtly apparent as it is in Shaun, the traditional influence of psychoanalysis on the Romeroesque is also redoubled in Dead Set. The human condition of a subject split between freedom and necessity not only produces an endless cycle of alternating pathologies of melancholia and neuroses but can, instead, produce a dark, sardonic, and wicked humor.[45] This humor is ultimately directed at notions of our own mortality and the tension between free ethical action and the fateful repetitive actions that underpin everyday relationships.[46] The classic Yiddish archetypes that com-modify humor with ideological awareness are essentially uncanny fools—a mixture of perversity and simplicity, of wisdom and stupidity, of familiarity and strangeness, of vulgarity and exactitude—who have an innate ability to speak the truth to power while often remaining mute, or refusing to engage in polite civility.[47] Arguably, in Dead Set all these traits are collapsed into the cast, crew, and the undead.

Freud's topology of the psyche is as present in Dead Set as it is in Shaun. Kelly, the crew runner who sees rationality and intelligence as the solution to the crisis, is ego; Patrick is super-ego, viewing the housemates as com-modities to provide enjoyment for the viewers. The housemates, with their unrepressed urges and desires and their lack of decorum, along with the rapacious undead, collectively represent the id, and the house—a space in which the id is given free rein—attracts both the television viewer and the zombie horde to itself.[48] Unfortunately for the cast, avoiding death at the hands of the undead is as impossible as fully embracing the excesses on offer in the Big Brother house while simultaneously avoiding eviction. If Shaun's undead are reminiscent of Romero's shambling cannibals in their satirizing of contemporary consumer and slacker culture,[49] those of Dead Set can be seen as an uncanny ideological bent that has no interest in the presentation of difference as viable commodity. Dead Set's undead kill and consume everybody, exhibiting an indifference to difference. Quite simply, like the gaze of the camera in *Big Brother*, everyone is a zero-sum universalized commodity. There are no differences; ideology gazes at everyone from a point at which the subject cannot see *it*. This gaze is exemplified at the end of *Dead Set* as a zombified Kelly is transfixed by a closed-circuit TV camera that, in turn, fixates the gazes of a myriad undead. In Brooker's take on post-ideology, the gaze no longer represents enjoyment by the viewing subject, but the autonomous object-gaze of the Big Other—the hegemonic ideology. If not openly humorous, the finale of *Dead Set* is acidulously ironic: Patrick, the obscene manager of this new form of enjoyment, can be simultaneously positioned as super-ego and uncanny fool, since he is repeatedly found to be the repository of some innate wisdom and the only member of the group to actually successfully die. Kelly, the only real moral and ethical character on the set, seemingly chooses suicide by throwing herself into a horde of zombies. In fact, however, the only way to free herself from the medium's hegemonic gaze, is to become uncanniness—that is, is to become *it*, and to look at herself from outside of her own body.[50]

In *Shaun* and *Dead Set*, the Romeroesque is used to parody post-ideology but, by engaging with the media's form, utilizes humor to question the fantasies that underpin our ideological investment in our everyday reality. Zom-coms should not be read as post-apocalyptic narratives of dystopian social realism, but as a redoubling of post-ideological cynicism. The humorous traits and flaws in our zom-com characters allow us to assess not just how they behave, but what we believe. The redoubling of the Romeroesque in *Shaun* and *Dead Set* creates anew the oscillation of ideological self-awareness between tragic myths and amusing fables that address our modern questions of infinitude in new and insightful ways. Similar to *Night of the Living Dead* and the literature of tragedy, there is no happy ending, or indeed survival, for the characters in *Dead Set*. There is no "working through" or making of history as there is for *Shaun*. Tragedy is not a warning of an avoidable dilemma; it is affirmation of a tragic human finitude—there is only the unending existence of the trauma of zombification and unquenched desire.

While the Romeroesque closure of *Shaun of the Dead* is far closer to that of *Dawn of the Dead* or *Day of the Dead*, its parallel to the cautionary model of fable is also uncannily cannibalized; there is no happy unification of ego, superego, and id as there is in so many folkloric tales. We are left wondering how long Shaun's happiness will last if, like Oedipus, he has to voluntarily blind himself to his nature. It is, in short, often in the process of ostracism and the accompanying unconscious desire to be accepted that the baseless absurdity of hegemonic rules and prohibitions becomes apparent. In laughter we glimpse the truth, that what we hold to be sublime can simultaneously be the very excrement we wish to escape.

Our flawed comic anti-heroes, fighting a revolutionary and uncanny undead, are really engaged in a conflict with their own Britishness, and by doing so overcome the limits of representation inherent in tragedy. Romeroesque comic anti-heroes may in fact be better suited to our notions of post-ideology than flawed tragic heroes are in addressing our repressed anxiety regarding human finitude. The laughter evoked by the undead is itself an uncanny form of infinitude and suggests a comic acknowledgment of our fate, rather than authentic tragic insistence. In doing so, it vocalizes the laughable inauthenticity of post-ideological injunctions. Given that mythic tragedy heroes, by definition, retain a sense of dignity throughout their travails, the solidarity of laughter shared with our post-ideological heroes is perhaps the only thing we have left.

Notes

1. The release of *Night* was a watershed moment, auguring the growing resistance to the daily realities of the late 1960s. *Night of the Living Dead* (1968), *El Topo* (1970), *The Harder They Come* (1973), *Pink Flamingos* (1972), *The Rocky Horror Picture Show* (1975), and *Eraserhead* (1977) became known as the classic Midnight Movies. See *Midnight Movies*.

2. Russell, *Book of the Dead*, 64–72, and Loudermilk, "Eating 'Dawn' in the Dark." John Carpenter considers that Romero did not only reinvent horror as a politicaly subversive genre but actually made independent filmmaking a credible and concrete form of media. Without Romero's *Night*, independent filmmaking as well as the horror genre as we understand it today would simply not exist. See Fallows and Owen, *George A. Romero: The Pocket Essential*, 12–13.

3. This was both due to technical limits of filmmaking and conceptual limits of visualizing monstrous Otherness. See Brougher, "Art and Nuclear Culture."

4. Russell, *Book of the Dead*, 64–71.

5. The most prominent concept to adorn the notion of Romero's zombies, and indeed the undead in horror generally, is the Freudian psychoanalytic concept of the uncanny—that what is familiar can at the same instant be unfamiliar, and thus be sublime and excremental at the same instant. Romero's zombies indeed exude the affects of the sublime and the excremental contemporaneously. It is pertinent to mention the theme of the "double" as integral to the evolution of the concept of the uncanny. Freud considered the "double" to be an important part of the ego's defense mechanism and accounts for man's fascination with his reflection, shadows, guardian spirits—an energetic denial of the powerful inevitability of death. This idea of "immortal soul" is the same desire that motivated the ancient Egyptians to the making of art in the lasting images of their dead. However, Freud considered that once

this desire had moved on from archaic man to modernity the double takes on a new aspect—from being an assurance of immortality the double becomes the harbinger of death and self-destruction. See Freud, *The Uncanny*, and Dolar, "I Shall Be with You on Your Wedding-Night."

6. In Romero's undead, death itself becomes uncanny—familiar, yet unfamiliar—a way of raising the trauma of subjective death into the light of a narrative of fantasy in order to keep it repressed. For Freud, denial of death had serious connotations: We surround ourselves with the fantasy narratives of death but then have no way of imagining our own deaths other than as spectators who survive it. As a result, Freud argued, on a psychic level the totality of the human unconscious could be convinced of its own immortality (see Rutherford, *Zombies*, 39–45, 88–89). It is worth noting here that in psychoanalysis the unconscious conceptualization of infinitude can induce a deep perturbation, trauma, and neuroses. For an interesting interpretation in film criticism see Žižek, *Pervert's Guide to Cinema*.

7. See Williams, *Cinema of George A. Romero*, 1–20, and *Nightmares in Red, White and Blue*.

8. Myths and fairy tales answer the eternal questions about what life is really like and the reality of the human condition. However, myths offer binary and definitive answers, while fables and fairy tales offer animistic modes of storytelling that help narrativize one's own experiences of the world in the form of a self-reflective worldview that conforms to one's own time and context. Myths also have a rigid finality and usually tragic narrative closure; fables, on the other hand, have a subtle finitude that is optimistic, happy, and open-ended. For an interesting Freudian analysis of the interplay of psychic and narrative tropes employed by both myth and fable, see Bettelheim, *Uses of Enchantment*, 35–41, 47–53. For an anthropological perspective, see Levi-Strauss, *Myth and Meaning*.

9. Paffenroth, *Gospel of the Living Dead*.

10. Romero was heavily influenced by horror comics during the 1950s. Not only is this evident in his visual style of storyboarding and editing but also thematically. Although the horror comics of the 1950s were viciously criticized during the McCarthy era by conservatives who claimed links between juvenile delinquency and comic book "trash-culture," they were more visually and thematically subversive of institutional values than mainstream critical media. Romero's explicit homage to EC Comics and the horror genre they created can be seen in *Creepshow* (1982). See Williams, *Cinema of George A. Romero*, 2–3, 17–23, 29–30, 83–98, 114–18, 120–27.

11. Loudermilk, "Eating 'Dawn' in the Dark."

12. Romero considers *Day* to be his personal favorite and the most technically accomplished zombie film of his oeuvre. This author agrees. For insightful interviews with Romero about his films, see Williams, *George A. Romero: Interviews*. For works that have unique insight into the production processes specific to Romero and that are written by fans who starred as extras in *Day*, see Gagne, *The Zombies That Ate Pittsburgh*, especially 147–91, and Karr, *The Making of George A. Romero's* Day of the Dead.

13. Whether slow, shambling zombies in the Romero mold, or fast, sprinting zombies of the new era of films, zombies share a particular revolutionary ethic. Once humanity is absent they appear to all get along—they don't do 'isms'; race and gender are of no import and it is as if they espouse a particularly inverted form of indifference to difference: "Become dead the same as us and we will be indifferent to your differences." For a discussion of the evolution of contemporary zombies in a post-9/11 world, where the zombie has had to grapple with its own familiarity, see Bishop, "Dead Man Still Walking." For a full discussion that traces the ideological roots of the zombie to Haitian operations of social repression and then details its evolution within an ideological apparatus by which the zombie can be seen as both symbolic of hegemonic and subversive ideological negations, see Bishop, *American Zombie Gothic*, particularly 52–72 and (for discussion of the evolution of the zombie as subject) 158–96.

14. Romero has again returned to the Romeroesque; however this time he has returned to its very roots by authoring a comic book series, *Empire of the Dead*, that parodies the origins of his undead as influenced by the uncanny vampires in Matheson's 1954 masterpiece, *I Am Legend*. Romero's comic series unfolds in epic fantasy style with a three-way conflict between zombies, humans, and vampires. See Williams, *Cinema of George A. Romero*.

15. Robert Kirkman, author and creator of *The Walking Dead*, is vocal about the anxiety-inducing nature of the narrative non-closure of Romero's films. Stating that the one and only thing he hates about zombie films is the ending, his ultimate goal for *The Walking Dead* graphic novel was to produce a narrative that never ended. Arguably this is an unconscious confirmation of the power and thrall of the Romeroesque; however, it is worth noting that *The Walking Dead* lacks any apparent capacity for inherent self-ridicule in the mold of the Romeroesque and thus lacks self-awareness of its origins as an ideological construct in and of itself. Viewed through the lens of the Romeroesque it could be argued to take itself too seriously (see Kirkman, et al., *The Walking Dead: Book 1*, 304). For an interesting insight into the workings of postmodern traumatic literature in a psychoanalytic context, see Ruti, *Singularity of Being*, 52–53 and 124–26.

16. Throughout his works Romero's zombies evolved, parodying and destabilizing his own conventions, growing to question the conditions—unfettered warfare, global capitalism, and voyeuristic modern technology—that organize social, cultural, and familial relations in the twenty-first century.

17. See Flint, *Zombie Holocaust*, and Kay, *Zombie Movies*.

18. Romero ironically feels that the popularity of zombies in contemporary pop culture is driven more by games from within pop culture than it has been by films as a mainstream cultural artifact. See Robey, "George A. Romero: Why I Don't Like The Walking Dead."

For the Romeroesque's influence on video games—in particular the *Call of Duty* franchise—see Webley, "The Supernatural, Nazi Zombies, and the Play Instinct." Also relevant are Flint, *Zombie Holocaust*, 169–77; Vuckovic, *Zombies!* 142–50; Backe and Aarseth, "Ludic Zombies"; Krzywinska, "Zombies in Gamespace"; and Bishop, *American Zombie Gothic*.

19. As in, "We split up with Liz tonight!"

20. He came to a party several years before—and is still there. However, in reminding Shaun that he has "work this morning" we are reminded that Ed's persistent presence in the house perhaps has some form of function for Shaun.

21. It is arguable that Brooker's writing style is in and of itself Romeroesque. From the use of music from *Dawn* in its appeals to somnambulistic viewers, to its overt commentary on and castigation of the British public's indiscriminate cannibalistic consumption of what he considers vapid television, Brooker's *Wipe* (and *Black Mirror*) series are well respected for their self-ridicule and self-parodying nature as they lampoon themselves for being a product of the very media they deride.

22. In an interview on the set of the production, Brooker remarked, "TV should scare people, should terrify people. . . . I hope kids stay up late and watch this and come away traumatized, and then fucking kill each other. In 15 years' time there's fewer fucking human beings in this rotting world. . . . Why do I always say things like that? . . . What is the matter with me? . . . I don't mean it!" (*Dead Set*, DVD extras).

23. Liu, "Psychoanalysis, Popular and Unpopular."

24. Dolar, "'I Shall Be with You on Your Wedding-Night.'"

25. A properly Freudian way to consider the uncanny is actually as a negation of a negation—in and of itself a downward spiral of negativity. This is an essential Hegelian reading of dialectical negation, where each negation carries an inscribed trace on the underside of its meaning of the prior negation.

26. This is what has prompted many cultural theorists to argue that the Romeroesque zombie is at the same time an object of comedy and horror and pity and envy. See, for example, Žižek, *Absolute Recoil*, 335–36.

27. Freud's repeated returns to the uncanny, however, did little to actually solidify a working theory of how these unique and codependent phenomena function as a human constellation of psychic affects, or how they coalesce in clinical praxis. As Dolar writes, we are left with a phenomena that is little more than a prolegomenon to the psychic functioning of the uncanny, and its relation to our slips, jokes, and the dreams that speak of the foundations of our daily lives, our ideologies, and ultimately the "kingdom of sense" that most of us choose to exist in. Dolar, "'I Shall Be with You on Your Wedding-Night.'"

28. Liu, "Psychoanalysis, Popular and Unpopular."

29. Ibid.

30. Ibid.

31. Ibid.

32. Ibid.

33. Ibid.

34. Ibid.

35. Jewish folkloric humor evolves around themes of earthiness and stubborn plebian pride, where personal acts of goodwill and praiseworthy ventures reveal the existence of fundamental flaws. Ibid.

36. Ibid., 220.

37. Liu, "Psychoanalysis, Popular and Unpopular," 221.
38. Wright, "'Why Would You Do That, Larry?'"
39. Abrami, *Psychoanalyzing Jewish Humor*.
40. See Gorer, *Exploring English Character*. It would seem that, given the vitriolic critiques of his work, Gorer was in fact unconsciously proved correct in his assertions. See, for example, "Book Reviews," *American Anthropologist* 58, no. 6 (October 2009), http://onlinelibrary.wiley.com/doi/10.1525/aa.1956.58.6.02a00290/pdf. See also Rutherford, *Zombies*, 90.
41. Žižek, *Sublime Object of Ideology*, 28–31.
42. Wright, "On Jewish Humor."
43. Critchley, *Ethics—Politics—Subjectivity*, 224.
44. It is worth noting that in traditional Greek thought the basic trait of human essence is translated by German philosophy as "uncanniest"; as in, to be the "uncanniest one,"—the innate human drive to cast oneself out of history, out of the homely. See Critchley, *Ethics—Politics—Subjectivity*, 222.
45. Critchley, *Ethics—Politics—Subjectivity*, 224–25.
46. Ibid., 228.
47. Ibid., 231.
48. In homage to *Dawn of the Dead*, Joplin suggests that zombies are attracted to the house because "this place used to be like a church to them," prompting another housemate, Marky, to retort: "Perhaps they can just smell bullshit." *Dead Set*, Brooker.
49. Watt, "Zombie Psychology," 59–88.
50. Žižek, *Absolute Recoil*, 215–16.

Bibliography

Abrami, Leo M. "Psychoanalyzing Jewish Humor." My Jewish Learning. N.d. http://www.myjewishlearning.com/article/psychoanalyzing-jewish-humor/#.
Backe, Hans-Joachim, and Espen Aarseth. "Ludic Zombies: An Examination of Zombieism in Games." *Proceedings of DiGRA 2013: DeFragging Game Studies*. 2013. http://www.digra.org/wp-content/uploads/digital-library/paper_405.pdf.
Bettelheim, Bruno. *The Uses of Enchantment: The Meaning and Importance of Fairy Tales*. 1975. New York: Vintage, 2010.
Bishop, Kyle William. *American Zombie Gothic: The Rise and Fall (and Rise) of the Walking Dead in Popular Culture*. Jefferson, NC: McFarland, 2010.
———. "Dead Man Still Walking: Explaining the Zombie Renaissance." *Journal of Popular Film and Television* 37, no. 1 (2009): 16–25.
Brougher, Kerry. "Art and Nuclear Culture." *Bulletin of the Atomic Scientists* 69, no. 6 (2013): 11–18.
Critchley, Simon. *Ethics—Politics—Subjectivity: Essays on Derrida, Levinas and Contemporary French Thought*. New York: Verso, 1999.
Dead Set. Directed by Charlie Brooker. London: Channel 4, 2008. DVD.

Doc of the Dead. Directed by Alexandre O. Philippe. 2014. London: Altitude Films, 2015. DVD.

Dolar, Mladen. "'I Shall Be with You on Your Wedding-Night': Lacan and the Uncanny." *October* 58 (Autumn 1991): 5–23.

Fallows, Tom, and Curtis Owen. *George A. Romero: The Pocket Essential.* Harpenden, UK: Oldcastle Books, 2009.

Flint, David. *Zombie Holocaust: How the Living Dead Devoured Pop Culture.* Medford, NJ: Plexus Publishing, 2009.

Freud, Sigmund. *The Uncanny.* 1919. New York: Penguin Classics, 2003.

Gagne, Paul R. *The Zombies That Ate Pittsburgh: The Films of George A. Romero.* New York: Dodd, Mead, 1987.

Gorer, Geoffrey. *Exploring English Character: A Study of the Morals and Behaviour of the English People.* New York: Criterion, 1955.

Karr, Lee. *The Making of George A. Romero's Day of the Dead.* Medford, NJ: Plexus Publishing, 2014.

Kay, Glenn. *Zombie Movies: The Ultimate Guide.* Chicago: Chicago Review Press, 2008.

Kirkman, Robert, Tony Moore, Charlie Adlard, and Cliff Rathburn. *The Walking Dead: A Continuing Story of Survival Horror, Book 1.* Berkeley, CA: Image Comics, 2006.

Krzywinska, Tanya. "Zombies in Gamespace: Form, Context, and Meaning in Zombie-Based Video Games." In *Zombie Culture: Autopsies of the Living Dead*, edited by Shawn McIntosh and Marc Leverette, 153–68. Lanham, MD: Scarecrow Press, 2008.

Levi-Strauss, Claude. *Myth and Meaning: Cracking the Code of Culture.* 1978. New York: Schocken, 1995.

Liu, Catherine. "Psychoanalysis, Popular and Unpopular." In *Concise Companion to Psychoanalysis, Literature, and Culture*, edited by Laura Marcus and Ankhi Mukherjee, 216–32. Malden, MA: Wiley-Blackwell, 2012.

Loudermilk, A. "Eating 'Dawn' in the Dark: Zombie Desire and Commodified Identity in George A. Romero's *Dawn of the Dead.*" *Journal of Consumer Culture* 3, no. 1 (2003): 83–108.

Midnight Movies: From the Margin to the Mainstream. Directed by Stuart Samuels. 2005. Troy, MI: Anchor Bay, 2007. DVD.

Nightmares in Red, White and Blue: The Evolution of the American Horror Film. Directed by Andrew Monument. 2009. New York: Kino Lorber, 2011. DVD.

Paffenroth, Kim. *Gospel of the Living Dead: George Romero's Visions of Hell on Earth.* Waco, TX: Baylor University Press, 2006.

Robey, Tim. "George A. Romero: Why I Don't Like The Walking Dead." *The Telegraph*, November 8, 2013. http://www.telegraph.co.uk/culture/film/10436738/George-A-Romero-Why-I-dont-like-The-Walking-Dead.html.

Russell, Jamie. *Book of the Dead: The Complete History of Zombie Cinema.* London: Titan Books, 2014.

Rutherford, Jennifer. *Zombies*. London: Routledge, 2013.

Ruti, Mari. *The Singularity of Being: Lacan and the Immortal Within*. New York: Fordham University Press, 2012.

Shaun of the Dead. Directed by Edgar Wright. Los Angeles: Universal Studios Home Entertainment, 2004. DVD.

Vuckovic, Jovanka. *Zombies! An Illustrated History of the Undead*. London: St. Martin's Griffin, 2011.

Watt, Stephen. "Zombie Psychology." In *The Year's Work at the Zombie Research Center*, edited by Edward P. Comentale and Aaron Jaffe, 59–88. Bloomington: Indiana University Press, 2014.

Webley, Steve. "The Supernatural, Nazi Zombies, and the Play Instinct: The Gamification of War and the Reality of the Military Industrial Complex." In *Horrors of War: The Undead on the Battlefield*, edited by Cynthia J. Miller and A. Bowdoin Van Riper, 201–17. Lanham, MD: Rowman & Littlefield, 2015.

Williams, Tony. *The Cinema of George A. Romero: Knight of the Living Dead*. London: Wallflower, 2003.

———. *George A. Romero: Interviews*. Jackson: University Press of Mississippi, 2011.

Wright, Benjamin. "On Jewish Humor." *Wright on Film*, November 26, 2012. http://wrightonfilm.com/2012/11/26/on-jewish-humor/.

———. "'Why Would You Do That, Larry?' Identity Formation and Humor in *Curb Your Enthusiasm*." *Journal of Popular Culture* 44, no. 3 (2011): 660–77.

Žižek, Slavoj. *Absolute Recoil: Towards a New Foundation of Dialectical Materialism*. New York: Verso, 2014.

———. *The Pervert's Guide to Ideology*. Directed by Sophie Fiennes. Performed by Slavoj Žižek 2012.

———. *The Sublime Object of Ideology*. New York: Verso, 2009.

~

CHAPTER FOUR

Undead in the City

The Vampire's Kiss (1988) and Its Kin

Gary D. Rhodes

It was a shock to me to turn from the wonderful smoky beauty of a sunset over London, with its lurid lights and inky shadows and all the marvellous tints that come on foul clouds even as on foul water.

—Jonathan Harker, in Bram Stoker's *Dracula* (1897)

In the country the darkness of night is friendly and familiar, but in a city, with its blaze of lights, it is unnatural, hostile and menacing. It is like a monstrous vulture that hovers, biding its time.

—W. Somerset Maugham, *A Writer's Notebook* (1946)

Like a moth to a flame, the vampire of fiction regularly yields to the temptation of the big city, and it is easy to understand why. If you want to feed—or at least need to feed—the city represents a trough, a seemingly endless supply of fresh blood, of victims to be hunted. Immediately after Bram Stoker's Dracula describes the "children of the night" to Jonathan Harker, he adds, "Ah, sir, you dwellers in the city cannot enter into the feelings of the hunter."[1]

The urban appeal and its influence on vampire lore most notably comes in Stoker's 1897 novel, with Dracula famously leaving his rural Transylvanian castle for London, eschewing his old world for something new. As Dracula tells Harker: "I long to go through the crowded streets of your mighty London, to be in the midst of the whirl and rush of humanity, to share its life, its change, its death, and all that makes it what it is."[2] If handwritten letters and published books preserve Dracula's history in his homeland, the typewriter, the phonograph, and the photograph do the same in England. Here is a change of eras, a change of scenery, and a change of reputation.

Too many in Dracula's homeland know him to be a vampire; in England, however, he can be anonymous. As he tells Harker:

> Well, I know that, did I move and speak in your London, none there are who would not know me for a stranger. That is not enough for me. Here I am noble; I am *boyar*; the common people know me, and I am master. But a stranger in a strange land, he is no one; men know him not—and to know not is to care not for.[3]

Dracula longs to be an unknown quantity; in fact, he even traffics under the pseudonym Count de Ville. Safety comes in numbers, both his own and his would-be victims. God save the Queen, as well as the Count, so to speak.

Even though he had never been to the city, Dracula was clearly susceptible to its lure, just as the Anglo-Irish Stoker must have been, moving to London and becoming manager for the famous actor Henry Irving. But neither Dracula nor his creator was the first to seize upon the possibilities of London, that metropolitan hub known to many in Great Britain simply as "The City."

In 1819, John Polidori's seminal short story "The Vampyre: A Tale" has Lord Ruthven, its titular nobleman, arriving in London as well. Polidori writes:

> His peculiarities caused him to be invited to every house; all wished to see him, and those who had been accustomed to violent excitement, and now felt the weight of ennui, were pleased at having something in their presence capable of engaging their attention.[4]

Unlike so many of those vampires who would follow in his wake, Ruthven's sojourn in London proves successful. At the story's end, he has successfully "disappeared," having "glutted" his "thirst" with the blood of a certain "Miss Aubrey."

Stoker's novel certainly became the more influential on the twentieth century, in part due to its many screen adaptations. For example, Tod Browning's *Dracula* (1931) focuses on London to the extent that it geographically compresses the real-life distance between the city and the seaside town of Whitby, transforming the latter into something of bedroom community to the former. Browning's version also eliminates Dracula's flight to Transylvania (as Stoker wrote it), and has Van Helsing (Edward Van Sloan) staking

Dracula (Bela Lugosi) on British soil. *Dracula's Daughter* (1936), Lambert Hillyer's sequel to the Browning film, has its title character (Gloria Holden) becoming a popular guest in London homes before her own vampirism is discovered by Dr. Garth (Otto Kruger), one of Van Helsing's students. One could quickly enumerate subsequent film adaptations in which Dracula believes London is particularly well-suited to sate his bloodlust: Alan Gibson's *The Satanic Rites of Dracula* (1973) and Mel Brooks's *Dracula: Dead and Loving It* (1995), for example.

Other adaptations find the Dracula character foregoing rural life for cities other than London, most famously the Dracula-inspired Orlok (Max Schreck) purchasing property in Bremen in F. W. Murnau's *Nosferatu* (1922). Later films drew upon America: The Dracula of Stan Dragoti's *Love at First Bite* (1979) chooses New York City as his destination. The title characters of Bob Kelljan's *Count Yorga, Vampire* (1970) and William Crain's *Blacula* (1972) travel to Los Angeles. And vampires Louis (Brad Pitt) and Lestat (Tom Cruise) appear in modern-day San Francisco in Neil Jordan's *Interview with the Vampire: The Vampire Chronicles* (1994).

Cinematic emphasis on vampires in cities is hardly peculiar, of course. By the time Tod Browning directed *Dracula*, nearly half of the American population lived in urban areas, and that number increased dramatically during the rest of the century.[5] The lure of the metropolis was hardly limited to vampires. In both the nineteenth and twentieth centuries, author Horatio Alger trained many an American to perceive relocation to the "big city" as the key to success. One could go from rags to riches in the space of a single novel, and while historians have not quantified the matter, it is safe to say that the majority of Hollywood film narratives, regardless of genre, are themselves set partly or wholly in cities. Indeed, it is fair to speculate that, even before a majority of Americans lived in cities, a majority of American film characters did. If they can make it there, they can make it anywhere.

For most of them, though, the city is hardly a utopia. What more clichéd commentary can be made about cities than how lonely they can be, ironically so, given their dense and sizeable populations? And yet, as is the case with so many clichés, here is truth—if not for all, then certainly at least for some. The potential lack of personal interaction does not, however, speak necessarily to the negative. As we learn from fiction (including, notably, film noir), the city is awash in sin and vice. Murder and crime rates possess as much power to frighten as any horror movie. There is no poverty of trouble, even if there is, at least in some neighborhoods, a poverty of wealth. Rather than characters in Alger novels, denizens of many urban centers can become—or at least feel like—numbers, cogs in an overpopulated machine, not unlike the workers in Fritz Lang's *Metropolis* (1927) and King Vidor's *The Crowd* (1928).

Time and again, cities quickly transform into nightmares, including for vampires. Cities are usually not all-you-can-eat buffets, but instead dangerous restaurants at which vampires wear out their welcome after just a few appetizers. Lord Ruthven might have left London with his glistening lips upturned into a smile, but the same was not true of most of those who followed, including Dracula and his progeny. For example, an urbane Dr. Seward might contact an expert in another city, like Dr. Van Helsing of Amsterdam (his home in Stoker's novel). Those in the city are (allegedly) more educated and learned than their rural counterparts. At first, that fact might place them at a disadvantage, given a predisposition against belief in the supernatural; however, even if they are slow to react, their knowledge usually allows them to rout or even destroy those bloodsuckers that dare mess with their cities.

In the novel, Dracula is found out; he must flee back to his homeland. The city proves too much; as Van Helsing declares, "This London was no place for him." Time and again, the vampire's attraction to the city is fatal. By the time of Alan Gibson's *Dracula A.D. 1972* (1972), the vampire dies in London not once, but—thanks to being reborn during a black mass held in the now-swinging modern city—*twice* in the running time of a single feature film.

Even before it destroys them, though, urban living does not fulfill its initial promise for vampires. In the Murnau film, for example, Orlok attacks no one other than Hutter's wife, the one with whom he can be most readily connected, given Hutter's visit to his castle in the Carpathians. In the Browning film, Dracula attacks only one random victim, a flower girl, before his attentions and teeth focus with razor-sharp precision on Lucy (Frances Dade) and Mina (Helen Chandler).

Here is yet another kind of repetition, one driven by generic recapitulation and the basic need for screen drama to introduce a limited number of characters. Orlok and Dracula do not turn the strangers in their respective destinations into crimson troughs. Instead, they concentrate on a limited number of victims, the very persons who are most likely to cause the vampires' undoing. "Brooklyn . . . I love this place," Maximillian (Eddie Murphy) announces in Wes Craven's *Vampire in Brooklyn* (1995), but like his undead forebearers, he hardly takes advantage of it, becoming all-too-enraptured by a particular woman. Despite the city's significance in its title, *Vampire in Brooklyn* is little more than a retelling of *Dracula*, with Maximillian arriving by boat from another land: Passage from a Caribbean island to New York supplants the voyage from Transylvania to England.

While the city has thus served as a regular setting for vampire cinema narratives, it has rarely been explored beyond serving as mere background and proving in the end its unfulfilled promise. The key exception is Robert Bierman's iconoclastic *The Vampire's Kiss* (1988), which transformed New York City into a major character, one so potent as to make unnecessary the need for any Sewards or Van Helsings. This much-overlooked film marked a notable departure from previous genre films, including those produced in its then recent past.

Vampire cinema of the 1970s largely focused on recapitulation of traditional tales, even while occasionally updating or parodying the same.[6] Consider, for example, such films as Jesús Franco's *Count Dracula* (1970), Peter Sasdy's *Taste the Blood of Dracula* (1970), Roy Ward Baker's *Scars of Dracula* (1970), and the aforementioned *Dracula A.D. 1972* and *The Satanic Rites of Dracula*, all of which starred Christopher Lee as Stoker's vampire. Likewise, there were *Blacula*, Paul Morrissey's *Blood for Dracula* (1974), and Dan Curtis's *Dracula* (1974). One can also note the decade's conclusion: Werner Herzog's *Nosferatu the Vampyre* (1979), John Badham's *Dracula* (1979), and the aforementioned *Love at First Bite*.

During the Reagan-era "Me" decade of the 1980s, vampire cinema notably changed, eschewing Dracula as a character and concentrating instead on modern urban vampires, whether in such comedies as Tom Holland's *Fright Night* (1985), Howard Storm's *Once Bitten* (1985), Richard Wenk's *Vamp* (1986), and Jimmy Huston's *My Best Friend Is a Vampire* (1987), or in such serious fare as Tony Scott's stylish *The Hunger* (1983) and Joel Schumacher's cult favorite, *The Lost Boys* (1987). Vampires were not only urban and modern, but also chic and fashionable: It was, after all, the 1980s that spawned the goth subculture.

Released near the end of the decade, *The Vampire's Kiss* was less a culmination of earlier vampire comedies or of the goth movement than it was a darkly humorous and largely original approach to the genre, so much so that it became best known as the film in which Nicolas Cage actually devoured a live cockroach on-screen. To the extent that it received much further comment, it was sometimes outrage at the workplace harassment to which Cage's character, Peter Loew, subjects his secretary Alva (Maria Conchita Alonso).

However, *The Vampire's Kiss* is at its most daring and original in its positioning of New York City as the antagonist to literary agent Peter Loew. Its power is particularly strong in the daytime: The film begins at dawn, with breath-like steam lifting into the sky off a number of buildings. Phallic skyscrapers and their spires appear regularly, from the opening to the closing images, sometimes depicted in slow, methodical tilts. The city is omnipresent: Even when Peter is in bed inside his own apartment, sirens can be heard and car headlights can be seen out of his window. The city is also inescapable: Peter leaves only once, to retrieve Alva from her home in Pelham, but immediately and unhappily returns to Manhattan in a city taxi.

New York City drains more than one character in the film. Alva tries to hide in Pelham to avoid the office. One secretary complains of work driving her crazy, so much so that she intends to sleep all weekend. And Peter nearly vomits after ranting about how work "never just goes away." He recites the alphabet to his psychiatrist, Dr. Glaser (Elizabeth Ashley), after complaining about a possibly misfiled literary contract; he starts with a sternly voiced "A, B, C," and ends by shouting "W, X, Y, and Z." As he does, the windows in the office allow the cityscape to remain in view.

Leaving a diner in disgust after hearing a woman describe a marriage proposal, Peter screams, "Fucking greasehole!" to everyone and no one. His comment is about the restaurant, but it might well serve as his overall opinion of Manhattan. On one occasion, he refers to the city as a "jungle." And the club where he makes a date to meet Jackie (Kasi Lemmons) is called Mondo Cane, which brings to mind Paola Cavara and Gualtiero Jacopetti's gritty and grimy 1962 "shockumentary" of the same name. *Mondo cane*, of course, translates into English as "a dog's world."

And so the confident appearance that Peter presents to Manhattan—whether in his affected voice, his expensive clothes, his announcement to Jackie that the city is his "kingdom," or his announcement of "checkmate" after moving a chess piece in his apartment—is a façade, which crumbles as the narrative progresses.

Peter Loew (Nicolas Cage) explaining to Dr. Glaser (Elizabeth Ashley) how easy it is to file documents in *The Vampire's Kiss* (1988).

In a sidebar Nicolas Cage wrote for an earlier essay of mine, he said the following of Peter Loew:

> Reading [*The Vampire's Kiss*], I took it as a story of a man who was losing his mind through loneliness and his own inability to experience love. It was the lack of love, plus the kind of loneliness and isolation that is so abundant in the contemporary world, that drove him over the edge.[7]

Viewing the film, it is difficult to deny Cage's assertion. Peter is surrounded by literally millions of people, but he is lonely, and an upper-class lifestyle cannot save him. Even at his office, he seems at a remove from his colleagues, working as he does in "foreign distribution."

But loneliness is only one of his problems. As his name suggests, Peter Loew has gone impotent. He is surrounded by phallic symbols in the city, and even in the sculptures in Dr. Glaser's office, but those do nothing to cure his illness. He blames his troubles on the fact he just "never found the right woman," but he is undeniably fond of Jackie. That said, they do not seem to have consummated their relationship; instead, he tells Dr. Glaser that he "wanted her, the same as always, to disappear. I wanted her the hell out of there." Glaser notes how quickly his desire for the woman vanished. As for Peter, he returns to his apartment and picks up a limp sock that he had removed the night of his incomplete encounter with Jackie.

During another session with Dr. Glaser, while talking about how easy it should be to file paperwork properly, he dramatically insists that nothing could or should be easier. "You just put it in!" he bellows, with the Empire State Building looming over his shoulder through her windows. "What could be easier?" And yet it is not easy for him. Instead, he finds himself sitting hunched over on his bed watching *Nosferatu* at night, his poor, limp posture providing a marked contrast to Orlok's rigidity.

Peter's obsession at work becomes an inability to find an old literary contract for a story called *Rattlesnake Hills*. Its title suggests a phallic world to which, not unlike Manhattan, he does not fully belong. In a twisted effort to regain control over his life, to find that which he has lost, to perceive himself as powerful, he mercilessly harasses a secretary named Alva, something that the all-male management of the literary agency callously laughs about. When Alva eventually locates the contract, Peter insists that it is "too late," a phrase that he repeats prior to his failed rape attempt. Nor can he shoot himself with Alva's gun, as he tries to do twice. Pulling the trigger with it inside his mouth does not bring death. He is literally firing blanks.

At the film's conclusion, when his crazed mind invents a new girlfriend named Sharon (Jessica Lundy), he remains unable to escape his sexual difficulties. Within minutes his initial joy at meeting her deteriorates into a fight. "Does this mean we can never have children?" the fabricated partner asks after learning what he has become. But *what* has he become?

Peter does not acknowledge his impotence. Rather, his mental descent conjures vampirism as a means to combat the city and all that it has taken from him. Vampirism holds the promise of restoring lost sexual strength and power, of ending his impotence and allowing him to be like those couples that he grudgingly admires from a distance.

After taking Jackie to his apartment at the beginning of the film, a bat flies into the room, thus becoming a manifest form of *coitus interruptus*. For Dr. Glaser, Peter recounts being in "mortal combat with a fucking bat," and is "damned" to discover that the activity aroused him sexually. Later, after meeting Rachel (Jennifer Beals) at a nightclub, Peter's disturbed mind imagines that she is a vampire who bites him on the neck. With her Medusa-like hair and animal-like behavior, she is the source of sexual pleasure. She is in charge, something that seems apparent even when Peter meets her at the club and says he "loves" her prominent, elongated earrings. Later, he imagines that Rachel prevents him from keeping his date with Jackie at Mondo Cane.

Rachel, so he believes, has turned him into a vampire. Soon Peter cannot see his reflection in mirrors, even though the audience certainly can. He complains of bright lights, closing the blinds in his office and wearing

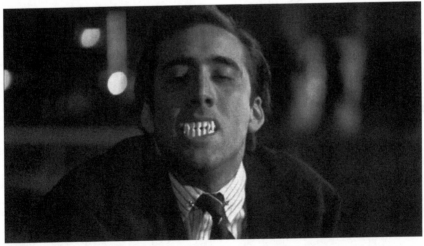

Peter with his fake vampire teeth.

sunglasses even while inside. As his mind becomes increasingly unhinged, he turns his sofa upside down to mimic a coffin lid. He emerges at night to eat a pigeon for fresh blood and attempts to mimic Orlok's stiff walk when exploring the streets.

Even as he gleans some pleasure from imagining Rachel feeding off of him, however, Peter realizes that his limitations continue. Unhappy with the minimal size of his own teeth, he purchases a pair of "cheapie plastic" vampire fangs. He does murder a victim (Jill Gatsby) while wearing them, but the act does not prove sexual conquest or even functionality. Peter assures the vampiric Rachel, "I can do it! I know I can do it!" But she spits on him in disgust, not unlike what a street mime does to her partner earlier in the film.

It is not long before the city dispels the fake vampire that is Peter Loew. Its power against his invented persona is apparent. While carrying a grocery bag containing a rigid baguette, Peter collapses on the sidewalk, helpless after seeing a neon crucifix. He flees without the baguette and is nearly hit by a car. And at the film's conclusion, Alva's brother Emilio (Bob Lujan) drives a wooden stake through Peter's body as punishment for the perceived rape of his sister. The stake is Peter's: Only moments earlier, he had placed it between his legs as a phallic extension when telling Sharon to leave him "the fuck alone."

The narrative of *The Vampire's Kiss* is enriched by its dreamlike qualities. We learn Peter is capable of lying; he tells Glaser he never saw Jackie again after the night of the bat attack, but in fact he visited an art museum with her. He is also capable of being confused and of having a poor memory. Was

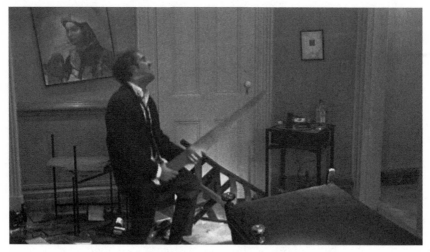

Peter with the stake used to kill him.

there *really* a bat in his apartment? And even if Peter believes there was, did Jackie *actually* see it? "This part, I don't know if it really happened, or I dreamt it later, or what," he tells Glaser of his arousal at fighting the bat. In his next session when Glaser brings up the subject, he says flatly, "I don't really know what you're talking about. I don't remember."

It is evident for many reasons that, while Rachel exists as a real woman who Peter briefly encounters at a nightclub, his insane mind invents Rachel the vampire. Even he is aware of this fact, at least once, when he brings coffee to her in bed only to discover she isn't there. And the audience is subsequently aware of this fact on repeated occasions, including when he opens his shower curtain to let her join him, but no one is there.

The Vampire's Kiss openly embraces its oneiric quality. "Sweet dreams," the vampiric Rachel tells Peter, for example. Then, at the end of the film, she notably says, "Dream of me." More notable is the parallel editing between Peter screaming, "What is happening to me?" and the frightened Alva on the subway to Pelham. Collecting donations on her train is a man singing an old Stephen Foster song:

> Beautiful dreamer, wake unto me,
> Starlight and dewdrops are waiting for thee;
> Sounds of the rude world, heard in the day,
> Lull'd by the moonlight have all pass'd away!
> Beautiful dreamer, queen of my song,
> List while I woo thee with soft melody;
> Gone are the cares of life's busy throng . . .

That Peter is trapped in a city in which the line between fantasy and reality are blurred is clear. But the dreamscape of *The Vampire's Kiss* is less a dream in any positive sense of the word than it is a nightmare, a darkly and insidiously comic nightmare about the city killing a man and the vampire persona he invents.

The Vampire's Kiss became the most extended meditation on urban vampirism in film history. Director Bierman brought the existentialist script to life by creating a bleak and relentless mise-en-scène, one that took full advantage of New York City, so much so that some of the extras on the city streets were real people who didn't even know they were in the movie.[8] And Cage's performance is a tour de force, likely the best of his career. It also represents one of the greatest examples of Expressionist acting in the sound era.

Regrettably, the film pleased few viewers, either on its original release or in the decades since. Perhaps horror and vampire fans were displeased that the movie does not feature a real vampire; the fact that publicity photos depicted Cage in a cape that he does not even wear in the movie might have added to the disappointment.

The Vampire's Kiss also had little discernible impact on subsequent vampire cinema, which largely resumed its prior use of the city in much the same manner as Stoker had in 1897. The asphalt jungle was not kind to the vampires of Ralph S. Singleton's *Graveyard Shift* (1990), Francis Ford Coppola's *Bram Stoker's Dracula* (1992), *Dracula: Dead and Loving It*, *Vampire in Brooklyn*, or—for that matter—to those who appeared in Stephen Norrington's *Blade* (1998) and Patrick Lussier's *Dracula 2000* (2000). The title character of Michael Almereyda's *Nadja* (1994) prefers Manhattan over the "village" that is Europe because of its nightlife. Like so many others, though, she must return to her quiet Transylvanian home.

To the extent vampires were even temporarily in control of the urban landscape, it would be in three screen adaptations of Richard Matheson's 1954 novel *I Am Legend*, where in each case, ironically, few humans remain alive.[9] But the general promise of the city to supernatural vampires remains largely unexplored. Abel Ferrara's *The Addiction* (1995) and Onur Tukel's *Summer of Blood* (2014) feature a sense of the potential randomness of vampire attacks that a city might suffer, though in the latter, the lead character Erik (Onur Tukel) still concentrates on using vampirism as the means to fornicate with his ex-girlfriend and one of his coworkers.

After *The Vampire's Kiss*, the most extensive exploration of the city in vampire cinema comes in Jim Jarmusch's *Only Lovers Left Alive* (2013). Here the vacant and decaying neighborhoods of Detroit serve as an outward sign of two vampires ill-suited to modern America. They exist on the periphery of life, just as their environment does: both are at some remove from the neon lights of the city's downtown. "So this is your wilderness?" Ava (Mia Wasikowska) asks Adam (Tom Hiddleston). His response: "Everybody left." The two vampires do as well, fleeing to Tangier after disposing of a victim's body. They fear discovery, and so their departure is not unlike that which so many prior vampires have made from so many other cities. Trade the new for the old, and with all speed.

Here is yet another reason to herald the uniqueness of *The Vampire's Kiss*. Its vampire is created in the city and by the city. He cannot trade the new for the old, the past for the present, or the rural for the urban. He is trapped and destroyed by the modernity that birthed him and then robbed him of his potency.

Peter Loew's madness was sadly normal enough that some of those real persons who became extras saw him as just another of the city's denizens. He is anonymous, as Dracula hoped to become in London, but that accomplishment is hardly an accomplishment at all. As Charles Baudelaire once wrote: "What strange phenomena we find in a great city, all we need do is stroll about with our eyes open. Life swarms with innocent monsters."

But the city does not swarm with all-you-can-eat blood buffets. And Horatio Alger does not have fangs. Beware the bright lights: thus hath the candle singed the moth.

Notes

1. Stoker, *Dracula*, 19.
2. Stoker, *Dracula*, 20.
3. Ibid.
4. Polidori, "The Vampyre: A Tale," 1403.
5. Monkkonen, *America Becomes Urban*, 72.
6. To be sure, one can also cite exceptions to the dominant pattern of vampire films of the 1970s, such as Richard Blackburn's *Lemora: A Child's Tale of the Supernatural* (1973) and George Romero's *Martin* (1977).
7. Cage, "Nicolas Cage Remembers," 281.
8. Robert Bierman speaks about this fact in the audio commentary that he and Nicolas Cage recorded for a DVD released by MGM in 2002.
9. The Richard Matheson novel *I Am Legend* has been adapted for the screen on three occasions: Ubaldo B. Ragona and Sidney Salkow's *The Last Man on Earth* (1964), Boris Sagal's *The Omega Man* (1971), and Francis Lawrence's *I Am Legend* (2007).

Bibliography

Cage, Nicolas. "Nicolas Cage Remembers *The Vampire's Kiss*." In *Dracula: The First Hundred Years*, edited by Bob Madison, 281. Baltimore: Midnight Marquee Press, 1997.

Monkkonen, Eric H. *America Becomes Urban: The Development of U.S. Cities and Towns, 1780–1980*. Berkeley: University of California Press, 1988.

Polidori, John. "The Vampyre: A Tale." In *The Broadview Anthology of British Literature*, edited by Joseph Black, et al., 1403–13. Peterborough, ON: Broadview Press, 2015.

Stoker, Bram. *Dracula and Other Horror Classics*. New York: Barnes & Noble, 2013.

~

CHAPTER FIVE

Beyond Fear in
The Book of Life

Discussions on Children,
Death, and Latinidad

Eric César Morales

Children's films and death form difficult pairings. Few can forget the scene in *Bambi* (1942) when the young fawn's mother is killed off-screen by a hunter's bullet, or the moment in *The Lion King* (1994) when Mufasa falls to his doom with Simba watching. While relatively short, such is the power of death in a children's film that these scenes have become part of our cultural consciousness and are ranked "among the top collective early childhood traumas," with the former being particularly criticized by psychologists.[1] In Jorge Gutierrez's animated feature, *The Book of Life* (2014), though, death is different—constant, yet occasionally darkly humorous. Filled with motifs of skulls, skeletons, murder, and eternal damnation—all that elicits dread—as well as the irreversible deaths of every relative of the protagonist, the film reflects many facets of the horror genre and the macabre. Yet, the film is billed as a children's adventure comedy, turning the stuff of nightmares into breathless laughter. In this essay, I explore what makes this approach to death different, and in the process, question the way the concepts of childhood, horror, and comedy are connected.

The film is set in the distant past, in the small town of San Angel, located in the "center of the universe," otherwise known as Mexico, where two adolescent best friends, Manolo Sánchez and Joaquín Mondragon, vie for the heart of their friend María Posada. Through a present-day framing narrative,

Mary Beth, a museum tour guide, reads their story from *The Book of Life* to a group of children, introducing the characters during the festivities of *Día de los Muertos* (Day of the Dead), a holiday where families visit the graves of loved ones to celebrate their lives. In the cemetery, La Muerte, goddess of the festive Land of the Remembered, and her former lover, the trickster Xibalba, god of the bleak Land of the Forgotten, agree to a wager: If Manolo weds María, Xibalba will stop meddling in the affairs of men, and if Joaquín does, La Muerte will trade realms. To improve his odds, Xibalba gives Joaquín the Medal of Everlasting Life, helping him grow into a valiant warrior. Meanwhile, Manolo, a musician at heart, reluctantly trains as a bullfighter to appease his father by continuing the legacy of his family. Years later, when María returns from studying in Spain, she is touched by Manolo's music and his compassion, demonstrated by his refusal to kill a bull. Threatened by their growing attraction, Xibalba murders María with a single snakebite, and then persuades Manolo to commit suicide so that he may follow her into the underworld. Upon hearing this, one of the museum children exclaims: "What is it with Mexicans and death!?" Good question.

In answer, I briefly explore the use of death in horror and children's films and then juxtapose the treatment of this subject matter with the Mexican folk celebration of *Día de los Muertos*, examining its unique engagement with death. I argue that by framing death within this tradition, the normally un-settling depictions of death, more regularly found in the horror genre, can be diffused, allowing for humor. In this way, *The Book of Life* is able to introduce a note of levity to a death-focused narrative, enabling death to become an accessible, enjoyable, cathartic, and healthy story for children.

Children, Horror, and Films

With its depictions of cemeteries, skeletons, murder, and suicide, *The Book of Life* may seem like an awkward choice for young audiences, but children's films can cover a remarkable range of subject material. In fact, while iden-tifying the defining characteristics of any genre is a daunting and never fully complete task, it is particularly so with children's films, because, as Ian Wojik-Andrews observes, "not all children's films are about children and not all films children see are just children's films. Defining a children's film, and thus the child viewer said film presupposes, is something of an impossibility."[2] Part of the problem is that conceptions and elaborations of "childhood" have a startling cross-cultural range. The subject of death, for example, may be introduced to children very cautiously in some cultures, but matter-of-factly in others. Yet a key aspect of children's films and literature is always pedagogy, principally cultural and social learning. Whether found in the screenwriter's hopes to impart a lesson or the child's desire to learn, there is always an element of moving from the unknown to the known. When designing films for impressionable young audiences, therefore, great care is taken in introducing difficult themes such as death.

Such considerations, however, do not cause filmmakers to shy away from death in children's films; quite the contrary. A 2014 study compared the on-screen deaths in the 45 top-grossing G- and PG-rated animated films with those in the 90 top-grossing adult dramas released between 1937 and 2013. Researchers found that half of the films aimed at adults included the on-screen deaths of important characters, while two-thirds geared toward children included such material, those proportions remaining relatively constant throughout the study years.[3] A 2001 study focusing on the highest-grossing and Academy Award–nominated U.S. films showed, additionally, that many films meant for children, while using death as a plot device, either failed to acknowledge death or avoided using "death terminology," suggesting that even though death was an intrinsic part of the films, American culture was skittish about directly discussing it with children.[4] Interestingly, a separate study found that of 23 deaths in 10 animated Disney films, 52 percent were likable characters while 48 percent were villains.[5] While the deaths of the villains in these films are largely anticipated and generally do not carry the same emotional impact on children, the deaths of likable characters may seem out of place and jarring.

Rather than being disturbing, however, those numbers are an indicator of the type of plot structure often utilized in such films: the *bildungsroman*, a coming-of-age narrative that requires characters to go out into the world alone so that they may mature and later reintegrate into society.[6] When the protagonist is a child, too young to feasibly leave home, adults who represent "home" are often eliminated, and, depending on how this is accomplished, the effect can be dramatic and unexpected. This type of death can be depicted through well-constructed, emotional cinematic moments,[7] or the death of a parental figure can simply be implied.[8] In *The Book of Life*, by the time we meet any of the core characters, they have already been touched by death: Joaquín's father was murdered by the bandit Chakal;[9] Manolo's mother died under unexplained circumstances; and, while not clearly stated, María's mother is assumed to have died as well, as she is completely absent from the narrative. The film's constant revisiting of death and the motifs associated with it, as well as its presentation of death as seemingly random, are what separate it from the majority of children's cinema, moving it into the realm of horror.

Children's films emphasize morality and hope, but the dramatic underpinnings and overarching themes of the horror genre are generally nihilistic. Horror pits man against forces bent on the destruction of social order, often utilizing a supernatural element as a catalyst. In so doing, it questions the foundations of what we know to be unequivocally human and forces us to deal with the fragile nature of existence. It is this struggle that is embodied in the archetypal "monster." If the monster can be vanquished completely, its defeat implies the possible restoration of the status quo; if it cannot, the idea that society can be overturned at any moment lingers with it.

At its core, the horror genre deals directly with anxiety,[10] and death is among the strongest sources of that anxiety, for as Freud reminds us, "we all know that we must eventually die, but this is a truth, and a concept, so abstract to us, that it lies well beyond the human mental capacity to truly grasp it."[11] As a result, motifs associated with horror films often revolve around death, whether in the form of settings that are eerily bereft of life, like abandoned buildings, deserted towns, and graveyards; or through the inclusion of harbingers of death such as skulls, skeletons, blood, snakes, and spiders. Death is such a constant presence in the genre that we watch horror films in anticipation of it, enthralled by the knowledge that anyone can die. In fact, we often eagerly wait for a hapless character to stumble into that one error that leads to their demise at the hands of a masked killer, an undead monster, or some supernatural force—threats that, like our own eventual deaths, exist outside of our everyday realities.

Similar to traditional horror films, death and its portents are ever-present in *The Book of Life*. For instance, the name of the goddess, La Muerte, literally translates as "The Death." She is depicted as a painted skeleton adorned in a striking, long red dress, wearing a matching, beautifully extravagant, sombrero lined with lit candles and decorated with skulls. Her counterpart, Xibalba, is a dark skeletal figure, also adorned with skulls and candles, and equipped with large black-feathered wings and a staff in the form of a two-headed snake. The opening scenes establish the deaths of the parents of the central characters and depict the spirits of seven other caretaker figures. By the halfway mark, we see María die, then Manolo. Near the end of the film, Manolo's father is murdered by Chakal, and his grandmother dies of a heart attack. Since the deaths of parental figures in children's films usually occur toward the beginning in order to force the protagonist into the world, the seeming randomness of when and how the characters die here is much more reminiscent of the horror genre. The film, however, is able to make death a consistent presence without it being a source of anxiety.

Many of the methods it uses to do this are familiar from other children's films: filling the screen with spectacular imagery, utilizing an apposition of saturated and unsaturated colors, shifting the camera away for a death scene that would potentially be gory, and using a soundtrack attuned to young audiences rather than the harsh and discordant sounds normally used to heighten fear in horror films. The film's principal and most effective technique, however, revolves around its use of *Día de los Muertos* as a lens through which to view death.

The Three Deaths

A product of Mesoamerican and Spanish cultures, *Día de los Muertos*, a uniquely Mexican holiday, is the most visible celebration in the country. People gather around private *ofrendas*[12] in their homes, attend lavish events in the city, and create festive displays in the cemetery in order to reunite with their departed loved ones. Gravestones are washed, painted, decorated with candied skulls, candles, flowers, *papel picado* (perforated paper), and mementos of the person's life. Musicians perform, and different types of food, particularly a bread called *pan de muerto* (bread of the dead), are left for the deceased to symbolically eat, as this is the one occasion of the year when the dead may enjoy the pleasures they knew in life.

Indigenous groups in Mexico have continuously observed versions of this festival for around 3,000 years. The Florentine Codex contains records of two Aztec feast days devoted to the dead: *Miccailhuitontli* and *Miccailhuitl*, translating as "Feast of the Little Dead Ones" and "Feast of the Adult Dead," with the period of festivities being given the name of *Tlaxochimaco* (The Offering of the Flowers) or *Xocotl Uetzi* (Fruit Falls). They are performed in honor of the Aztec goddess Mictecacihuatl, also known as the Lady of the Dead. While these events were originally held during the summer, Spanish colonizers in the sixteenth century moved them to October 31 through November 2 to coincide with the Roman Catholic triduum festival of Allhallowtide: All Saints' Eve, All Saints' Day, and All Souls' Day—although some celebrations begin as early as October 27.[13] In some regions of Mexico, the earlier divisions between feast days for children and adults are still honored, November 1 being dedicated to children and November 2 to adults, with the former being a more private affair and the latter more public.

In the context of these celebrations, dying is not to be feared. As Mexican author Octavio Paz once said: "The word death is not pronounced in New York, Paris, or in London, because it burns the lips. The Mexican, in contrast, is familiar with death, jokes about it, caresses it, sleeps with it, and celebrates it. It is one of his favorite playthings and his most steadfast love."[14] Indeed, skulls, skeletons, and other symbols of death take center stage in Mexican culture during this time in order to act as a reminder that death is meant to be embraced and celebrated as a part of life; even the presence of flowers, particularly the ubiquitous use of the marigold, fulfills this role because their wilting speaks to the brevity of life.

One of the reasons this holiday is so successful at disempowering the un-settling aspects of dying is that its roots are predicated on the Aztec belief of three deaths: the death of the physical body, the death of the spirit—when the body is buried—and the death of the soul, occurring when no one re-mains to remember or welcome the soul home.[15] In the Aztec belief system, where people are sent after death depends on how they died: Warriors who expired in battle accompany the rising sun in the morning, women who passed away in childbirth join the setting sun, victims of drowning are sent to the paradise of Tlalocan, and the majority of individuals engage in a four-year voyage with the dog-faced god Xolotl or his avatar, through the nine levels of the underworld of Mictlan,[16] ruled by Queen Mictecacihuatl and King Mictlantecuhtli.[17] In rendering this holiday for film, director Gutierrez took some liberties with this complex cosmology, effectively creating a new mythology for an international audience.

The rulers of the underworld are the characters La Muerte and Xibalba. The former is a composite of three interrelated Mexican icons: the Aztec Goddess Mictecacihuatl, represented as a skeletal body; La Calavera Catrina, a zinc etching by José Guadalupe Posada depicting a female skeleton wear-ing an ornate hat;[18] and Santa Muerte (Saint Death), a folk saint tradition-ally pictured as a female skeleton cloaked in a long robe. The Aztec God Mictlantecuhtli is subsumed by the character of Xibalba, which is the name attributed to the underworld of Quiche Maya mythology.[19] Additionally, La Muerte is introduced as being fashioned from "sweet sugar candy," contrasted with Xibalba who is made of "tar and everything icky in the whole world." This characterization of foodstuff versus non-foodstuff has a layered mean-ing, for many of the skulls used in decorating altars for the *Día de los Muertos* festivities are sugar skulls, made with meringue powder and icing. Applying this practice to La Muerte, the goddess of the Land of the Remembered and the earthly embodiment of death, literally makes death sweet. Describing Xibalba, the god of the Land of the Forgotten who represents the third death, as "everything icky" then reinforces the notion that being forgotten is what is unpalatable.

The multiple realities of the afterlife are also condensed into three distinct worlds: the Land of the Remembered, the Land of the Forgotten, and the

The rulers of the underworld, La Muerte and Xibalba.

Cave of Souls. The Land of the Remembered, located directly under San Angel, is similar to the living world, but more vibrant, beautiful, and festive. Unlike Mictlan, it is implied that everyone gains access immediately upon death. By contrast, the Land of the Forgotten represents the third death—the death of the soul—and is shown as a desolate wasteland where souls turn to ash, slowly fading away. The Cave of Souls, invented for the film, is said to exist at the edge of the Land of the Remembered, guarded by an enormous unnamed creature resembling depictions of Xolotl. A god, known as the Candle Maker, resides in the cave to take care of the candles that represent each individual life—a clear reference to the votive candles used in the Day of the Dead and in other Roman Catholic traditions. Throughout these adaptations, however, the treatment of death remains consistent and effectively advances the narrative.

When Manolo commits suicide, he does it by allowing Xibalba's two-headed snake to bite him on each foot, but upon arriving in the Land of the Remembered and reuniting with his deceased relatives, including his mother, Manolo discovers Xibalba in charge and learns that María still lives. Xibalba then explains through a flashback scene that the single snakebite María endured only put her in a sleep death, and when Joaquín leaned in to kiss her forehead, the Medal of Everlasting Life he wore touched her and she awoke. With Manolo dead, María then agreed to marry Joaquín so that he would stay to protect the city from Chakal, making Xibalba the winner of the bet. Incensed at this knowledge, Manolo, his mother Carmen, and his paternal grandfather Luis, all animated as painted and clothed skeletons, undergo a series of trials to search out La Muerte and set things right. In the process, Manolo proves his purity and courage to the cave guardian and then meets the Candle Maker, who informs him that Chakal is currently on his way to San Angel and will kill everyone in the village, leaving no one to remember any of its inhabitants. Finding La Muerte thus becomes a quest to prevent their third deaths, with their souls hanging in the balance.

While the idea of eternal damnation is the most anxiety-inducing and horrific concept in the film, it also implicitly engages with what death actually means in Mesoamerican culture and how it affects the worldview of some present-day Mexicans. Physical death is simply a passing from one reality to another, entailing a temporary separation from loved ones broken by the yearly celebrations that permit brief reunions. When the living re- member their lost loved ones, death is not final; by living with courage and conviction, making positive impressions on people, our own demise can be postponed. This effectively helps allay the fear of death, which is further mitigated by humanizing skeletons with clothing so that death is seen as deserving of respect, familiar and manageable.

Comedy in Children's Animated Films

By neutralizing the elements of horror through the underlying philosophies of *Día de los Muertos*, the film is then free to effectively employ traditional conventions from children's animated films, such as cartoonish antics, ir- reverent behavior, wordplay, pop-culture references, and, most importantly, love. Yet, although death is no longer presented as a strong source of anxiety, the pairing of it with this mythology continues to push new boundaries by expanding the ways in which humor can be created in an animated film.

According to Susan Ohmer, "Animation [is] the cinematic medium with perhaps the greatest potential for humor and transformation."[20] It allows for an expansive spectrum of visual storytelling techniques, as narratives can be set in any time or place, actual or imaginary. It also enables characters to take on exaggerated physical proportions in order to emphasize specific per- sonality attributes, and for their bodies to be easily manipulated—stretching, snapping back, being jammed into impossibly tight spaces, or with individual parts being rearranged to no lasting ill effect.

This elasticity of the characters is particularly prevalent in children's cartoon series, where the death of a character is highly unlikely. We can thus watch classic characters such as Wile E. Coyote run into a wall at 100 miles an hour, only to be flattened into a pancake, with little concern for his well-being because he quickly pops back into shape. Since the physical damage is benign, it functions as harmless diversion, providing an endless source of physical comedy. Mainstream animated children's films are often set, however, in a world where death is a likely possibility. A result of this is that animators lose full access to the types of sight gags that the painted picture so readily exploits. When Mufasa falls from the cliff, he dies—there is no bouncing back, no laughter, just shock.

In *The Book of Life*, however, the dead do not leave the narrative and are, instead, able to transcend the physical limitations imposed upon the living, allowing leeway in how their bodies can be used for humor. For instance, when Manolo arrives in the Land of the Remembered, his introduction to his deceased relatives involves being thrown off a bridge, flung between buildings from one cousin to the next, and even dismembered in midair. It ends with him effortlessly reassembling himself as he lands in a standing position in front of his uncle, completely unscathed. In a similar vein, upon meeting the cave guardian, Manolo's paternal grandfather Luis is decapitated and his body flung off screen, but, rather than respond with pain or fear, Luis exclaims: "Hey, my arthritis—it's gone!" For the next few scenes, he simply exists as a dismembered head, carried by his daughter-in-law Carmen, who even resorts to flinging the head in the air to get a bird's eye perspective of Manolo's battle with the cave guardian. When they all reunite with La Muerte, the goddess returns Luis's body, garnering only a response of "Great . . . my arthritis is back," which, at this point, has become a running gag. Thus, through the incorporation of the mythology, death allows the type of serious dramatic scenes that landed Manolo in the afterlife, as well as the playful ones where bodies become props for sight gags and slapstick.[21]

The film's treatment of death as lacking in finality means that even the severity of dying can be mocked. A perfect example of this is Manolo's grandmother. When Manolo refuses to kill a bull, arguing with his father that music, not bullfighting, is in his heart, his grandmother, not looking up from her knitting, responds with: "Kids these days, with their long hair and not killing stuff." Similarly, after her heart attack, when she dies and appears in the Land of the Remembered, her surprised husband Luis asks, "Mamá, what are you doing here?" To which she replies, "Eh, cholesterol," still knitting, not even missing a stitch.

For the moments where the topics of death and its grisly trappings are not easily diffused, the film relieves latent anxiety by switching between narrative formats: the primary narrative set in a Mexican past and the framing narrative set in a contemporary museum, presumably in the United States. While the use of this storytelling structure is invaluable for providing necessary exposition to foreign audiences, it also allows for the reactions to the *Día de los Muertos* imagery, and the potentially unsettling contents of death in the story, to be given a voice. For instance, in looking at the displays, one wide-eyed child states, "So many skulls," and, on hearing of María's death, another child loudly exclaims, "What kind of story is this? We're just kids!" These expressions of shock and awe are in such startling contrast to the events occurring in the main narrative that they make manifest any fears viewers may reasonably have, allowing for cathartic release. This reaction of horror then not only dissipates, but is also turned into humor, for as Immanuel Kant describes, "laughter is . . . the sudden transformation of a strained expectation into nothing."[22] With this method, the supernatural and more chilling elements of the story are then kept at a safe distance from the more mundane events expressed in the museum. The result is a film that effortlessly jumps in and out of the macabre.

Following the Heart

In these ways, through the progression of the film, elements of the horror genre become de-horrified and recontextualized into the Mexican celebration of *Día de los Muertos*, which also provides further venues for humor. As previously stated, however, one of the primary components of children's films is the pedagogical focus, and in this particular example, the resolution hinges on Manolo's internal battle over whether to be a bullfighter like his ancestors, or follow his passion by becoming a musician. His skill in both venues is formidable. This plot device, though, reaches a crescendo when, in order to win back his life, he agrees to a wager with Xibalba where he must triumph over his deepest fear: battling, all at once, every bull his family has ever killed.

With the whole of the underworld watching, Manolo maneuvers through the thousands of bulls who then coalesce into one large skeletal monster engulfed in flames; all the while, above, Chakal advances on the city. Although struggling, Manolo dodges an attack from the beast, its horns impaling a wall as he is flung across the arena with his sword and guitar landing in the dirt before him. Manolo stands, sees his reflection in the blade of the sword, and then reaches for his guitar instead, looking down to read the inscription María had engraved on it when they were children: "Always play from the heart." The crowd, dismayed, begins genuflecting, praying for his soul, but Manolo sings to the bull—a song of apology for the murders perpetrated by his family against the beast, continuing even as he is further attacked. When the song comes to a conclusion, the beast rests, accepts the apology, and with Manolo's touch, it disintegrates into wilted leaves. Manolo, now said to be the greatest bullfighter in the history of the Sánchez family, refrains—even with the fate of his entire world in the balance—from killing a bull. In the

The three friends, triumphant.

process, he finds the strength to be himself, overcoming that which was truly his greatest fear.

With that message, the narrative firmly situates itself within the domain of children's films and the coming-of-age genre. It encourages one to not fear death, respect the taking of a life, and be true to the inner self. While doing so, the film also makes *Día de los Muertos* and the cultural attitudes underlying it accessible to a large audience, successfully adding a more diverse presence to the landscape of children's cinema. Like the children in Mary Beth's tour group, the film encourages the audience to not fear death and to accept it as a natural and inevitable part of life, one that can be met with courage, a warm memory, a smile, or even laughter.

Manolo, of course, wins back his life, teams with Joaquín to save the town, then weds María and lives happily ever after, except that each of his family members remains dead. In keeping with the cross-cultural message about death, though, neither Manolo nor the film regards this as a tragedy or even cause for sadness. As La Muerte says in the end, "The world keeps spinning, and the tales keep turning, and people come and people go, but they're never forgotten. And the one truth we know, it held true one more time—that love, true love, the really, really good kind of love never dies."

Notes

1. King, "The Audience in the Wilderness," 62.
2. Wojik-Andrews, *Children's Films*, 7.
3. Colman, et al., "Cartoons Kill," 2.
4. Schultz and Huet, "Sensational! Violent! Popular! Death in American Movies."
5. Cox, Garrett, and Graham, "Death in Disney Films," 274.

6. Joseph Campbell also delineates this structure in his work, *The Hero with a Thousand Faces* (1949), in which he introduces the monomyth concept of a hero's journey, requiring that a hero go through the primary stages of separation, initiation, and return.

7. As seen in *Bambi* (1942), *The Land before Time* (1988), *The Fox and the Hound* (1981), *The Lion King* (1994), *The Hunchback of Notre Dame* (1996), *Tarzan* (1999), *Brother Bear* (2003), *Finding Nemo* (2003), and *How to Train Your Dragon 2* (2013).

8. As seen in *The Little Mermaid* (1989), *Beauty and the Beast* (1991), *Lilo and Stitch* (2002), *The Princess and the Frog* (2009), *How to Train Your Dragon* (2010), *Rio* (2011), *Frozen* (2013), and *Rio 2* (2014). *Rio* is, perhaps, the perfect example of implied death. The central protagonist, Blue, is introduced as a playful fledgling blue macaw in his nest in Brazil and is then captured by poachers, eventually raised in Minnesota. There he discovers he is the last male of his species, suggesting that his parents and any possible siblings were brutally killed by the poachers. To my knowledge, this is the first children's film that begins with an implied genocide.

9. Joaquín's mother is also not mentioned or shown throughout the film, so she may be dead as well.

10. Wells, *The Horror Genre*, 3.

11. Freud, *Art and Literature*, 364.

12. Literally translating as "offerings," this refers to the use of an altar where gifts are placed for deceased family members.

13. Mendoza Covarrubias, "Día de los Muertos," 403.

14. Quoted in Brodman, *Mexican Cult of Death*, xii.

15. Mendoza Covarrubias, "Día de los Muertos," 403.

16. León-Portilla, *Aztec Thought and Culture*, 124–26.

17. Ibid., 99.

18. In the Spanish release of the film, the character of La Muerte is named La Catrina, adding further credence to this theory.

19. Fitzsimmons, *Death and the Classic Maya Kings*, 48.

20. Ohmer, "Laughter by Numbers," 123.

21. It is worthwhile to note that Manolo's three mariachi friends, who represent the archetypal fools, have a bit more leeway in using their bodies for sight gags, not completely confined by the same restrictions of the other living characters.

22. Kant, Immanuel, 1911 [1790], *Critique of Judgment*, James Creed Meredith (tr.). Oxford: Clarendon Press. First Part, sec. 54. http://plato.stanford.edu/entries/humor.

Bibliography

Brodman, Barbara. *The Mexican Cult of Death in Myth, Art and Literature*. Bloomington, IN: iUniverse, 2011.
Colman, Ian, Mila Kingsbury, Murray Weeks, Anushka Ataullahjan, Marc-André Bélair, Jennifer Dykxhoorn, Katie Hynes, Alexandra Loro, Michael S. Martin,

Kiyuri Naicker, Nathaniel Pollock, Corneliu Rusu, and James B. Kirkbride. "Cartoons Kill: Casualties in Animated Recreational Theater in an Objective Observational New Study of Kids' Introduction to Loss of Life." *BMJ* [*British Medical Journal*] 349 (December 2014): 1–7. doi: http://dx.doi.org/10.1136/bmj.g7184.

Cox, Meredith, Erin Garrett, and James A. Graham. "Death in Disney Films: Implications for Children's Understanding of Death." *Omega* 50, no. 4 (2005): 267–80.

Fitzsimmons, James L. *Death and the Classic Maya Kings*. Austin: University of Texas Press, 2010.

Freud, Sigmund. *Art and Literature* (The Pelican Freud Library, vol. 14). Harmondsworth, UK: Penguin Books, 1985.

King, Margaret J. "The Audience in the Wilderness: The Disney Nature Films." *Journal of Popular Film and Television* 24, no. 2 (1996): 60–68.

León-Portilla, Miguel. *Aztec Thought and Culture: A Study of the Ancient Nahuatle Mind, Vol. 37*. Norman: University of Oklahoma Press, 2012.

Mendoza Covarrubias, Alexandra. "Día de los Muertos (Day of the Dead)." In *Celebrating Latino Folklore: An Encyclopedia of Latino Cultural Traditions*, edited by María Herrera Sobek, 403–13. Santa Barbara, CA: ABC-Clio, 2012.

Ohmer, Susan. "Laughter by Numbers: The Science of Comedy at the Walt Disney Studio." In *Funny Pictures: Animation and Comedy in Studio Era Films*, edited by Daniel Ira Goldmark and Charles Keil, 109–26. Berkeley: University of California Press, 2011.

Schultz, N. W., and L. M. Huet. "Sensational! Violent! Popular! Death in American Movies." *Journal of Death and Dying* 42 (2001): 137–49.

Wells, Paul. *The Horror Genre: From Beelzebub to Blair Witch, Vol. 1*. London: Wallflower Press, 2000.

Wojik-Andrews, Ian. *Children's Films: History, Ideology, Pedagogy, Theory*. New York: Taylor & Francis, 2000.

PART II

~

HORROR, IN THEORY

~

CHAPTER SIX

The Humor of
William Castle's Gimmick Films

Murray Leeder

On November 3, 1996, Roger Ebert's "Movie Answer Man" column contained an irate letter from a Rob Wolejsza of Astoria, New York, about his frustrations at a revival screening of *The Exorcist* (1973) at Radio City Music Hall:

> Although I enjoyed the film, I noticed that the intensity seemed to be lacking, thanks to the audience, which laughed and applauded at the most inopportune moments (i.e., the vomit scene and during the climactic exorcism itself). They even managed to giggle when x-rays of Regan's brain flashed on the screen! Admittedly, there were a few lighter moments, but it seemed as though every ten minutes something tickled the audience. *The Exorcist* is not your run-of-the-mill horror flick; it borders on the spiritual at times and is hardly worthy of snickering.[1]

Ebert suggested that the reaction stemmed from two factors: "(1) laughter is a common reaction among those too touched or embarrassed to reveal true emotion, and (2) unsophisticated audiences consider any sign that a movie is dated (period dialog, references, clothes) to be a laugh cue."[2] If horror films show their age more readily than other kinds of films, this does not necessarily mean they lose their power as a result. As Pauline Kael wrote of *Nosferatu* (1922): "Every horror film seems to become absurd after the passage of years and many before—yet the horror remains."[3] Who is to say that those spectators of *The Exorcist* did not still experience the film as horror even while they laughed?

Wolejsza indicts the audience for not taking an appropriately reverential attitude to a classic film. But other explanations seem possible, like a cinephile audience laughing in pleasure at reaching favorite moments, or an audience familiar only with parodies like *Repossessed* (1990) and thus inevitably viewing the original through a comic lens. Furthermore, the gross-out moments of *The Exorcist*, notably the vomiting scenes, disclose a connection between horror and comedy through excess and viscerality. As William Paul states, "If *The Exorcist* were in fact a comedy a priest getting hit by flying pea soup might provoke comments of 'gross' among all the laughter."[4]

Laughing in a horror film is not necessarily laughing *at* a horror film and may even pay tribute to a film's effectiveness. This is what Ebert suggests first, though it may not be inability to "reveal true emotion" so much a reaction to undesirable bodily reactions. Novelist Craig Shaw Gardiner notes that an exquisitely mounted horror sequence, like the "bus" sequence in *Cat People* (1942), might end with audience laughter, but that this is the laughter of relief and surprise.[5] Many times I have witnessed students in classes on horror laughing at those effective moments when the film gets the better of them, seemingly as a strategy to regain their own subjectivity.[6] As Carol J. Clover describes it,

> a "good" moment (or film) is one that "beats" the audience, and a "bad" moment (or film) is one in which, in effect, the audience "wins." Judged by the plot alone, the patterns of cheering and booing seem indiscriminate or unmotivated or both. It is when they are judged by the success or failure of the film to catch the audience by surprise (or gross it out) that the patterns of cheering and booing fall into place.[7]

The cheering and booing Clover describes are frequently intermixed with laughter, which is far from *verboten* in the context of the horror film, in part because of the heightened emotional and visceral reactions for which the audience is primed.

Finally, Wolejsza's letter implies that there is a kind of horror film that seems okay to laugh at, in contrast to the reverent silence one presumably must bring to *The Exorcist*. The focus here is instead on horror films where it is perfectly appropriate—where one is even encouraged—to laugh: the quirky pictures made by the "Master of Gimmicks," the "Abominable Showman," director William Castle. In a previous essay,[8] I wrote about Castle as an inheritor to the "exhibitionist" mode of audience address typical of early cinema and the Cinema of Attractions,[9] with Castle's authorial image as a kind of *monstrateur*, to borrow André Gaudreault's term for the showman/

magician who blurs diegetic and non-diegetic space through his gimmicks and his fondness for direct address.[10] In this essay I examine Castle's cheerfully irreverent and unabashedly fun gimmick films, which are notable for their capacity for inducing laughter alongside perfectly complementary chills.

Abominable Showmanship

Mixing horror and humor is by no means unique to Castle, but perhaps his particular brand is. Having also made more serious thrillers (1964's underrated *The Night Walker*), as well as more overt comedies like *The Old Dark House* (1963), *Let's Kill Uncle* (1966), and *The Spirit Is Willing* (1967), his reputation rests on low-budget gimmick films from the late 1950s and early 1960s.[11] These include *Macabre* (1958), where Castle insured the audience against death by fright; *House on Haunted Hill* (1959),[12] with the flying skeleton "Emergo"; *The Tingler* (1959), where "Percepto" motors buzzed the behinds of select audience members as the entire theater was treated to a non-diegetic "Scream Break"; *13 Ghosts* (1960) with the color process "Illusion-O" and its "ghost-viewer"; *Homicidal* (1961), with a "fright break" that allowed audience members the option of leaving if they were too scared to see the ending and its shocking twist; and the "Punishment Poll" in *Mr. Sardonicus* (1961), where the audience putatively decides the fate of the villain. By *Strait-Jacket* (1964), Castle had moved on to stunt casting in place of gimmickry, in this case a wildly unhinged Joan Crawford.

In addition to his famous gimmicks, Castle made himself into a "Living Trailer," a larger-than-life public persona who took charge of the marketing of his own films with an unusual directness. His first-person trailers were lower-rent analogues of Hitchcock's celebrated trailers—replacing Hitchcock's dry British archness with an American carnival barker's naked perversity, promising the unprecedented scares his pictures would deliver and warning off the faint of heart. At his frequent public promotions, where he often arrived in a hearse or coffin, he would make statements like, "Ladies and gentlemen, please do not reveal the ending of *Homicidal* to your friends, because if you do they will kill you, and if they don't, I will."[13] From *The Tingler* on, Castle did first-person introductions to his films from "inside" them, both building his authorial cult of personality and blurring the line between diegetic and audience space in a way that paralleled many of his gimmicks. His films are laughed at now—as they were when first released—by design, much in the manner of a carnival funhouse. On the commentary track for the documentary *Spine Tingler! The William Castle Story* (2007), Castle's daughter Terry Castle indicates her father "didn't take these things seriously. . . . The whole thing was done in a campy way and he knew it was campy and he was having fun with it."

Castle was an unapologetic purveyor of fun, unafraid to appeal to laughter and horror, sincere and spontaneous. His irreverent approach would come to characterize a generation of auteurs who often credit him as an influence, notably John Waters, John Landis, Robert Zemeckis, Joe Dante, Sam Raimi, and Stuart Gordon, who observed that "you'll never find an audience that wants to laugh more than a horror audience."[14]

Books like *The Golden Turkey Awards* tag Castle's gimmick films as "bad films."[15] Such films, we know, inspire laughter or ridicule. Noël Carroll writes: "Often a very bad horror film . . . will provoke thunderous laughter . . . that can be explained by suggesting that the fearsomeness of the monster has not been sufficiently projected, often because of inept or outlandish make-up and special effects."[16] But few, I think, would describe the skeleton in *House on Haunted Hill* or the wonderful plastic-tendrilled lobster-thing that is the tingler as "failed monsters," or think of Castle's gimmick films as unsuccessful horror films because they are funny. The tone of Castle's gimmick films is larkish and fun, and it seems more prudent to think of them as successful horror-comedies than failed horror. In *House on Haunted Hill* and

Vincent Price adds horror and humor to *House on Haunted Hill* and *The Tingler*.

The Tingler, this tone is amplified by Vincent Price, the consummate camp performer and "male diva,"[17] who manages a delicate balance between serious commitment to the plot and tongue-in-cheek detachment. Castle also allied himself with "serious" writer Robb White—screenwriter on five of his films, who did not recall their collaborations fondly[18]—and a strange mix of sophistication and carnivalesque fun results from this meld of authorial impulses. Indeed, perhaps due to the partnership of White and Castle, there is a curious mismatch in films like *House on Haunted Hill* and *The Tingler* between the films' juvenile format and some of their thematic elements (including venomous, disintegrating marriages and even drug use, *The Tingler* being the first film to depict LSD usage).

Kids Gone Wild

Horror producers in the 1950s often used comedy to defuse criticism of their films. James H. Nicholson—cofounder, with Samuel Z. Arkoff, of American International Pictures—said,

> In our concept of each of our monsters, we strive for unbelievability. Teenagers, who comprise our largest audience, recognize this and laugh at the caricatures we represent, rather than shrink in terror. Adults, more serious-minded perhaps, often miss the point of the joke.[19]

Castle's gimmicks depend on a Cinema of Attractions–esque mode of near-direct address and on his young audiences who were more receptive than adults. *The Tingler*'s Dr. Chapin (Vincent Price) says, "I've been trying to frighten myself but nothing works. It isn't that I'm too intelligent, just too grown-up. Kids can scare themselves by lying in the dark and making ghosts out of chairs, but we can't." In a variation on Poe's "Annabel Lee," children are praised not for their ability to *love* innocently but to *fear* innocently, and to embrace the carnivalesque "fun factor" of its project.

"Fun" is a deceptively packaged term, bound up with concepts like pleasure, leisure, *jouissance*, or entertainment, but synonymous with none of them.[20] An anonymous reviewer for my aforementioned Castle article noted it led them to revisit *House on Haunted Hill* and *The Tingler*, and that they "hadn't had as much fun in years." It is a tacit admission that even scholars are not—and should not—be immune to fun (and increasingly, are not pretending to be); we are missing key features of a text if we ignore the "fun factor." Linda Williams argues that the once-dominant strain of semiotic/psychoanalytic film theory, bent on questioning and denying visual pleasure of all sorts, estranged scholarship from important ludic qualities of *Psycho* (1960)—Hitchcock's most Castle-esque film—which some have claimed was inspired by *House on Haunted Hill*,[21] and which Hitchcock regarded as "a *fun* picture."[22]

The Tingler is Castle at his most audacious. It is shrewdly and openly constructed to solicit audience response—especially screaming. It involves pathologist Dr. Chapin discovering that the feeling of tingles down your spine—*frisson*—is actually a living organism, a parasite that feeds off fear. This "tingler" is powerful enough to kill, but is generally subdued by screaming. However, a giant tingler—a kind of plasticky lobster/millipede monster—grows in the body of Martha Higgins (Judith Evelyn), ironically a deaf-mute who therefore cannot scream. Freed by Dr. Chapin's experiments, the gigantic tingler wreaks havoc among patrons of a silent movie repertory theater. *The Tingler*'s horrific/comic interest in things abject, corpses, interiors made exterior, and involuntary bodily reactions marks it as an ancestor to the 1970s and 1980s gross-out films that Paul characterizes as "offer[ing] a real sense of exhilaration, not without its disturbing quality, in testing how far they can go . . . how far they can push the boundaries to provoke a cry of 'Oh, gross!' as a sign of approval."[23]

The Tingler begins with Castle standing in front of a blank movie theater screen delivering a first-person precautionary statement:

> I feel obligated to warn you that some of the sensations, some of the physical reactions, which the actors on the screen feel, will also be experienced, for the first time in motion picture history, by some members of this audience. I say certain members because some people are more sensitive to these mysterious electronic impulses than others. These unfortunate sensitive people will at times feel a strange tingling sensation. Others will feel it less strongly.

Castle here refers to the film's main gimmick, Percepto. Vibration devices were prewired to certain seats (not all of them, thus encouraging patrons to attend again and again in hopes of getting the full effect) which buzzed at certain points in the film, giving the spectators in those seats the impression of being electrocuted (a theme in the film, which starts with an execution by electric chair).

The Tingler's climactic sequence is the "Scream Break," when the tingler gets loose in the movie theater during a screening of *Tol'able David* (1921). Dr. Chapin and the perverse theater owner, Ollie Higgins (Philip Coolidge), try to find it, but it has actually crawled into the projection booth. We see *Tol'able David* freeze and disintegrate and then the shadow of the tingler inch across the screen. At this point the pretense of narrative integration falls away in favor of one of the most extreme examples of direct audience address the Hollywood system can possibly produce. The screen turns to black and the voice of Vincent Price announces: "Ladies and gentlemen, do not panic! But scream! Scream for your lives!" At this point, the Percepto-wired seats buzzed continuously while screams on the soundtrack (presumably) overlapped with those of the patrons. At the end of the "Scream Break," Price announces, "The tingler has been paralyzed by your screaming. There is no more danger. We will now resume the showing of the movie." At this point, *The Tingler* restarts and Ollie and Chapin head to the projection booth to contain the now-inactive tingler, subdued by the audience's participation like an anti–Tinker Bell.

In the DVD extra, "Scream for Your Lives: William Castle and *The Tingler*," horror aficionado Bob Burns describes his experience of the "Scream Break":

> The theater was just pandemonium for a few seconds, because it was totally in the darkness. That's when they set these things off under the chairs, and they started hitting sporadically these different little vibrators . . . and then finally a collective scream [came up] from about everybody. And by then the whole theater's screaming and yelling all over the place. It's contagious! Everybody's laughing, I mean it was like a big party in the theater.

The title of William Paul's *Laughing Screaming* is literalized in the bacchanal of the Scream Break, in which laughter and screams naturally converge, as they often seem to.

Similarly, at the conclusion of *House on Haunted Hill*, Annabelle Loren (Carol Ohmart) is assailed by what she believes to be the reanimated skeleton of her murdered husband, Frederick (Price), rising from a pit of acid. In fact, Frederick is still alive and the skeleton is a fake he is controlling. Originally, the skeleton was coordinated with "Emergo," a glowing plastic skeleton that was meant to flutter out from the front of the screen and hover over the audience. John Waters recalls:

> The kids went wild. They screamed. They threw popcorn boxes at the skeleton. Most importantly, they spent their allowance and made the film a huge hit. Was this not the first film to utilize audience participation to an absurd length? It certainly seemed more fun to me than dressing à la Brad and Janet and throwing rice at the screen.[24]

Not all theaters put Emergo and the other Castle gimmicks into practice, and even among those that did, the execution was very uneven. John Landis recalls, "It was the tackiest thing. It was a paper skeleton on a string that came over the audience," whereas Joe Dante says, "Mine was one of the few theaters that actually had a real skeleton . . . once kids found out that it was happening, they would come back with slingshots and popcorn boxes. That was a pretty expensive gimmick."[25] Even without the benefits of Emergo, the skeleton sequence is laughter inducing. While her husband's voice taunts her, the skeleton confronts Annabelle. She screams repeatedly, and the hilarious absurdity of the situation is heightened by the fact that the skeleton looks very fake—too clean, spindly, and fragile. When the skeleton pushes her into the pool of "acid," the moment is hilarious because there seems no way any skeleton, fake or otherwise, could do this. But one suspects that Castle was happy with audiences laughing at it as part of the carnivalesque environment his gimmick films generated—happy with any vocalized audience reaction. It seems reasonable to say that without Castle, there would be no *Rocky Horror Picture Show* (1975), at least not in its ritualized midnight movie incarnation.

Subversive Shivers?

Castle's memoir, *Step Right Up! I'm Gonna Scare the Pants Off America* (1976)—its title alluding to the carnival roots of Castle's gimmick style[26] while simultaneously containing fecal and sexual connotations—contains several comic anecdotes about the gimmicks backfiring, all of which have a subversive edge to them. One tells of an early screening of *House on Haunted Hill* in which the wires supporting the Emergo skeleton snapped and it fell into the audience. Says Castle, "The kids rose from their seats, grabbed the skeleton and, hollering, bounced it up into the air. The theatre was a madhouse!"[27] He also talks about a screening of *The Tingler* in Philadelphia, where a burly truck driver "got so angry when the motor under his seat gave him a shock, that he ripped out the entire seat in a rage, and threw it at the screen. Five ushers had to control him."[28] Castle insists that his gimmicks have an element of risk and randomness to them. One anecdote takes us back to where we started: with unsanctioned audience reactions, albeit of a kind very different from the chuckling of patrons watching *The Exorcist*:

> A week before *The Tingler* opened in Boston, *The Nun's Story*, starring Audrey Hepburn, was playing. During a matinee filled with women, the bored projectionist decided to test the "Tingler" equipment. He pushed on the switch during a scene where Hepburn and the nuns were praying. The proper Bostonian ladies got the shock of their lives.[29]

The sadistic anecdote invests B-movie gimmickry with a sort of carnivalesque power—potent enough to upset the space of an uptight audience of "proper Bostonian ladies" and of an Academy Award–nominated prestige picture. It invokes the paracinematic sensibility laid out by Jeffrey Sconce, which embraces "bad taste" and "trash" for the subversive power to trouble the confines of "high culture."[30] It also implies a certain "colonization" of the mainstream cinematic space by low-grade horror that speaks to the generic regimentation of audience reactions: hushed silence for dramas (pierced only by an occasional cathartic gasp), screams for horror films (and laughter for "fun" horror films like Castle's, but presumably not for prestige ones like The Exorcist). Waters writes of the alleged Boston incident, "I'm sure Audrey Hepburn never got such a vocal reaction before or after this 'electrifying' screening,"[31] contrasting a cinematic icon of gentility and taste with Castle's vulgar and visceral shocks.[32] These outlandish ideas subvert the blandness of Hollywood's "prestige" products with trash gimmicks. Whether this was a real subversion is another question.

In Dante's Matinee (1993), the self-promoting gimmick director Lawrence Woolsey (John Goodman) is an amalgam of Castle and other horror/science fiction directors of the 1950s and 1960s. Dante, who was 12 years old when House on Haunted Hill and The Tingler were released, valorizes Castle/Woolsey for delivering exactly what the giddy young audience wants: "It's hard to believe you're a grown-up," the youths tell Woolsey at one point. This transgression, however, is of a very circumscribed variety and Woolsey, a cuddly emblem of American capitalism's most benign aspects, is ultimately a figure of comfort and security, even as his gimmicks (including real electric shocks) are more intense than Castle's. Woolsey figures himself as a rescuer of children and becomes one in reality—his movies end, after all, while the horrors of reality never do.

Yet, Matinee still suggests transgression of another sort. When Woolsey denounces the Hollywood studios as dinosaurs that do not understand the public and its real needs as well as he does, the moment is ironic; we know full well that Woolsey (or Castle) is the dinosaur. But it allows openness to a parallel history of cinema, one allowing purveyors of unapologetic and direct fun a place in the center, rather than pushing them to the margins.

We seem to have had a Castle renaissance of late. His name is casually cited when discussing vibrating theater chairs,[33] and bloggers endorse him as "a fucking visionary."[34] An article on the humor website Cracked opines, with reference to The Tingler, "I don't think anybody actually thought a crazy fear monster was crushing their spine, but you can't tell me that's not a thousand times more fun than, say, anything that happened in Avatar."[35]

Fascinatingly, this new adulation often positions Castle as a visionary auteur from a purer time, before a jaded audience faced an endless slate of new cinematic advances that fail to shake up the format as ostentatiously as something like *The Tingler*, leaving it primed for good old-fashioned low-tech gimmickry. As "kettlechips," a commenter on the *Cracked* article, states: "The 'Tingler' shtick sounds WAYY too fun for something that could exist today . . . one complaint [about the physical buzzing] would ruin it for everyone else."[36] Perhaps this is the same "nostalgic fantasy of audiences charmingly naïve enough to be taken in by such ridiculous hijinx . . . when one could still zap audience members in the ass with bolts of electricity without getting sued" that Sconce finds in *Matinee*.[37] It is obviously the case that some cinema-goers are looking to Castle in much the same way as John Waters did: as a figure whose refreshingly direct DIY gimmickry can still be invoked to deflate the grandiose pomposity of Hollywood excess.

To Laugh or Not to Laugh?

And was *The Exorcist* really all that different? It too is a piece of what Adam Lowenstein calls "spectacle horror"[38] with the sequences of vomiting and head-spinning and spider-walking (the latter restored in the 2000 reissue) moments not so far removed from the Fright Break, or the attack of the skeleton on Mrs. Loren. The difference resides more in cultural legitimacy than anything else. And the hype machine surrounding *The Exorcist* was rife with ballyhoo: rumors of strange occurrences on the set, whispers that the film itself was cursed, (false) rumors that Linda Blair suffered a nervous breakdown from the strain of the part, and, most Castle-esque of all, rumors of patrons fainting, vomiting, and even pregnant women miscarrying from the shock of the film . . . all carefully managed by the studio.[39]

In 2010, the *Telegraph* ran an article with the headline "Horror Film Gene That Makes Some Scream While Others Laugh: The Secret of Why Horror Films Make Some People Scream in Terror While Others May Simply Laugh Has Been Revealed." It uses *The Exorcist* as its major example: "While many screamed and some even fainted in cinemas at scenes of spinning heads and shaking beds, others simply laughed. A particular variant on the 'COMT' gene affects a chemical in the brain that is linked to anxiety, [scientists] have found."[40] The article describes a study by the University of Bonn that tested 97 women by "showing them three different types of pictures—emotionally 'pleasant' ones of smiling babies and cute animals, 'neutral' ones of items like electric plugs or hairdryers, and 'aversive' ones of weapons or injured victims." The conclusion of the study was that certain people are genetically predisposed to feel fear at the sight of certain images and others are not. No horror films were used during the tests and, despite the presence of a picture of Linda Blair in the header, the author of this article seems merely to have placed that spin on the article for sensation's sake. To appeal to genetics to explain something as culturally entrenched as horror is dubious, but I find it telling the article raises laughter—again, the idea of people laughing at *The Exorcist*—as the stock response to not being horrified by something (as opposed to indifference, or perhaps a mode of engagement detached from physical reactions). So stubbornly we seem to cling to these oppositions: laughing *or* screaming, horror *or* comedy. Why not both? Do we need a visit from *The Tingler* to remind us that they need not be separate?

Notes

Special thanks to Johnson Cheu, John A. Dowell, Cynthia Miller, and A. Bowdoin Van Riper.

1. Roger Ebert, "Movie Answer Man, 11/03/96."
2. Ibid. Laughing at older films is not a new phenomenon; as early as 1949, Béla Balázs wondered, "Why are old films funny?" (Balázs, *Theory of the Film*, 36).
3. Kael, *5001 Nights at the Movies*, 534.
4. Paul, *Laughing Screaming*, 292.
5. Gardiner, "Blood and Laughter," 94.
6. Aalya Ahmad similarly describes how "[s]tudents screamed, howled, jumped and laughed at their and others' reactions" during screenings in her "The Monstrous Feminist" class (Ahmad, "When the Women Think," 69).
7. Clover, *Men, Women and Chain Saws*, 202.
8. Leeder, "Collective Screams."
9. As originally delineated by Gunning in "The Cinema of Attraction," generally retitled "The Cinema of Attractions" on reprints.
10. For use of this term in the horror context, see Heffernan, *Ghouls, Gimmicks, and Gold*, 8. I developed the reading of Castle as a *monstrateur* in "Collective Screams" (especially 778–79).
11. A highly prolific filmmaker, Castle directed dozens of B-films, mostly crime thrillers and Westerns, even before his first gimmick film, *Macabre* (1958).
12. Numerous sources, including Castle's own memoirs, name the film as *The House on Haunted Hill*, but the film's own title sequence lacks a "The."
13. *Spine Tingler! The William Castle Story.*
14. Carroll, "Horror and Humor," 146.
15. Medved and Medved, *The Golden Turkey Awards.*
16. Carroll, "Horror and Humor," 157.
17. See Benshoff, "Vincent Price and Me."

18. White, "An Outspoken Conversation with Robb White."

19. Doherty, *Teenagers and Teenpics*, 160.

20. See Rutsky and Wyatt, "Serious Pleasures."

21. Colavito, *Knowing Fear*, 273.

22. Williams, "Discipline and Fun," 353. Compare Matt Hills's assertion that "theoretical approaches to horror have explained (away) the genre's pleasures by invoking their own disciplinary and theoretical norms" (*Pleasures of Horror*, 2).

23. Paul, *Laughing Screaming*, 20.

24. Waters, "Whatever Happened to Showmanship?" 56.

25. Quoted in Jones, *Clive Barker's A–Z of Horror*, 222.

26. The linkages to the carnival inevitably evoke the "carnivalesque" overturning of roles through chaos and laughter associated with the Russian literary theorist Mikhail Bakhtin and his reading of the medieval carnival and its social function. Significantly, Angela Ndalianis notes: "Remnants of the carnival tradition . . . later were adjusted to meet the demands of new commercial needs in the form of amusement parks, penny arcades, burlesques, and film genres such as comedy and horror" (Ndalianis, *The Horror Sensorium*, 109).

27. Castle, *Step Right Up!* 149. Robb White tells a similar story of greater transgressive potential, locating the incident in a test screening with "twenty-two big producers—I mean, John Huston and people like that. We sat them down and ran the picture, and then this skeleton came out floating over them. Well, they thought it was great, until the line snapped and the skeleton fell straight on top of them [*laughs*]! They all got up and walked out!" (White, "An Outspoken Conversation with Robb White," 64).

28. *Step Right Up!* 152.

29. Ibid. *Step Right Up!* is full of entertaining episodes of dubious veracity, but in this case the dates at least seem to check out: *The Nun's Story* debuted July 18, 1959, and *The Tingler* on July 29, 1959.

30. Sconce, "'Trashing' the Academy."

31. Waters, "Whatever Happened to Showmanship?" 57.

32. Waters goes on to suggest that Hollywood ought to revive Castle's style gimmickry: "Even highbrow, critically acclaimed Oscar winners could up their grosses. Drag enthusiastic members of the *Reds* audience before mock Senate hearings in the lobby. Close down the concession stand for *Gandhi* and let the patrons get into the spirit of the thing by starving to death." Ibid., 58.

33. Bracken, "Will These Home-Theater Chairs Change the Way You Watch Movies in Your Living Room?"

34. Millar, "William Castle, Part One."

35. Sims, "5 Great Moments from the World's Craziest Filmmaker."

36. Ibid.

37. Sconce, "Movies," 289–90.

38. Lowenstein, "Reintroduction to the American Horror Film."

39. Kattelman, "'We Dare You to See This!'"

40. Adams, "Horror Film Gene That Makes Some Scream While Others Laugh."

Bibliography

13 Ghosts. Directed by William Castle. 1960. Los Angeles: Columbia/Tristar Video. 2009. DVD.

Adams, Stephen. "Horror Film Gene That Makes Some Scream While Others Laugh." *Telegraph*, August 10, 2008. http://www.telegraph.co.uk/news/2535221/Horror-film-gene-that-makes-some-scream-while-others-laugh.html.

Ahmad, Aalya. "When the Women Think." In *Fear and Learning: Essays on the Pedagogy of Horror*, edited by Aalya Ahmad and Sean Moreland, 56–74. Jefferson, NC: McFarland, 2013.

Balázs, Béla. *Theory of the Film: Character and Growth of a New Art*. 1949. Translated by Edith Bone. New York: Dover, 1970.

Benshoff, Harry M. "Vincent Price and Me: Imagining the Queer Male Diva." *Camera Obscura* 23, no. 1 (2008): 146–50.

Bracken, Mike. "Will These Home-Theater Chairs Change the Way You Watch Movies in Your Living Room?" *Movies.com*, October 2, 2013. http://www.movies.com/movie-news/tremor-fx-home-theater-chairs-vibrate-to-onscreen-action/13701.

The Busy Body. Directed by William Castle. 1967. San Diego, CA: Legend Films. 2008. DVD.

Carroll, Noël. "Horror and Humor." *Journal of Aesthetics and Art Criticism* 57, no. 2 (Spring 1999): 145–60.

Castle, William. *Step Right Up! I'm Gonna Scare the Pants Off America: Memoirs of a B-Movie Mogul*. 1976. New York: Pharos, 1992.

Clover, Carol J. *Men, Women and Chain Saws: Gender in the Modern Horror Film*. Princeton, NJ: Princeton University Press, 1992.

Colavito, Jason. *Knowing Fear: Science, Knowledge and the Development of the Horror Genre*. Jefferson, NC: McFarland, 2008.

Doherty, Thomas. *Teenagers and Teenpics: The Juvenilization of American Movies in the 1950s*. Boston: Unwin, 1988.

Ebert, Roger. "Movie Answer Man, 11/03/96." *RogerEbert.com*. http://www.rogerebert.com/answer-man/movie-answer-man-11031996.

The Exorcist. Directed by William Friedkin. 1973. Los Angeles: Warner Home Video. 2011. DVD.

Gardiner, Craig Shaw. "Blood and Laughter: The Humor in Horror Film." In *Cut! Horror Writers on Horror Film*, edited by Christopher Golden, 91–100. New York: Berkeley, 1992.

Gunning, Tom. "The Cinema of Attraction: Early Film, Its Spectators and the Avant-Garde." *Wide Angle* 8, no. 3–4 (1986): 63–70.

Heffernan, Kevin. *Ghouls, Gimmicks, and Gold: Horror Films and the American Movie Business, 1953–1958*. London: Duke University Press, 2004.

Hills, Matt. *The Pleasures of Horror*. London: Continuum, 2004.

Homicidal. Directed by William Castle. 1961. Los Angeles: Columbia/Tristar Video. 2009. DVD.

House on Haunted Hill. Directed by William Castle. 1959. Culver City, CA: Columbia/TriStar Video. 2009. DVD.

Jones, Stephen, ed. *Clive Barker's A–Z of Horror*. New York: HarperCollins, 1997.

Kael, Pauline. *5001 Nights at the Movies*. New York: Picador, 1982.

Kattelman, Beth. "'We Dare You to See This!' Ballyhoo and the 1970s Horror Film." *Horror Studies* 2, no. 1 (2011): 61–74.

Leeder, Murray. "Collective Screams: William Castle and the Gimmick Film." *The Journal of Popular Culture* 44, no. 4 (August 2011): 773–95.

Lowenstein, Adam. "Reintroduction to the American Horror Film." In *The Wiley-Blackwell History of American Film, Volume 4*, edited by Cynthia Lucia, Roy Grundmann, and Art Simon, 154–76. Malden, MA: Wiley-Blackwell, 2011.

Macabre. Directed by William Castle. 1958. Los Angeles: Warner Archives. 2010. DVD.

Matinee. Directed by Joe Dante. 1993. University City, CA: Universal Pictures. 2010. DVD.

Medved, Michael, and Harry Medved. *The Golden Turkey Awards: The Worst Achievements in Hollywood History*. New York: Perigee, 1980.

Millar, Will. "William Castle, Part One." In *Advent of the Zombie Holocaust* (blog), June 24, 2012. http://inadventofthezombieholocaust.blogspot.com/2012/06/william-castle-part-one.html.

Mr. Sardonicus. Directed by William Castle. 1961. Los Angeles: Columbia/Tristar Video. 2009. DVD.

Ndalianis, Angela. *The Horror Sensorium: Media and the Senses*. Jefferson, NC: McFarland, 2012.

The Night Walker. Directed by William Castle. 1964. Universal City, CA: Universal Pictures. 1996. Video.

The Old Dark House. Directed by William Castle. 1963. Los Angeles: Columbia/Tristar Video. 2009. DVD.

Paul, William. *Laughing Screaming: Modern Hollywood Horror and Comedy*. New York: Columbia University Press, 1994.

Rutsky, R. L., and Justin Wyatt. "Serious Pleasures: Cinematic Pleasure and the Notion of Fun." *Cinema Journal* 30, no. 1 (Fall 1990): 1–19.

Sconce, Jeffrey. "Movies: A Century of Failure." In *Sleaze Artists: Cinema at the Margins of Taste, Style and Politics*, edited by Jeffrey Sconce, 273–309. Durham, NC: Duke University Press, 2007.

———. "'Trashing' the Academy: Taste, Excess, and an Emerging Politics of Cinematic Style." *Screen* 36, no. 4 (1995): 371–93.

Sims, Chris. "5 Great Moments from the World's Craziest Filmmaker." *Cracked*, January 27, 2013. http://www.cracked.com/blog/5-great-moments-from-worlds-craziest-filmmaker_p2/.

Spine Tingler! The William Castle Story. Directed by Jeffrey Schwartz. 2007. Culver City, CA: Columbia/TriStar Video. 2009. DVD.

The Spirit Is Willing. Directed by William Castle. 1967. Toronto: Mongrel Media. 2012. Blu-Ray.

Strait-Jacket. Directed by William Castle. 1964. Los Angeles: Columbia/Tristar Video. 2009. DVD.

Strawn, Linda Mae. "Interview with William Castle." In *Kings of the Bs: Working within the Hollywood System: An Anthology of Film History and Criticism,* edited by Todd McCarthy and Charles Flynn, 287–301. New York: Dutton, 1975.

The Tingler. Directed by William Castle. 1959. Culver City, CA: Columbia/Tristar Video. 2009. DVD.

Waters, John. "Whatever Happened to Showmanship?" *American Film* (December 1983): 55–58.

White, Robb. "An Outspoken Conversation with Robb White." Interview by Tom Weaver. *Film Fax* 18 (1990): 60–65, 94–95.

Williams, Linda. "Discipline and Fun: Psycho and Postmodern Cinema." In *Reinventing Film Studies,* edited by Christine Gledhill and Linda Williams, 351–78. London: Arnold, 2000.

~

CHAPTER SEVEN

"We're Not All Dead Yet"

Humor amid the Horror in James Whale's Bride of Frankenstein

Martin F. Norden

During a late-1940s revival of Bride of Frankenstein, a spectator was so caught up in the film's delectable frissons that she barely noticed several latecomers who had slipped in behind her near the back of the theater. As Bride unfolded, however, she became increasingly annoyed by their behavior; the latecomers were actually laughing at the film. Believing they were mocking the 1935 Universal horror-fest, she finally turned back to the group and addressed its presumed leader, a slender, tall, impeccably groomed man in his late 50s. "If you don't like the show," she huffed, "you can damn well leave!" Little did she know that the chuckling fellow to whom she had just given a piece of her mind was James Whale, the Englishman who had directed Bride of Frankenstein more than a dozen years earlier.[1]

Whale, who enjoyed retelling this anecdote in his later years, clearly relished the intentional humor that he, his screenwriters, and his actors had woven into Bride so many years before. As history has shown, though, he was by no means the only person to have savored the film's comedic pleasures. Indeed, when the movie began playing in theaters across the United States during the spring of 1935, numerous critics immediately hailed it as a first-rate horror film that had something extra going for it: it was, well, funny. For example, Roland Barton wrote in the Independent Exhibitors Film Bulletin that Whale's film was "as good as the original Frankenstein in horrors, with an added touch of humor," adding that it "will completely engross almost any audience with its fine interplay of comedy and imaginative drama." A Boston Globe reviewer wrote that Whale "has built up a spine-chilling production, enlivened by carefully spaced comedy-relief." Hollywood-based syndicated writer Douglas Churchill whimsically suggested that a more appropriate title for the film might have been *Fun in a Morgue*.[2]

As *Bride* made its way around the globe later that year, international critics had a more mixed response to it; however, they appreciated its humor as a means of making the horrific subject material more palatable. A London *Times* reviewer disliked *Bride*'s fright-inducing aspects ("the sole purpose of this film is to horrify," the critic sniffed, lamenting that the actors' talents were "wasted on a production with so ignoble a motive") but praised its comedic moments; without them, the critic wrote, *Bride* "would be an intolerably morbid affair with its preoccupation with murder, the coffin, and the grave." A scribe for the *Sydney Morning Herald* wrote that Whale "treats the unpromising theme with admirable balance, keeping it poised somewhere between farce and ugly melodrama." A reviewer for the Shanghai-based *China Press* was more charitable, writing that *Bride* "is the type of film which requires a distinctive sense of humor and enjoyment and of its type is first rate."[3]

What makes *Bride of Frankenstein* funny? How does its humor interact with and inform the film's scarifying aspects? Why did Whale and his colleagues wish to lace it with humor in the first place? These are easy questions to ask but difficult ones to answer. It's important to note that quite a few critics who wrote about the film during its initial release didn't acknowledge its humor at all,[4] and those who did often did not agree on what it was they found funny. Critics in subsequent decades detected additional layers of humor in the film, far different from those observed by their journalistic counterparts in 1935. Lyn Phelan, writing in 2000, described it as "a strangely beautiful and great horror film," that had come to be seen as "a camp classic brimming with a knowing, sexually loaded humour."[5]

This essay examines *Bride of Frankenstein*'s exceptionally wide range of comedic dimensions, including those revealed in scenes that Whale filmed but decided to cut and scenes described in the screenplay that were never filmed.[6] Though these moments did not find their way into the release version of the film, they do shed further light on the filmmaker's attitudes and intentions. *Bride*'s comedic dimensions included not only surface-level comic relief and Hollywood in-jokes, but also veiled (and not-so-veiled) references to such primal issues as sexuality, gender, and religion. Due to the strictures of Hollywood's Production Code, then strictly enforced, Whale and his screenwriters, William Hurlbut and John Balderston, had little choice but to cloak their humorously subversive views on these issues in oblique words and images. This strategy, however, helped to make the film a rich viewing experience by inviting the audience to read between the lines and is key to *Bride of Frankenstein*'s decades-long status as a cult classic.

Origins

Not surprisingly, Universal's decision to make *Bride of Frankenstein* can be traced to the overwhelming success of the film's predecessor, *Frankenstein*, in 1931. "Smacko, socko, loco went the house records, from border to border and coast to coast," as Universal publicist Joe Weil colorfully described *Frankenstein*'s success in the trade language of the day. Producer Carl Laemmle Jr. could barely contain his glee over the film's boffo box office. "Remember my prediction about *Frankenstein*?" he chortled shortly after the film swept the nation. "We hit them with that one, didn't we? We've started a cycle of crime and horror stories and we're going to continue along that line." He elaborated: "Mystery and crime, if they are presented from an original and unusual point of view, are always interesting. The cycle we started with *Dracula* and *Frankenstein* can go on indefinitely. It doesn't have to lose its flavor and go out of favor like the gangster pictures."[7]

Laemmle, widely known in the industry as "Junior" Laemmle, had recently stepped down as Universal's production head and wanted his first independently produced film for the studio to be a sequel to *Frankenstein*. He also wanted *Frankenstein*'s director, James Whale, to helm it. What Junior did not anticipate, however, was Whale's reluctance to involve himself in a follow-up to the huge box office hit. The Briton privately told his colleague, screenwriter R. C. Sherriff, that he wanted nothing to do with the sequel, then tentatively titled *The Return of Frankenstein*. Said Whale of Laemmle and producers in general:

> They're always like that. If they score a hit with a picture they always want to do it again. They've got a perfectly sound commercial reason. *Frankenstein* was a goldmine at the box office, and a sequel is bound to win, however rotten it is. They've had a script made for a sequel and it stinks to heaven. In any case I squeezed the idea dry on the original picture, and never want to work on it again.[8]

Despite his initial rejection of what he termed "this horrible *Frankenstein* sequel,"[9] Whale eventually gave in and agreed to direct the film. He decided to develop the project as a "hoot," however, and had, in the words of biographer James Curtis, "no intention of making a straight sequel to *Frankenstein*."[10]

Whale began working with newly recruited scenarists Balderston and Hurlbut on a thorough revision of the script, and one of their first tasks was to create a new story from the ashes of *Frankenstein*'s conclusion: the Monster's fiery death in an old windmill. "The producers realized they'd made a dreadful mistake," said Boris Karloff, who played the shambling Frankenstein creation. "They let the Monster die in the burning mill. In one brief script conference, however, they brought him back alive. Actually, it seems he had only fallen through the flaming floor into the millpond beneath, and now could go on for reels and reels!"[11]

After injecting life back into the Monster—an action strikingly appropriate for this particular storyline—Whale directed Balderston and Hurlbut to return to the Mary Shelley novel for additional narrative ideas. They obliged by harvesting a number of developments involving Shelley's Monster that hadn't been used in the first film, including his encounter with a blind man in the woods, his newfound ability to speak, and his insistence that Frankenstein create a mate for him. However, Whale was not especially interested in creating a faithful adaptation (his *Frankenstein* of 1931 had migrated far from the source material) and encouraged the writers to mine these developments for their comedic possibilities.[12]

Even before the heavily revised script was ready, Whale began assembling a cast consisting largely of actors with whom he had worked before. They included some of the original *Frankenstein* performers—principally Boris Karloff as the Monster, Colin Clive as Henry Frankenstein, and Dwight Frye as his grave-robbing assistant, Karl[13]—and actors who had worked with Whale on other movies such as *The Old Dark House* (1932) and *The Invisible Man* (1933). He believed this latter group of actors—including Ernest Thesiger as a wily and seductive scientist, Una O'Connor as an apoplectic maid, and E. E. Clive as a harrumphing Burgomaster—would contribute significantly to the film's comedic dimensions.

With Whale's guidance and participation, Balderston and Hurlbut completed a shooting script in early December 1934. Junior Laemmle approved the script and, following the new Hollywood protocol, submitted it to the Production Code Administration, the intra-industrial regulatory board, for final approval before shooting could begin. PCA head Joseph Breen raised a number of concerns about the film's script, mainly ones related to religion, free love, and the brutality of some of the Monster's scenes. After Whale and Laemmle addressed these issues, production began in early January 1935 and continued into March.

The resulting film ran about 90 minutes and was shown to preview audiences during the first week of April. After the previews, Whale decided to eliminate several scenes that he felt drifted too far from the main narrative. Much to Junior's dismay, they included scenes that had accentuated the film's horrific qualities; one featured the ghoulish Karl plotting to murder his hateful aunt and uncle by making it look as if the Monster did it, another showed the Monster giving a severe and possibly fatal beating to the Burgomaster, and still another showed Karl murdering Henry Frankenstein's fiancée, Elizabeth (Valerie Hobson). Junior was concerned that the film was becoming less of a horror film and more of a comedy, but Whale prevailed. "I have no sympathy with gruesomeness on the screen apart from fantastic imagination," the director commented.[14] The final film, its name changed from *The Return of Frankenstein* to *Bride of Frankenstein*, clocked in at about 75 minutes.

The film begins with a short prologue that depicts *Frankenstein* author Mary Shelley (Elsa Lanchester) in conversation with Lord Byron (Gavin Gordon) and Percy Bysshe Shelley (Douglas Walton) while a storm rages outside. The filmmakers included the prologue to help explain how the Monster avoided incineration at the end of *Frankenstein* and perhaps also to give their film something resembling a literary cachet. In addition to providing a bit of low verbal comedy (Gordon rolls his r's in an extremely exaggerated way while uttering lines such as "I take great relish in savoring each separate horror—I roll them over on my tongue"), the prologue introduces the audience to the film's ample ironic humor; in response to Lord Byron's invitation to look out the window at the storm, Mary declines by gently replying, "You know how lightning alarms me." Audiences familiar with the lightning-driven pyrotechnics of the *Frankenstein* films would doubtless have chuckled at that comment.

The main point of the prologue, however, is to allow Mary to spin a sequel to her famous novel for Lord Byron, her husband, and of course the audience. As visualized by Whale and cinematographer John Mescall, her explanation resembles an extended flashback that takes up the remainder of the film.

After the Monster has escaped the burning windmill and murdered several people in the process, Elizabeth nurses her fiancé, Baron Henry Frankenstein, back to health from his traumatic ordeal. Their bed of tranquility is abruptly ruptured by the appearance of Dr. Septimus Pretorius (Thesiger),[15] Henry's quirky and elderly mentor who, like his star pupil, has stolen corpses in pursuit of an unholy quest: the artificial creation of life. He proposes to Henry that they work together to form another creature and shows him the results of some of his own experiments: a half-dozen miniature people—homunculi—grown from seed. Despite some misgivings, Henry is intrigued and tentatively agrees.

Meanwhile, townspeople led by their Burgomaster capture the Monster and carry him hog-tied to the local prison. They chain him to a prison chair, but within seconds of his captors' departure the Monster breaks his bonds through sheer preternatural strength. He escapes into the woods, where he encounters a nameless blind Hermit (O. P. Heggie). Believing the Monster simply to be a rather large mute, the Hermit takes him under his wing and begins a modest socialization process for him; he teaches him to speak and introduces him to the joys of music and friendship, as well as good food, drink, and cigars. They enjoy an idyllic life together until two hunters happen upon the Hermit's cottage, spy the Monster, and begin struggling with him. Chaos ensues.

Forced to flee again, the Monster accidentally encounters Pretorius in a crypt and is pleased to learn that the scientists plan to create a mate for him. However, the plans have gone awry; Henry, still shaken from the disastrous results of his previous experiment, has second thoughts and wants to back out of the collaboration. Undaunted, Pretorius enlists the Monster to convince Henry to reconsider. The Monster obliges by abducting Elizabeth and holding her captive until Henry and Pretorius make a woman for him. The scientists eventually create a Monstress (Elsa Lanchester, in a dual role) stitched together from cadavers and brought to life with lightning.[16] Yet, in an unanticipated turn of events, the Monstress rejects the Monster and is drawn to Henry. In response, the devastated Monster orders Henry and Elizabeth to escape before pulling a lever that obliterates the laboratory, himself, the Monstress, and Pretorius.

Views from 1935

Within this narrative framework, Whale and his screenwriters were able to leaven their grotesque story with considerable doses of humor. The most easily identifiable material—indeed, the most frequently observed by critics in 1935—is the surface-level comic relief provided by two Whale favorites in secondary roles: O'Connor as a screechy housekeeper named Minnie, and Clive as the blowhard Burgomaster.

The script describes Minnie as "a dour, cadaverous calamity howler." As she surveys the burning remains of the old windmill near the beginning of the film, the script calls for her to watch "the gruesome disaster with a grim satisfaction; it is meat and drink to her—she has a lust for horror—her aged emotions are fed and glutted on violence, obscenity and death."[17] O'Connor, dressed in traditional Tyrolean *tracht* topped with a ribbon-festooned headdress, played the role to the hilt. "Well, I must say, that's the best fire I ever saw in all me life!" she cackles lustily. Later, after everyone else has gone to the Frankenstein castle to deliver the unconscious Henry, she stays behind at the mill, presumably to continue feeding her bloodlust. The Monster, who has just murdered the parents of the girl he killed in *Frankenstein*, suddenly looms behind her. It's a classic comic moment that hinges on low-level dramatic irony; we see him but she does not. She turns, realizes who's behind her, and then races back to the castle, screaming at the top of her lungs.

Whale and his writers gave O'Connor a number of choice lines of dialogue. After the villagers have captured the Monster and shackled him to a chair in the town jail, for instance, Minnie peers through the bars of a window and says to anyone who'll listen, "I'd hate to find him under my bed at night. He's a nightmare in the daylight, he is." Well acquainted with O'Connor's actorly talents, Whale allowed her to improvise whenever possible. Shortly after the villagers have captured the Monster, for example, the Burgomaster orders several men to bind him. Whale then cut to a close-up of a wild-eyed Minnie, who calls out to the men with dialogue not in the script: "You want any help there? I'll bind him!"

Another example occurs earlier in the film, when a mysterious pounding on the castle's front door shatters the relative quiet of the Frankenstein

Una O'Connor as Minnie, the wild-eyed maid, provided much of *Bride of Frankenstein*'s comic relief.

manor. According to the script, Minnie was merely to say "Who's there?" and "What's all this?" in response to Pretorius's excessive knocking.[18] Whale and O'Connor improvised a bit of dialogue that allowed her character to comment on several characters, including the as-yet-unseen Pretorius. The improvisation included these lines: "All right. All right! Don't knock the castle over. We're not all dead yet." By relying on O'Connor's comedic skills to build up the scene, Whale created a moment similar to the famous Porter scene in *Macbeth* (Act II, Scene 3), in which a drunken porter complains about Macduff's zealous knocking at the gate of Inverness. As with the Porter scene, Minnie's door-answering moment helps relieve the strong tension that's been building.

Critics overwhelmingly praised O'Connor's work. "Una O'Connor walks away with the feminine honors for as neat a bit of acting as has come to our eyes and ears for some time," raved the *Hollywood Reporter*, while *Motion Picture Daily* observed, "Una O'Connor, as a frightened maid, gives a great performance." Critics in New Zealand and Australia were especially impressed. "The inimitable Una O'Connor as Minnie successfully relieves the tension," wrote a critic for Auckland's *New Zealand Herald*, while the critic's colleague at the *Auckland Star* opined that the actress provided "a welcome vein of comedy." A writer for the Sydney-based periodical *Truth* observed she was "always a clever performer" who "rates high for her frantic display of terror, running like a spectre through the play."[19]

Though his presence in the final version of the film was severely curtailed by several subplot excisions, the handlebar-mustachioed actor Clive was likewise up to the challenge of his comic role: the Burgomaster, described in the script as "pompous" and "officious."[20] Clive's job was essentially to play the character as a windbag largely oblivious to the threat posed by the Monster. The self-important Burgomaster doesn't hesitate to take credit for the Monster's capture ("You may thank your lucky stars they sent for me to safeguard life and property"), tells the weeping Minnie to "shut up," and expresses his frustration when the townspeople don't do as he says. "I get no cooperation, none at all!" he laments. He's not even convinced that the person they've been pursuing is a monster. "This strange man you call a monster is dead. Monster, indeed," he scoffs. Indeed, his "Monster, indeed" line becomes a virtual refrain in the film. After the incarcerated Monster breaks his chains, tears down his cell door, and starts shredding another in the jail's dungeon, Whale created another bit of dramatic irony by cutting to a scene outside the jail in which the Burgomaster addresses the curious townspeople. "Go to your homes. Just an escaped lunatic," he assures them. "Quite harmless." The film then cuts back to the Monster, who finishes demolishing the second door and emerges onto the street. Everyone panics, including the know-it-all Burgomaster. Critics appreciated Clive's comic work in these and other scenes.[21]

The performances of O'Connor and Clive weren't the only things in *Bride* that 1935 reviewers tagged as comedic; another was the strange little scene in which Pretorius shows off his collection of miniature creations to Henry. In fact, this was the only scene that the *Philadelphia Inquirer*'s Mildred Martin identified as humorous. Calling *Bride* "a gorgeous and grotesque sequel," she wrote that "the sequence devoted to the squeaking little king, queen, bishop and mermaid he has grown from seeds and keeps in pickle jars is delightfully humorous and original."[22]

Martin was referring to the rather charming comedy arising from the scene's special effects cinematography and altered soundtrack in which three of the miniature characters—a King, a Queen, and an Archbishop—chatter in chipmunk-like unintelligible voices. (The others, a Devil, a Ballerina, and a Mermaid, remain mute.) The scene deserves a closer look, for it features a different kind of humor with which Martin may not have been entirely familiar: inside jokes that Hollywood denizens, if not the general public, would have understood. For example, the King is a Henry VIII look-alike who, after munching on a chicken leg, escapes from his jar and tries to break into the Queen's jar. Not coincidentally, Elsa Lanchester's husband, Charles Laughton, who was friends with Whale and had worked with him on the 1932 film *The Old Dark House*, had won an Oscar in March 1934 for playing the title role of *The Private Life of Henry VIII*. Los Angeles audiences could hardly miss the connection; *Private Life* ran April 17–19, 1935, in a brief revival at Los Angeles's Pantages Theatre immediately before the premiere of *Bride* in that same venue.

Whale and his screenwriters attached insider humor to some of the other homunculi. Moments after showing off the King, the Queen, and a dozing Archbishop (the latter of whom, once awakened, objects strongly to the King's amorous advances to the Queen), Pretorius presents a miniature Devil and remarks: "There's a certain resemblance to me, don't you think?" The resemblance is not so surprising; the actor who played the Devil, Peter Shaw, was Thesiger's stand-in on the *Bride* set.

The Mermaid, who Pretorius impishly describes as "an experiment with seaweed," was played by Josephine McKim, a champion swimmer who won three medals at the 1928 and 1932 Olympics. Her character is the only homunculus fully submerged in water, likely a nod to her recent athletic achievements. However, Whale's decision to represent her that way may have been a sly reference to something else; McKim had recently garnered notoriety in Hollywood for performing nude in an underwater swimming scene in *Tarzan and His Mate* (1934).

Though Pretorius shows off six individual creations to Henry, a wide shot in the scene reveals a seventh jar inhabited by a toddler in a high chair. In a bit that Whale cut from the final film, Pretorius introduces the youngster, played by short-stature actor Billy Barty, by saying, "I think this Baby will grow into something worth watching." The script describes the toddler as "looking as if it might develop into a Boris Karloff" and in the midst of tearing a flower to pieces.[23] This action was perhaps a reference to an infamous scene in *Frankenstein* in which the Monster and a little girl he has just befriended toss daisies into a lake; when they run out of flowers, the Monster, with childlike logic, continues their game by throwing the girl into the lake, too. Though Whale evidently thought the "Baby" moment too bizarre or silly to include in the final version of the film, it too had a sense of the in-joke to it.

In addition to suffusing the scene with inside references, Whale and his screenwriters further sought to lighten the scene by having one of Pretorius's grave-robbing assistants accidentally walk in just as Pretorius is showing off his specimens to Henry. After Pretorius throws him out, the chap rushes home and rouses a fellow grave-robber from a drunken sleep. "He is the Devil I tell you," the agitated fellow blurts out, "and now he's got a lot of little devils all in bottles, no higher than that! It's witchcraft! He ought to be burned at the stake!" Supremely nonplussed, the other ghoul merely turns over in his bed and mutters, "Oh, go and bury your grandmother."[24] Perhaps falling flat when it played on the screen, the scene ended up on the cutting room floor alongside the Barty Baby material.

One additional *Bride* scene tickled the funny bone of contemporaneous reviewers. Describing the movie as "a curious blend of brutality and comedy," a critic for the *Hartford Courant* discussed only one instance of its humor: the scene in which the nameless, blind Hermit teaches the Monster to speak and shares the pleasures of good food, drink, cigars, and music. "It is at this point that the action borders on the slapstick," the *Courant* critic wrote, a comic urge that would be fully realized in Mel Brooks's burlesque of the scene in *Young Frankenstein* almost 40 years later.[25]

Bride's Hermit is a notable example of a disability-related movie stereotype known as the "Saintly Sage." Enjoying some popularity in 1930s and 1940s films, the Saintly Sage is usually shown as a blind older person who exudes wisdom and spirituality, and, with ham-handed filmmakerly irony, "sees" (i.e., understands) things that sighted people do not.[26] In other films of the time, such as *The Devil Doll* (1936), *Heidi* (1937), *Saboteur* (1942), and

The Enchanted Cottage (1945), the seer-like Sage isn't played for laughs. In *Bride of Frankenstein*, however, the situation is open to debate. Despite the Hermit's wisdom and compassion, he too is arguably a source of humor. His piety, accentuated by an organ rendition of Schubert's "Ave Maria" on the film's soundtrack, comes across as excessive and overwrought to the point of parody. In addition, his prayer of thanks to God for sending him a friend "to be a light to mine eyes and a comfort in time of trouble" is rendered highly ironic minutes later; far from serving as a "comfort," the Monster struggles violently with two wayward hunters who have stumbled upon the Hermit's cottage. Whale ratcheted up the irony by having the cottage go up in flames during the struggle, about a minute and a half after the Hermit had assured the Monster that "fire is good."[27]

Modern Assessments

The humorous situations involving Minnie and the Burgomaster, Pretorius's miniatures, and the Hermit tell only part of the story of *Bride of Frankenstein's* comedy. For contemporary audiences, the humor in *Bride* emanates mainly from subjects buried, so to speak, beneath its surface: namely, issues of religion, gender, and sexuality. By 1935, with the Breen office cracking down on anything resembling controversial subject matter in the movies, Whale and his screenwriters had little choice but to submerge their decidedly nonmainstream views. No doubt they enjoyed the creative challenges inherent in such an undertaking.

It is reasonably clear, for example, that Whale and his writers were bent on making a mockery of organized religion throughout the film. An indication of their attitudes may be found in a line of dialogue that never made it to the final film. The script originally called for Pretorius to utter the following line to Henry during the homunculi scene noted above: "Leave the charnel house and follow the lead of nature . . . or of God—if you are fond of your fairy tales."[28] The Breen office found this statement offensive, and so, during the shooting, Whale changed the latter part of the line to "or of God, if you like your Bible stories." However, Ernest Thesiger's sneering delivery of the line leaves little doubt about the filmmakers' perspectives.

Far more conspicuous than this dialogue deletion is the film's frequent and bizarre association of the Monster with Christ imagery. Most famously, angry villagers capture the Monster early in the film, tie him to a pole, and, after binding his arms at the wrist above his head, raise him up above the crowd.

As a number of second-wave *Bride* critics have pointed out, the Monster's pose at this moment is similar to a standard crucified Christ image. It is a striking piece of iconography and, as it turns out, hardly coincidental; the script describes the moment in these terms: "To get the Monster into the cart the mob has to rear him up, and for a moment we see him raised against the sky, a terrible but pathetic sight—friendless, persecuted and almost crucified." The "almost" is appropriate; it's not quite the classic crucifixion pose but very close.[29]

Other examples abound. A crucifix on a wall in the Hermit's cottage is framed conspicuously behind the Monster's right shoulder and glows with an otherworldly light while the Hermit thanks God for sending him a friend. The Hermit pointedly directs his prayer to God the Father, in essence praising that paternalistic figure for sending his only begotten son. Later, after escaping the Hermit's burning cottage, the Monster wanders through a graveyard past a life-sized crucified Christ sculpture: a "Christus," as the script calls it.[30] According to the screenplay, the Monster views the figure on the cross as a fellow sufferer and tries to rescue it; the Breen office objected to this moment, however, and what's left in the scene is the Monster toppling a nearby statue of a bishop before crossing directly in front of the Christus and descending into a crypt.

Narratively, the film manifests strangely twisted parallels to the Christ story. Christ, the misunderstood good outsider, is crucified, thus sacrificing himself for the greater good, and is resurrected; the Monster, the misunderstood bad outsider, begins as dead, is resurrected at the start of the film, is crucified but defeats that crucifixion, enters a tomb instead of triumphantly emerging from it, and then sacrifices himself as well as Pretorius and the Monstress at the end of the film for the sake of Henry and Elizabeth. (On an extra-filmic level, he is of course resurrected again in the next film in the cycle, 1939's *Son of Frankenstein*, and countless productions thereafter.) It's as if the filmmakers took the ingredients that make up the Christ and Frankenstein stories and tossed them into a blender to see what comically sacrilegious material would result. They were no doubt beside themselves with giddiness when they learned that their Christianity-defiling film would have its world premiere on, of all days, Good Friday.[31]

Comic renderings of gender and sexuality also permeate *Bride of Frankenstein*, a point that *Philadelphia Inquirer* critic Mildred Martin hinted at in her 1935 review when she noted in passing that *Bride* "injects sex into already feverish material with strangely disturbing results." She had no idea how on-target she was with her brief comment; as a number of more recent commentators have argued, the film is replete with a potent blend of sexual/gender-related subtexts including homosexuality, bisexuality, necrophilia, incest, and the Oedipus complex.[32] These subtexts are best explained as a series of triangulated relationships among the *Bride* characters. Of them, the triangles that are played mostly for laughs are Elizabeth/Pretorius/Henry, Pretorius/Monster/Monstress-to-Be, and Henry/Monster/Monstress, each of which is discussed below.

Elizabeth/Pretorius/Henry

Three of the film's central characters may readily be seen as embodiments of heterosexuality, homosexuality, and bisexuality respectively. The threat that Pretorius poses to Elizabeth and Henry's relationship is revealed early in the film, when Elizabeth, on her would-be wedding night, describes to Henry an apparition she has seen: "It comes, a figure like Death, and each time he comes more clearly, nearer. It seems to be reaching out for you, as if it would take you away from me." At the height of her delirious narrative, someone begins pounding on the castle door. It's Pretorius, whom Minnie tartly describes to Henry and Elizabeth as "a very queer-looking old gentleman."[33] Characterized by horror author Clive Barker as "an archetypal old queen,"[34] Pretorius is unmistakably Elizabeth's rival and wants to take Henry away from her; there is little question that his attempt to persuade Henry to work with him is a seduction, pure and simple. Giving Elizabeth a thoroughly disgusted look, Pretorius insists on being alone with the young baron. The first thing he says to Henry after she has reluctantly departed is that "we must work together" to create artificial life. He also states that he and Henry "have gone too far to stop, nor can it be stopped so easily." Henry objects to the proposition, but, after Pretorius tells him that he too has created life, the younger scientist is intrigued and drops his opposition. That very evening, when Henry and Elizabeth would otherwise be sharing their first night as husband and wife, Henry abandons her and eagerly runs off with Pretorius to the latter's abode.

Pretorius's suggestive dialogue continues into the next scene, in which he reveals his miniature humans to Henry as proof of his fecundity, "now that you are my partner." He attempts to ply Henry with alcohol—"Do you like gin? It's my only weakness"—and later observes, "My experiments did not turn out quite like yours, Henry, but science, like love, has her little surprises." After showing off his homunculi, Pretorius mock-laments to Henry that size does matter: "Normal size has been my difficulty. You did achieve size. I need to work that out with you."

Dr. Septimus Pretorius (Ernest Thesiger, left) escalates his seduction of Dr. Henry Frankenstein (Colin Clive) late in the film.

Pretorius/Monster/Monstress-to-Be

It's obvious that Whale and his writers designed Pretorius as an outrageously fey character, and Thesiger's performance contributed greatly to their concept of him. Much of the film's campy humor can be traced to the actor's work, particularly his utterances of certain key lines. The humor is especially evident in a scene that hints at a Pretorius/Monster/Monstress-to-Be triangle: the infamous crypt scene. At Pretorius's direction, two ghouls have just retrieved the corpse of a 19-year-old woman and cleaned off its bones. Happy with the results, Pretorius dispatches the repulsed ghouls ("This is no life for murderers," one of them whimpers while exiting) and settles down to a bizarre candlelight dinner next to the pristine skeletal detritus of the young woman. A goofy, off-key piano motif plays on the soundtrack while Pretorius laughs maniacally to himself, but his pleasure is soon punctured by the Monster's sudden appearance. Far from being startled, Pretorius merely turns to him and says matter-of-factly, "Oh! I thought I was alone." He is completely unsurprised that the Monster can speak and even offers him a cigar, saying cigars are his only weakness—a line that contradicts his earlier statement to

Henry about gin. In response to the Monster's now-famous necrophilous utterance, "I love dead—hate living," Pretorius sagely observes, "You are wise in your generation." Abetted by the script and Franz Waxman's eccentric musical score, Thesiger dryly but thoroughly nails the comedy in this scene.

Henry/Monster/Monstress

Another of *Bride*'s triangulations humorously hinges on one of the movie's key ambiguities: the true identity of the bride of Frankenstein. Though the film has often been advertised as *The Bride of Frankenstein*, its formal title is *Bride of Frankenstein*,[35] and the absence of the definite article raises the possibility of more than one mate for Henry: Elizabeth, Pretorius, even the Monstress. The Monstress would not ordinarily be included among Henry's potential brides were it not for a conspicuous excision from the film and a particular line of dialogue left in. Whale originally planned to have Karl murder Elizabeth and bring her body to the laboratory after Henry and Pretorius commission him to fetch a fresh female corpse. The director ultimately judged this narrative development as too macabre and filmed a brief replacement scene in which Karl murders an anonymous young woman; had Whale included the original scene, however, the film would have merged two contenders for the title role into one.[36] As for the problematic line of dialogue, it occurs immediately after the doctors have brought the Monstress to life; as a wedding-bell motif by Waxman plays on the soundtrack, Pretorius proudly introduces her as "the Bride of Frankenstein." Though audiences have often associated the name "Frankenstein" with the Monster over the years, it actually refers only to the tormented doctor who created him. If its usage here isn't a mistake, then Pretorius views the new creature as Henry's bride, not the Monster's (unless of course he is referring to himself with the line). His pronouncement hints at a symbolically incestuous relationship between the Monstress and Henry, since the latter character is a father figure for the former. The filmmakers enhanced this potential relationship by heavily implying that the Monstress is attracted to Henry; she locks eyes with him several times and nearly swoons in his presence. After signaling her disgust for the Monster with several eardrum-rupturing shrieks, she even shields Henry with her body when the Monster begins his final rampage. Since Henry is also a father figure for the Monster—indeed, the latter's bitter hatred for Henry invites an Oedipal reading of their relationship—the movie doubly complicates the situation with its suggestion of a potentially incestuous relationship between the Monstress and her "brother," the Monster. Of course, it's a relationship that never happens after the carnage that follows her rejection of his clumsy romantic overtures.

Conclusion

Bride of Frankenstein brims with all sorts of humor: comic relief, Hollywood in-jokes, irony, thinly disguised jabs at religion, and comic takes on non-mainstream sexuality and aberrant procreation. Indeed, the film is founded on the darkly humorous premise that two entities made up of previously dead bodies are about to be united in holy matrimony. The concept proved problematic for Universal when it came time to promote the quirky film, but, much to the studio's credit, it decided to satirize the conventional Hollywood love story in many of its advertisements. Promotional images included the Monster in silhouette cradling an attractive young woman whose shapely legs are exposed beneath her traditional bridal gown, for example, while others featured the Karloff and Lanchester characters staring longingly into each other's eyes. In other publicity, the studio even kiddingly identified itself with Henry and Pretorius; a two-page spread appearing in the April 6, 1935, issue of *Universal Weekly* depicted the scientists' laboratory and sported the headline, "Here is where Universal created 'The Bride of Frankenstein' for you!"[37]

Though *Bride of Frankenstein* was a studio film involving the talents of dozens of people, it is safe to conclude that it was largely the vision of one person: James Whale. As an A-list director at Universal, Whale had considerable leeway in the creation of the film; he worked closely with his screenwriters, contributed significantly to the script, handpicked the cast, and developed numerous concepts for the settings, costumes, and other elements of what we now call production design. According to the film's editor, Ted Kent, Whale "had complete control from beginning to end. I don't believe he could have worked any other way." As we ponder the film's peculiarities and consider its exquisite balance of humor and horror, we have Whale's insistence on thorough creative control to thank. I agree with Whale biographer James Curtis, who argued that the control Whale maintained "is arguably the only way he could have achieved such a perverse—and captivating—mix of comedy and horror."[38]

Notes

1. The anecdote is recalled in Curtis, *James Whale*, 127; and in Manguel, *Bride of Frankenstein*, 28.

2. Roland Barton, "As I See Them," *Independent Exhibitors Film Bulletin*, May 22, 1935, 8; "New Films Reviewed," *Boston Globe*, May 4, 1935, 12; Douglas W. Churchill, "Reviews of the New Films," *Jamaica* (NY) *Daily Press*, Screen and Radio Weekly section, April 28, 1935, 13.

3. "New Films in London," *Times* (London), July 1, 1935, 14; "Film Reviews," *Sydney Morning Herald*, July 22, 1935, 6; "Karloff Again Shines in New Film Thriller," *China Press*, September 12, 1935, 5.

4. Sample adulatory reviews, none of which mentions the film's humor, include Nelson B. Bell, "'The Bride of Frankenstein' Causes Goose Flesh and Shudders at RKO-Keith's," *Washington Post*, May 3, 1935, 22; Frank Nugent, "The Screen," *New York Times*, May 11, 1935, 21; Martin Dickstein, "The Screen," *Brooklyn Daily Eagle*, May 13, 1935, 8; and Red Kann, "Insiders' Outlook," *Motion Picture Daily*, April 26, 1935, 2.

5. Phelan, "Artificial Women and Male Subjectivity," 173.

6. The film's shooting script (hereafter identified as "script") is reprinted in its entirety in Riley, *The Bride of Frankenstein*. The script is dated December 1, 1934, and features a rather odd pagination scheme; each of its eight sequences begins with an alphabetic letter and has its own set of page numbers.

7. Joe Weil, "Hold Your Breath!—the Bride of Frankenstein Is Coming!?!" *Universal Weekly*, February 23, 1935, n.p.; Laemmle cited in "A Chat with Laemmle Jr.," *New York Times*, April 3, 1932, X6.

8. Cited in Sherriff, *No Leading Lady*, 269.

9. Ibid.

10. Curtis, *James Whale*, 118.

11. Quoted in Mank, "Production Background," 26.

12. See Mank, "Production Background," 27. For a discussion of some key differences between the novel and the films, see Winner, *Autonomous Technology*, 306–17.

13. There's some question of the Frye character's identity in the screenplay. Though others in the film consistently refer to him as Karl (an oblique reference to Carl Laemmle Jr. perhaps), the script identifies him at various points as Fritz, Karl, Nephew, and First Ghoul.

14. Whale, cited in "Director of 'The Bride of Frankenstein' Tells All," undated Universal publicity material, reprinted in Riley, *Bride of Frankenstein*, n.p. See also Mank, "Production Background," 34.

15. Pretorius's first name is not actually mentioned in the film; however, Henry refers to him as "Professor Septimus Pretorius" in the script (B13).

16. Strangely, the script does not bestow any name upon the female Monster; it simply identifies her with such terms as "the figure" and "she." I have employed the term "Monstress" to distinguish her from the character played by Boris Karloff (identified as "Monster" in the script). See script, H18–H24.

17. Ibid., A10.

18. Ibid., B10.

19. *Hollywood Reporter* comment cited in Mank, 34; "Motion Picture Daily's Hollywood Preview," *Motion Picture Daily*, April 9, 1935, 6; "Entertainments," *New Zealand Herald* (Auckland), September 2, 1935, 15; "Film Programmes Reviewed," *Auckland Star*, August 31, 1935, 14; "Screen's Weirdest Lovers," *Truth* (Sydney, NSW, Australia), July 21, 1935, 29.

20. Script, D1.

21. For samples of reviews that highlighted his comedic work, see "Theater Reviews," *Buffalo Courier-Express*, May 3, 1935, 8; "Reviews of the New Feature Films," *Film Daily*, April 11, 1935, 9; and "Screen's Weirdest Lovers," *Truth* (Sydney, NSW, Australia), July 21, 1935, 29.

22. Martin, "Stanley, 'Bride of Frankenstein,'" *Philadelphia Inquirer*, May 10, 1935, 17.

23. Script, B25.

24. Ibid., B29.

25. "Karloff Plays Horror Role in Poli Film," *Hartford Courant*, May 25, 1935, 18. For a close analysis of these two scenes, see Norden, "From Sage to Gene."

26. For further discussion of this disability-related stereotype, see Norden, *Cinema of Isolation*, 131–33.

27. The script called for a moment in which the Monster lies on a bed and the Hermit kneels by his side in prayer. In his fictionalized treatment of Whale's life and career, Christopher Bram speculates that Whale approved of a shot in which the Hermit appeared to be performing fellatio on the Monster. See Bram, *Father of Frankenstein*, 133–34.

28. Script, B26.

29. Clarens, *An Illustrated History of the Horror Film*, 69; Greenberg, *The Movies on Your Mind*, 215–16; Baumgarten, "*Bride of Frankenstein*," 23–24; script, C6.

30. Script, F8.

31. In particular, it opened in Chicago's Palace on Good Friday, April 19, and in Los Angeles's Pantages Theatre on Saturday, April 20.

32. Martin, "Stanley, 'Bride of Frankenstein,'" *Philadelphia Inquirer*, May 10, 1935, 17; Norden, "Sexual References in James Whale's *Bride of Frankenstein*"; Young, "Here Comes the Bride"; Phelan, "Artificial Women and Male Subjectivity."

33. According to the screenplay, a death figure actually appears: "A shadowy, ghost-like figure of Death, in grave sheet windings appears in the shadows at the window" (Script, B8). In the final film, though, we cut right to Pretorius pounding on the door.

34. Barker, quoted in *She's Alive!: Creating the Bride of Frankenstein* (1999), a film produced, written, and directed by David J. Skal.

35. The film's title is listed as *Bride of Frankenstein* (no *The*) in both the film's opening credits and its copyright entry with the Library of Congress. See *Catalog of Copyright Entries, Part 1, Group 3: Dramatic Compositions and Motion Pictures* 8, nos. 1–12 (Washington, DC: U.S. Government Printing Office, 1936), 132.

36. See Ackerman, "Foreword," 17. A photograph from the discarded scene is included on page 16.

37. Numerous examples of Universal's advertising and publicity materials for *Bride* are included in an unpaginated 12-page section of the Riley anthology that begins after page 42.

38. Kent, cited in Curtis, *James Whale*, 237.

Bibliography

Ackerman, Forrest J. "Foreword." In *The Bride of Frankenstein, Universal Filmscripts Series, Classic Horror Films, Volume 2*, edited by Philip J. Riley, 15–17. Absecon, NJ: MagicImage Filmbooks, 1989.

Baumgarten, Marge. "*Bride of Frankenstein.*" *CinemaTexas Film Notes* 13, no. 1 (September 7, 1977): 21–25.

Bram, Christopher. *Father of Frankenstein*. New York: Dutton, 1995.

Clarens, Carlos. *An Illustrated History of the Horror Film*. New York: Capricorn Books, 1976.

Curtis, James. *James Whale*. Metuchen, NJ: Scarecrow Press, 1982.

———. *James Whale: A New World of Gods and Monsters*. Boston: Faber & Faber, 1998.

Greenberg, Harvey. *The Movies on Your Mind*. New York: Saturday Review Press, 1976.

Manguel, Alberto. *Bride of Frankenstein*. London: British Film Institute, 1997.

Mank, Gregory W. "Production Background." In *The Bride of Frankenstein, Universal Filmscripts Series, Classic Horror Films, Volume 2*, edited by Philip J. Riley, 25–36. Absecon, NJ: MagicImage Filmbooks, 1989.

Norden, Martin F. *The Cinema of Isolation: A History of Physical Disability in the Movies*. New Brunswick, NJ: Rutgers University Press, 1994.

———. "From Sage to Gene: A Comparison of the 'Blind Hermit' Sequences in *Bride of Frankenstein* and *Young Frankenstein*." *Echoes and Mirrors: Comparative Studies in Film* 1, no. 1 (January 1994): 4–11.

———. "Sexual References in James Whale's *Bride of Frankenstein*." In *Eros in the Mind's Eye: Sexuality and the Fantastic in Art and Film*, edited by Donald Palumbo, 141–50. Westport, CT: Greenwood Press, 1986.

Phelan, Lyn. "Artificial Women and Male Subjectivity in *42nd Street* and *Bride of Frankenstein*." *Screen* 41, no. 2 (2000): 161–82.

Riley, Philip J., ed. *The Bride of Frankenstein, Universal Filmscripts Series, Classic Horror Films, Volume 2*. Absecon, NJ: MagicImage Filmbooks, 1989.

Sherriff, R. C. *No Leading Lady: An Autobiography*. London: Victor Gollancz, 1968.

Winner, Langdon. *Autonomous Technology: Technics-out-of-Control as a Theme in Political Thought*. Cambridge, MA: Massachusetts Institute of Technology Press, 1977.

Young, Elizabeth. "Here Comes the Bride: Wedding Gender and Race in *Bride of Frankenstein*." In *The Dread of Difference: Gender and the Horror Film*, 2nd ed., edited by Barry Keith Grant, 359–87. Austin: University of Texas Press, 2015.

~

CHAPTER EIGHT

Abbott and Costello Meet Frankenstein (1948)

Laughing in the Face of an Uncertain Future

Deborah Carmichael

"*Monsters of Menace vs. the Masters of Mirth*"

—Universal-International promotional material

Abbott and Costello typically receive little comment in discussions of film comedy, and even less in studies of horror movies, yet *Abbott and Costello Meet Frankenstein* (1948) demonstrates the duo's skill in navigating both genres. As with many of their other films, they also negotiate the issues and uncertainties of the times. Bud Abbott, the quintessential straight man, and the lovable, bumbling Lou Costello enjoyed a long collaboration with writer John Grant, who mixed gags with contemporary concerns. The obvious examples of this practice are the duo's service films starting with *Buck Privates* in 1941. Lou, often befuddled by circumstances thrust upon him, defines the plight of the little guy, delighting audiences when he ultimately prevails, even if only by accident. In *Abbott and Costello Meet Frankenstein*, Chick (Bud Abbott) and Wilbur (Lou Costello) are working stiffs who become entangled in the hunt for classic monsters who have infiltrated American shores. In an unusual plot turn, Lou Costello becomes a roly-poly object of desire for not one, but two women. Audiences, familiar with the team from vaudeville, the Kate Smith Hour on weekly radio, and their 21 previous films, relished this juxtaposition of their favorite comedians with supernatural adversaries. Both laugh-producing and eerie, the film sets the scene for an unusual conglomeration of mayhem, both monstrous and comic.

Plotting Renewed Success

By 1948, box office returns for horror films had declined, as had the popularity of Abbott and Costello, especially after the mixed response to two 1946 projects (*Little Giant* and *The Time of Their Lives*) that did not feature Abbott and Costello working as a comedy team and so disappointed audiences expecting to see familiar, laugh-inducing routines. In that year the duo slid out of the Top 10 moneymakers at the box office, finishing at number 20. Returning to the beloved characters from *Buck Privates*, the team's first film of 1947 (*Buck Privates Come Home*), proved more popular, as did their second, *The Wistful Widow of Wagon Gap* (1947). Abbott and Costello began to regain their popularity, ranking 16th at the box office for 1947. By the end of 1948, exhibitor polls recorded their films at number three in earnings. Certainly the atrocities of World War II weighed heavily on the minds of moviegoers, and while some argue that filmic distractions were a welcome respite, others felt there had been too much of a good thing. There had been hundreds of horror-themed B movies in the theaters during the 1940s—Universal alone had released well over 50—and Abbott and Costello had made more than 20 comedies. This level of screen saturation, along with renewed spending opportunities and new priorities for American consumers, forced studios to rethink plans for new releases.

Wrestling with a decline in the horror genre that had once guaranteed profits for the studio, Universal executives and producers began brainstorming ideas to bolster movie attendance. If one monster could elicit fearful screams from an audience, studio executives reasoned, then surely two creatures could double the terror. Jeffery Miller reports that screenwriter Curt Siodmak had made the suggestion as a joke, but found himself writing the first plot for this new concept.[1] Universal released its first monster combo, *Frankenstein Meets the Wolf Man* (1943), starting what has been called a "monster rally" in the film industry.[2] Universal followed up with *House of Frankenstein* (1944), which promised moviegoers the thrill of five menacing monsters: the Wolf Man, the Frankenstein Monster, Dracula, the Hunchback, and the Mad Doctor. In 1945, the five reunited in *House of Dracula*. Combining horror and comedy, Columbia Pictures released a Boris Karloff and Peter Lorre film, *The Boogie Man Will Get You* (1942). Cashing in on the popularity of Karloff's Broadway performance in *Arsenic and Old Lace*, the film combined a mad scientist, a mysterious house, and a zany cast. The success of the multi-monster films, and of Abbott and Costello's own encounter with haunting hijinks in *Hold That Ghost* (1941), led Universal-International to begin planning their own horror-comedy film in which Bud and Lou would meet Dracula, Frankenstein's Monster, and the Wolf Man. Three monsters plus one popular comedy team would, studio executives hoped, equal novelty and increased admissions at the box office.

The project was originally titled *The Brain of Frankenstein*, but after many iterations, it became *Abbott and Costello Meet Frankenstein*, trading on the popularity of both the comedy team and the monster. Although other horror/comedy films had been released earlier, this film draws from two established cinematic traditions: Universal's classic monsters and Bud and Lou's expected hilarity. Unlike earlier combinations of screams and laughter, *Abbott and Costello Meet Frankenstein* also engages with the anxieties and concerns of a postwar America reassessing peacetime social roles, particularly for women, and contemplating an uncertain future with looming ideological and nuclear threats. Bud and Lou, while not erasing the uncertainties, provided zany shenanigans to ameliorate the apprehensions of the era.

Balancing Fright and Frolic

Many film critics see the comic insertion of Abbott and Costello as the end of the time-honored horror narrative.[3] Lon Chaney Jr. has been quoted as lamenting, "Abbott and Costello ruined the horror film; they made buffoons out of the monsters."[4] However, as Janet Staiger has argued, "Hollywood films have never been 'pure'—that is, easily arranged in categories."[5] Where there is no purity, there can be no hybridity. Locating the quintessential movie as an exemplar of a film genre remains imprecise, if not impossible. As Rick Altman has outlined, the idea of a film genre shifts depending on the situation. For the producers, genre is a "blueprint" or "formula," a shorthand for describing a project. For the director, genre motifs offer a "structure as [a] formal framework." For distributors and exhibitors, genre provides a convenient "label" to use in promotion. For the audience, genre suggests a "contract" for anticipated response.[6] In the case of *Abbott and Costello Meet Frankenstein*, genre served the needs of Universal executives who "just wanted it done quickly so they could release it and make money off of it."[7] Posters promoting the film communicated both the comedy and the horror, displaying a headline, in a scary font, that read, "It's a grand New idea for FUN!" The monsters, depicted using stylized drawings, chase Abbott and Costello, who are represented by head shots with frightened expressions pasted onto cartoon bodies. The incongruous "labels" offered by the poster's text and images signaled to the moviegoer that the "contract" for the audience for this film would be a unique experience, offering shrieks of both terror and laughter. Similar cartoon representations appeared in the opening credits for the film, giving audiences an unexpected, comic introduction to Universal's iconic monsters.

The incongruity embodied in the poster is, according to Nöel Carroll, a key element linking horror and humor in the horror-comedy genre. For Carroll, horror occurs when incongruity creates "fear and disgust" in abnormal associations such as those between wolf and man or dead and undead. "Central to the classification of a fiction as . . . genre-horror is that it contains a monster designed to arouse emotions of fear in the audience in virtue of its harmfulness, and that of revulsion in virtue of its impurity."[8] The monsters in *Abbott and Costello Meet Frankenstein* perform in ways consistent with their previous horrific representations, while providing comic opportunities for Bud and Lou. The pair's incongruous antics evoke laughter from audiences that mitigates any such fear or revulsion.[9] Lou, in one of his signature catchphrases, reminds audiences that he is a "baaaad boy," underscoring the comic roots of his misbehavior.

Those comic roots grew in burlesque and vaudeville where physical comedy was the norm. Louise Peacock looks specifically at the realm of slapstick comedy, in which physical danger or threat of injury is seen as comic. Framing her explication as "recognition, embodied understanding, evaluation of pain, and appreciation," she develops the process that leads to laughter.[10] She notes that comic genre cues and the recognition of a known comic creates laughter from physical funny business. Slapstick in this film provides a point of release as tensions build to the physical harm Dracula intends for Wilbur. When Chick (Abbott's character) thumps Wilbur during the film, the humor is welcomed and recognized as part of the performers' standard routine, but the boundaries between comedy and horror often are more porous in *Abbott and Costello Meet Frankenstein*, shifting rapidly even within a single scene as terror gives way to laughter, which is quickly replaced with new terrors and new gags.

With Abbott and Costello enjoying top billing in the title, the scales could easily have been tipped to comedy at the expense of the possibilities for terror. The monsters maintain their vintage roles, however, with the exception of one comic double-take when the Frankenstein Monster first sees Wilbur. The set design, lighting, and music also establish the expected horror-film atmosphere. With the exception of those set in the freight office where Wilbur and Chick work and the hotel where they reside, every scene evokes a dark, gothic world full of mysterious foreboding. The principal settings include a "House of Horrors" attraction that trades on ghoulish historical figures, a masquerade ball that takes place in the midst of a forbidding wilderness, and a haunted castle set on a secluded island. These frightening sets are filmed in low light, with an abundance of shadows in which danger might lurk. In McDougal's House of Horrors, for example, Dracula (Bela Lugosi) and the Monster (Glenn Strange) disappear into the shadows as Wilbur tries to convince Chick that he has actually seen them. Frank Skinner's film score adds to the suspense and provides audible cues for the duo's encounters with danger. The visual and tonal darkness that pervades the film despite the light-hearted antics of the comic duo establishes the oppressive possibility of peril. All of these elements of performance, set design, lighting, and music establish a tension between horror film conventions and expectations of laughter.

Between Humor and Horror

The opening scene of the film immediately creates a dark mood of apprehension. The title card announces London, and Big Ben tolls through the fog-shrouded streets. Lawrence Talbot (Lon Chaney Jr.), anxiously peers into the night sky as he desperately tries to complete his call from London to enlist American allies in his mission to stop the delivery of Dracula and Frankenstein's Monster to La Mirada, Florida, where McDougal (Frank Ferguson) is scheduled to take possession of them, believing that they are new mannequins for his House of Horrors. Talbot's call reaches the freight office where Wilbur and Chick work as deliverymen, but the warning message goes undelivered; the full moon appears and Talbot—still on the phone—transforms into the Wolf Man, whose growls and snarls only confuse and annoy Wilbur. Hanging up the phone, Wilbur and Chick are not yet aware that the crates, which contain the *real* monsters, are already in their care. The foreign infiltration of the United States has begun, and this sneak attack from abroad will require two American working stiffs to thwart it.

By the time Talbot arrives in La Mirada, a series of scenes at the freight office have shown Wilbur and Chick unloading baggage and commercial shipments, establishing them as hard-working, if none too bright. At one point, Wilbur points out to McDougal that he works 16 hour days as a union man, and—when McDougal snorts in disbelief—explains that he belongs to *two* unions. Much of the action at the freight office is punctuated by slapstick gags, including Wilbur's acrobatics atop the monsters' crates, but the sequence at the freight office also establishes that Bud and Lou are portraying wage earners: not businessmen like McDougal, aristocrats like Count Dracula, or intellectuals like McDougal's scientist-ally, Dr. Sandra Mornay (Lenore Aubert). An attractive brunette, Mornay teases Chick with sexual innuendo and is affectionately solicitous toward Wilbur when he is hit in the head by falling luggage. Mornay's attention to the giddy Wilbur bewilders the more worldly Chick (Lou rarely gets the girl, least of all a beautiful European vixen), but when he laments that he "doesn't get it," she responds that "you never will." What neither of the duo realizes is that Sandra is responsible for bringing Dracula and the Monster to America, and that they, like McDougal—who believes he has scored a business coup—are all dupes in her evil plot, which drives the horror narrative of the film. When she reminds Wilbur that they will attend a masquerade ball together, it hints at her later unmasking.

Dark elements of classic horror combine, incongruously, with comedic riffs during the sequence in McDougal's House of Horrors, a tourist attraction that frightens its paying customers by displaying lifelike depictions of torture and death. Wilbur encounters both Dracula and the Monster in scenes that introduce the undead—played straight and menacing—into classic Abbott and Costello routines. Soon after the comedy duo arrives at McDougal's museum, a storm knocks out the electricity, establishing a spooky setting that also offers the reprise of the "Moving Candle" gag first used in *Hold That Ghost*. Wilbur first acts as an odd stand-in for Van Helsing, the vampire expert created by Bram Stoker in *Dracula* and featured as the Count's nemesis on screen. Stoker describes Van Helsing as a metaphysician with a noble visage; Wilbur is none of these, but he is assigned the responsibility of reading the histories of both monstrosities, producing laughter as his fear grows more apparent. Packing crates creak; a candle slides precariously as crate lids slowly open; a hand reaches from under a coffin lid. The causes of Wilbur's terrified yelps are apparent—especially after staring into Dracula's hypnotic eyes, he knows that horrific beings have infiltrated Florida—but Chick sees nothing each time he responds to Wilbur's cries for help. The shots shift rapidly between frightening creatures and comic routines in this sequence, ending with Wilbur and Chick headed off to jail having lost McDougal's valuable exhibits. Dracula and the Monster, who have been spying on the misdirected proceedings, watch everyone depart before stepping from the shadows to make their escape.

The sinister plot of Dracula and Dr. Mornay is fully exposed in the next sequence, which takes place on a densely forested island dominated by a gothic castle containing an ominous laboratory. Dracula morphs from an animated bat to a formidable caped vampire, and Dr. Mornay is revealed to be a mad scientist whose "curious operations" have led to police pursuit in Europe. Some critics have labeled the monsters in the film as stand-ins for Nazis,[11] but the film draws no such connection, and Universal's trio of monsters certainly predate U.S. involvement in World War II. Count Dracula's plan

The comic and the monsters (Lou Costello, Bela Lugosi, and Glenn Strange).

to restore the Monster with a new brain establishes an evil plot unfolding in America rather than an enemy abroad and points to an uncertain future rather than events of the past—all more consistent with the Red Scare than with the just-concluded war. Dracula's desire for a brain that is "simple and pliable" and that will "obey like a trained dog" gives the knowing audience, if not a loud guffaw, at least a chuckle. It also, however, suggests the growing awareness of a communist threat unfolding in 1948. As James Burnham wrote in 1947, "What distinguishes Communism is that terror constitutes the force upon which it is founded, and deliberate deception the content of its myth."[12] The success of Dracula's nefarious plan relies, like communist subversion, on the concealment of his identity and motives.

Dr. Mornay represents a different kind of threat to the American social and cultural order. She is developed beyond the boundaries of the stock "mad scientist" character and presented as a woman confident in her intellect and medical skills. Regardless of her intentions, she is a capable surgeon who has deciphered Frankenstein's notes on life and death. The success of Dracula's plan rests on her expertise, as he emphasizes when they meet. She is also a professional woman, and the film suggests that her unnatural occupation is her downfall. By 1944 many government agencies were trying to plan for postwar employment problems. The increase in working women across all occupations, including laboratories, posed a serious dilemma. Interviews with company managers indicated their hope that the women would "evaporate" from the work force. Many offered this solution: "Looking ahead beyond the present emergency, a suggested solution is to limit women to occupations that will not compete with those of men."[13] Sandra Mornay presumes to defy Dracula, maintaining her position as scientist, but although she declares that her will is as strong as Dracula's, she succumbs to his hypnotic powers and becomes his vampire slave rather than a partner in his plan. Sandra has not "evaporated," but her presumptuousness has been neutralized. She has been put into her proper position as a woman in postwar America, relinquishing her career and independence.

With the horror plot clearly established, Talbot unexpectedly arrives at Chick and Wilbur's hotel, hoping to enlist their cooperation in his goal of destroying the monsters. The relationship among the three—established amid snappy one-liners about American men as lascivious "wolves"—is uncomfortable. Wilbur, having firmly asserted that "I saw what I saw, when I saw it," is pleased when Talbot confirms that Dracula and the Monster are real, but Chick believes that both Talbot and Wilbur are delusional. Talbot begs to be locked into his room, knowing that the autumn moon will cause his transformation.[14] Later Wilbur foolishly ignores the warnings and enters Talbot's room. Stalked by the Wolf Man through the hotel suite, the horror is dispelled by Wilbur's dumb luck when he unwittingly moves out of harm's way just in the nick of time—a moment of comic relief after the deadly serious conversation between Dracula and Sandra in the previous sequence. The hotel scene closely illustrates Peacock's slapstick theory. The audience, recognizing both the suspenseful horror-film cues and the comic persona of Lou Costello, understands the possible pain that Wilbur might experience and evaluates those possibilities, finally delighting in the comic deferral of the horrific. Wilbur returns to the safety of his hotel room, where he will soon encounter more subtle dangers in the form of feminine wiles.

The film cuts to a brief expository scene to identify Joan Raymond (Jane Randolph), an attractive blonde insurance investigator who becomes the next woman to complicate Wilbur's romantic life. Sent "from the home office" to determine what happened to the missing freight (Dracula and the Monster), she indicates, through her body language and teasing smile, that her investigatory technique includes seductive manipulation. A confident, professional woman like Dr. Mornay, she too will be removed from the workforce by the end of the narrative, resolving the postwar social dilemma of how to make the workplace (once again) a "man's world." As Linda Eisenmann notes, "Fearful of economic pressure from returning soldiers, political and social leaders encouraged women to act as responsible citizens by leaving the labour force and rededicating themselves to family."[15] Joan, modeling this process, eventually reverts to an acceptable, postwar role.

Sandra Mornay now appears again, visiting Wilbur and Chick—who are evidently unable to afford or unable to find a postwar home—at their hotel room. Again, to the dismay of Chick, she lavishes affection on Wilbur, asking him to "come by at sunset" for their date for the masquerade ball and implying that Dracula will be a dangerous third wheel. Sandra explains that she is not the woman who posted bail for the pair, as they had assumed, and she departs with a sultry farewell for the smitten Wilbur, who assumes the succeeding knock at the door is her, returning for a goodbye kiss. Eyes closed, mouth puckered in anticipation of the kiss, he is startled to discover he is now being kissed by Joan Raymond, who reveals that *she* posted their bond and asks Wilbur if he believes in love at first sight. Chick is now beside himself with confusion and jealousy as Joan and Wilbur agree to meet in the lobby to select masquerade costumes together. With two dates for the ball that night, Bud and Lou have ample material for jokes and wordplay, banter running through much of the film to milk the humor of Wilbur as "romantic" lead.

The pair check on Talbot before the shopping trip and assume that his disheveled appearance and the destruction of his room are the results of an all-night drunken bender. When Talbot explains his lupine affliction, Wilbur wisecracks, "I'm kind of a wolf myself." In attempting to convince the duo to help destroy Dracula, Talbot describes the mission as a date with Destiny. Wilbur suggests that Destiny can be Chick's date for the evening. This hotel sequence is primarily comic but, as throughout the film, there remains an apprehensive undertone, especially in anticipation of the masked ball, an opportunity for appearances to become even more deceiving.

Masquerading Monsters, Masquerading Women

With the narrative exposition complete, *Abbott and Costello Meet Frankenstein* moves quickly to hysterically terrifying and laugh-inducing action while underscoring the tensions between Sandra and Joan. Arriving at the island castle, Wilbur, Chick, and Joan rapidly make important discoveries. Professor Stevens (Charles Bradstreet), the earnest-but-unperceptive assistant to Dr. Mornay, welcomes the threesome. Joan immediately discovers that *she* believes in love at first sight when she meets the handsome professor, beginning her journey from independent woman to conventional, victimized female. Dressed in a white, Grecian-style gown for the ball, Sandra descends the grand staircase, coolly greeting Joan, who is dressed as a gypsy—albeit a glamorous one. Their costumes disguise their true identities: Sandra would be more appropriately dressed in black, and Joan, the insurance company employee, is anything but a gypsy. The women withdraw upstairs to "powder their noses," using that time to spy on each other. Joan, still with some investigative initiative intact, rifles through Sandra's bureau drawers, discovering Victor Frankenstein's notebook and thus Mornay's connection to unnatural experimentation. Sandra, meanwhile, finds Joan's insurance-company identification card in her evening bag and realizes that her plans for reanimating the Monster could be compromised. Both women have taken on deceptive identities in both costume and personae. The dark (brunette) woman will be punished for her transgressive occupation by death at the hands of the Monster. The life of the fair (blonde) woman is spared, but she ends the movie in a subservient role as helpmate to Professor Stevens, whose manly resourcefulness saves the fair maiden from the Monster. Women with autonomous agency will be subdued; proper social roles will be restored. Patriarchal hegemony prevails at film's end.

Left alone downstairs, Wilbur and Chick decide to investigate the castle after a phone call from Talbot informs them that they are on "Dracula's island"—a claim Chick dismisses as "phony baloney." Creeping down the basement stairs together, Wilbur leans on the stair wall and spins into a hidden room, where he unwittingly ends up on the lap of the Monster. Comedy once again releases the tension of the horror, as Wilbur's comic alarm at his position sends him scurrying toward Dracula just as the Count emerges from his coffin. Locating the secret panel, Wilbur spins back to the stairs, where Chick has seen and heard nothing. The scene is thus a reprise of the "Changing Room" routine from *Hold That Ghost*, in which Lou experiences the room in its transformed state, but Bud sees nothing out of the ordinary. Evil creatures lie hidden just beyond the revolving wall, but the comic turn defuses the threat.

In the next scene, both Wilbur and Chick encounter Dracula, who introduces himself as "Dr. Lejos," the alias he is using in America. Wilbur, though he knows that Dracula exists, does not see through the disguise, since Dracula has been careful to conceal his face behind his cape at each encounter. In fact, when "Lejos" comments on Wilbur's brains, the would-be donor is quite flattered and flustered. Chick, meanwhile, has no reason at all to suspect that the charming European aristocrat is a blood-sucking monster. Lejos/Dracula extends the joke as he sends the pair off to the masquerade ball with a comment about "making the most of life—while it lasts," and a knowing look at Wilbur. To facilitate his goals, Dracula suggests that Sandra and Wilbur take a second boat to the party. Sandra, using a common feminine complaint, declares she has a headache and will not be going to the festivities. Knowing that there is an investigation afoot, and recognizing that Stevens has become too curious about the wealth of lab equipment, she warns Count Dracula that proceeding with the surgery will be too dangerous, which leads to the battle of wills ending in her vampiric infection and enslavement.

The masquerade ball scene that follows is festooned with paper lanterns, illuminating a crowd of dancers costumed as everything from cowboys to turbaned pashas—an ideal setting for humor based on concealed identities. Wilbur, for example, is attacked by McDougal, who is dressed as the devil and enraged at the loss of his "exhibits" and the profits they might have generated. Chick asks McDougal to hit Wilbur again, in front of a witness—a knight in shining armor—and McDougal obliges, but the witness's vision is blocked by a slipping visor and Wilbur is pummeled again, to no purpose. As is often the case, Costello suffers the physical consequences when one of Abbott's plans goes awry. The familiar comedic gag defuses the terror, but only briefly. Soon after, while searching for Wilbur and Chick, Talbot finds them in a locker room in their masquerade costumes, masks in hand. Chick, the disbeliever, has chosen a werewolf mask, unwittingly mocking Talbot. Wilbur, meanwhile, appears in caped, formal evening attire and a Mr. Hyde mask, unwittingly mirroring Dracula's appearance.

The masquerade ball's intimation that true identities can be masked or false ones invented to cloak dark intentions, and that appearances can be perversely deceiving, is underscored in the next scene by the appearance of Dracula, accompanied by a zombie-like Dr. Mornay. The Count quickly leads Joan onto the dance floor, ordering Sandra to walk with Wilbur. If Mornay, the woman who has learned the secrets of life and death, cannot resist Dracula's power, then Joan has clearly met her doom. Being led down the garden path, both literally and figuratively, Wilbur stops to pick a rose, but instead of offering it to Sandra, he fidgets with it until he pricks his finger. Professing her love, Sandra tells Wilbur she "wants to be in his blood." Wilbur's dawning understanding of his predicament is reflected in his growing terror and underscored by Costello's celebrated "fright face." Sandra appreciatively describes Wilbur as "so round, so firm, so fully packed," a phrase familiar to contemporary audiences as an advertising slogan for Lucky Strike cigarettes and as a line in a song whose lyrics used advertising slogans to describe a woman. The description underscores an important aspect of the team's comedy—Lou Costello's childish, feminized behavior set against the masculine pragmatism of Bud Abbott—and adds a further contrast in the masculinized behavior of Sandra Mornay, who plans to control Wilbur's body. This juxtaposition reinforces the stereotypical bifurcation of feminine emotion and masculine rationality, but the Abbott and Costello films ultimately invert the traditional reliance on logical problem solving, making Lou, whose intuition leads to successful and humorous plot resolutions, the hero. It is Wilbur, not Chick, who can see and can identify the foreign threats lurking in the shadows.

Before Wilbur's resistance to Sandra's hypnotic spell is fully tested, the evil enchantment is broken by the shouts of Chick and Talbot searching for Joan, and comic chaos ensues. Sandra rushes away as Wilbur, Chick, and Talbot all go crashing through the underbrush in different directions. Law enforcement officers and the posse of partygoers are all pursing the wrong suspects. Talbot falls to the ground as his moonlit metamorphosis begins; Wilbur discovers him and—mistaking him for a costumed Chick, relaxing when he should be searching—begins to pummel him. Talbot, now in wolf form, attacks and Wilbur runs for his life back to the party. Meanwhile, McDougal is almost killed by a Wolf Man, which he identifies (correctly) as Chick. Wilbur rushes up and, still confused, berates Chick for attacking him moments before. Another chase ensues with police and bloodhounds on the trail of the innocent duo. While fleeing, Wilbur encounters Dracula, who transforms into a bat and chases him to the boat where a now-hypnotized Joan is being kept. As Dracula returns to his human form, Chick observes Wilbur's reaction to the vampire's power and swoons himself. Dracula has been unmasked; Chick now knows that the creature truly exists and that the sinister infiltration is real. Racing through the wilderness, Chick discovers Talbot—who has also eluded his pursuers—and they agree to join forces in an attempt to save Wilbur and Joan. These shadowy scenes underscore the terror plot of hidden threats, misidentification, and the eventual awareness of the dangers concealed in a classic, frenzied chase sequence leavened by brief moments of comic relief.

The film then cuts to the shadowy castle, where Wilbur pleads for release and Sandra responds by promising Wilbur that he will live forever after a "simple operation"—transferring his brain into the Monster's body. She thus dispels any illusions of affection for Wilbur and makes plain her intention to physically harm him. Interrupted by her erstwhile lab assistant, Stevens, who has discovered both a captive Joan and the Frankenstein journal, she ruthlessly dispatches him by bashing his head with a fire extinguisher. Dracula rises from his coffin to begin the preparations for the ghoulish operation, but Wilbur—injecting humor—warns the Monster: "I've had this brain for 30 years and it hasn't worked right yet." Throughout the movie, in the direst of situations, Wilbur provides the joke work—the comic relief from repressed tensions that reach chilling levels.

While Dracula and Sandra wheel the Monster into the lab, Talbot rushes in to tend to Stevens, while Chick works to free Wilbur. Again, a quick gag eases the terror. Wilbur mimes his discomfort as Chick hands him the heavy rock he has used to break the lock imprisoning his pal. Chick not only moves the rock from Wilbur's hand, but he also apologizes: a rarity in an Abbott

Lou, held captive for his brain.

and Costello movie, and so an ironic, unexpected gag. Escaping the castle seems to end the danger, but Stevens demands that they return to save Joan. Wilbur declines, preferring to prepare the boat for their escape rather than rush back into danger, but Dracula finds him and a hypnotized Wilbur skips back to the castle. Chick, Talbot, and Stevens arrive at the dock with Joan, only to discover that Wilbur has vanished again.

The film's tone now swings from comic mayhem back to horror as Wilbur's would-be rescuers spot the pulsing lights in the laboratory window and realize that the fatal surgery is imminent. Racing into the lab, Talbot grabs Sandra's arm as she is about to apply the scalpel to Wilbur's scalp. Dracula lunges for Chick, who holds him off with a chair, like a lion tamer at the circus. As Sandra comes to and prepares to attack Chick with her scalpel, he swings the chair behind him, unwittingly knocking her out cold once again—a comic move in the midst of danger. Throwing the chair at Dracula, Chick rushes out the door with the vampire in pursuit. It seems Wilbur is about to be freed from the gurney where he is restrained but Talbot, his rescuer, looks into the moonlight and becomes the Wolf Man yet again. Dracula returns, and the Wolf Man attacks him with the gurney, on which Wilbur remains strapped.

Despite the high stakes and potentially deadly consequences in this battle of undead creatures, watching Wilbur pushed back and forth between them is one of the funniest routines in the film. It climaxes with Dracula retreating from the operating room with the Wolf Man racing behind him, while Wilbur is left to spin in dizzying circles, inadvertently bumping into the electrical equipment that reanimates the Monster. Chick arrives to free Wilbur just as the Monster breaks free from his restraints, leading Wilbur to ask: "Do you believe me now?" The once-covert threat posed by the monsters is now fully revealed: The horrifying fiends are clear and present dangers, and the hulking Monster is alive and menacing. Sandra, conscious again, attempts to command and control the Monster—a final act of hubris that (in a scene reminiscent of earlier Universal horror films) ends when the Monster throws her out the window and she falls to her death on the rocky shore below.

The Monster then turns his attention to Wilbur and Chick. His powerful, lumbering stride is as frightening as it was in his first film appearance, but the chase through the castle is a fast-paced comedy of errors. Barricading a door with a heavy bed and putting their shoulders to the door leads to a comic failure, as the door opens into the hallway. Flinging open another door, Chick and Wilbur encounter Dracula and the Wolf Man fiercely battling. Sneaking up behind the Monster, the pair push him into a room and lock him in, only to have him punch Wilbur through the heavy door. (In fact, Lou missed his mark, and he was indeed hit by Glenn Strange.) Wilbur skillfully pulls a velvet tablecloth from a sideboard, leaving everything in place. With a quick look of satisfaction with his trick, Wilbur throws the tablecloth around his body and covers his face. The Monster responds as if seeing Dracula, but the effect is destroyed when Wilbur drops his disguise, and says to Chick: "He thinks I'm Dracula!" They flee, still pursued by the Monster, as Dracula and the Wolf Man—still locked in combat—tumble to their (apparent) deaths in the waters below the castle. With one threat left, the team slams the castle door behind them, but the Monster soon knocks it off its hinges and ambles over it. Running through the main gates of the castle grounds, Chick takes time to lock them, only to have the Monster rip them asunder, and relentlessly, menacingly continue his pursuit, seemingly unstoppable.

McDougal and the sheriff arrive at the island's pier and find the men they hope to capture running toward them. When McDougal responds that yes, he still wants his exhibits, Wilbur shouts, "Here comes one of them now!" Seeing the Monster headed for them, anger turns to fear, and both lawman and businessman leap from the dock and furiously swim away. The comic interlude thus gives way to the final scene of the horror plot, as Wilbur struggles to untie the boat from the dock and the Monster begins to throw barrels down at the pair. Joan and Stevens set the pier afire and escape as the Monster turns and walks into the flames, apparently perishing as (in a scene reminiscent of the climax of *Frankenstein*) the burning structure gives way beneath him. The nightmarish battle is over, the terrifying threat has been removed, but the movie does not have the happy ending—the return to normalcy—that would be expected in either a horror or comedy film.

Wilbur scolds Chick that, next time he says he saw something, Chick should believe him. Chick, knowing what *he* has seen, replies: "Oh relax, now that we've seen the last of Dracula, the Wolf Man, and the Monster, there's nobody to frighten us anymore." A cigarette seems to light itself, and a mysterious voice responds in disappointment that he can't "get in on the fun." "Allow me to introduce myself," the disembodied voice says, "I'm the Invisible Man." The frightened duo leap from the boat and swim frantically away. Rather than a tidy resolution, the film ends with a new, invisible threat that *neither* Wilbur nor Chick can see—a new creature potentially even more dangerous than the three monsters just encountered.

Conclusion

Throughout *Abbott and Costello Meet Frankenstein*, temporary escapes and rescues appear to resolve the perils, and the comic relief repeatedly mitigates the grim mood of horror, yet—as the final "appearance" of the Invisible Man underscores—additional terrors always remain. The pleasures of chills and chuckles provide no final resolution; unseen dangers persist. As Altman has proposed, genre can perform a ritual function, providing "imaginative solutions to a society's real problems."[16] In the case of *Abbott and Costello Meet Frankenstein*, navigating between the genres of horror and comedy offers an imaginative framework within which to consider postwar anxieties. The intertwined horror and comic narratives, relying on genre conventions from each, create a space to work through the postwar dilemmas of gender roles and communist infiltration. The war is over, prosperity has created a growing middle class, and happy days are here again, but the new era has disturbing undercurrents that create uneasiness. Although the film seems to settle the question of women in the workforce by removing them from their professional roles through love or violence, fear that a communist fifth column may be at work on American soil remains unresolved at the film's end. Andrew Tudor sees popular culture in general, and the horror genre in particular, as both "reflection and articulation" of "social constructions." In the case of horror films, genre conventions shape "landscapes of fear."[17]

Mixing comedy and horror, *Abbott and Costello Meet Frankenstein* offered a path through the "landscape of fear" present in postwar America, but ultimately the horror remained.

Bud Abbott and Lou Costello had dropped off the list of Top 10 Hollywood moneymakers, but *Abbott and Costello Meet Frankenstein* became one of Universal-International's most profitable films. In 1948 the comedy team was voted into the Top 10 in the Exhibitors' Poll for the first time since 1944.[18] Comic horror played well across the country, won acclaim for the stars, and spawned a series of sequels. The film earned additional recognition early in the twenty-first century. Each year the Library of Congress releases a list of movies to be added to the National Film Registry for being "'culturally, historically or aesthetically' significant motion pictures."[19] In 2001, *Abbott and Costello Meet Frankenstein* was added to the registry, ensuring that the "monsters of menace and the masters of mirth" will survive.

Notes

1. Miller, *Horror Spoofs of Abbott and Costello*, 17.
2. Weaver, Brunas, and Brunas, *Universal Horrors*, 323.
3. Odell and Le Blanc, *Horror Films*, 19.
4. Furmanek and Palumbo, *Abbott and Costello in Hollywood*, 175.
5. Staiger, "Hybrid or Inbred," 6.
6. Altman, *Film/Genre*, 14.
7. Miller, *Horror Spoofs of Abbott and Costello*, 3.
8. Carroll, "Horror and Humor," 152.
9. Ibid., 157.
10. Peacock, "No Pain: No Gain," 95.
11. Stephen Cox and John Lofflin, quoted in Miller, *Horror Spoofs of Abbott and Costello*, 62.
12. Burnham, *The Struggle for the World*, 63.
13. Seward, "Sex Roles in Postwar Planning," 181.
14. The script of *The Wolf Man* (1941) established that this shape-shifting occurs "when the autumn moon is bright"; the sequels changed the line to "when the moon is full and bright," but *Abbott and Costello Meet Frankenstein* uses any bright moon.
15. Eisenmann, "Educating the Female Citizen," 133.
16. Altman, *Film/Genre*, 27.
17. Tudor, *Monsters and Mad Scientists*, 5.
18. Stedman, "Abbott and Costello: Who's on First?" 30.
19. "In December 2001, Librarian of Congress James H. Billington announced the titles of the twenty-five motion pictures to be added to the National Film Registry." "Archival News." *Cinema Journal* 41, no. 3 (2002): 124.

Bibliography

Abbott and Costello Meet Frankenstein. Directed by Charles Barton. 1948. Universal City, CA: Universal-International Pictures. 2000. DVD.

Altman, Rick. *Film/Genre*. 1999. London: British Film Institute, 2004.

Burnham, James. *The Struggle for the World*. New York: John Day, 1947.

Carroll, Nöel. "Horror and Humor." *Journal of Aesthetics and Art Criticism* 57, no. 2 (1999): 145–60.

Eisenmann, Linda. "Educating the Female Citizen in a Post-war World: Competing Ideologies for American Women, 1945–1965." *Educational Review* 54, no. 2 (2002): 133–41.

Furmanek, Bob, and Ron Palumbo. *Abbott and Costello in Hollywood*. New York: Perigee Books, 1991.

Miller, Jeffery S. *The Horror Spoofs of Abbott and Costello: A Critical Assessment of the Comedy Team's Monster Films*. Jefferson, NC: McFarland, 2000.

Odell, Colin, and Michelle Le Blanc. *Horror Films*. Harpenden, UK: Pocket Essentials, 2001.

Peacock, Louise. "No Pain: No Gain—The Provocation of Laughter in Slapstick Comedy." *Popular Entertainment Studies* 1, no. 2 (2010): 93–106.

Seward, Georgene H. "Sex Roles in Postwar Planning." *Journal of Social Psychology S.P.S.S.I. Bulletin* 19 (1944): 163–85.

Staiger, Janet. "Hybrid or Inbred: The Purity Hypothesis and Hollywood Genre History." *Film Criticism* 22, no. 1 (1997): 5–20.

Stedman, David. "Abbott and Costello: Who's on First?" *What Dreams Are Made Of: Movie Stars of the 1940s*, edited by Sean Griffin, 12–32. New Brunswick, NJ: Rutgers University Press, 2011.

Tudor, Andrew. *Monsters and Mad Scientists: A Cultural History of the Horror Movie*. Oxford: Blackwell, 1991.

Weaver, Tom, Michael Brunas, and John Brunas. *Universal Horrors: The Studio's Classic Films, 1931–1946*. Jefferson, NC: McFarland, 2007.

~

CHAPTER NINE

Humor in Vampire Films

The Vampire as Joker

Mary Y. Hallab

Horror movies are rarely *intended* to be comic. But vampires are innately ridiculous, and I am often amazed that filmmakers can get us to take them seriously. Horror and humor are closely related, though, as both depend on the sudden apprehension of the incongruous, the unpredictable, and the impossible in order to achieve their desired affects. When considered in this way, effective horror often teeters on the edge of the absurd. In Hammer Studios' 1958 production of *Dracula*, for example, Christopher Lee's stunning version of the Count, bursting into a room in a violent fit of rage, may elicit shocked laughter that the filmmakers hadn't anticipated. Indeed, Dracula's dark, flamboyant vampire outfits seem to generate humor, as well as horror or fear. Our sense of humor (supposing that we have one), piqued by the incongruities of the film (those clothes!), leads us to pause temporarily before we become fearful. We experience a split second of doubt: Is this funny? Or is he dangerous?

Unintentional humor in such movies as the early *Dracula* (1931) and *Nosferatu* (1922) may release or, conversely, actually reinforce, the creepy effect of scenes such as Nosferatu rising straight up from his coffin. Obviously, this does not apply only to brief funny moments. It also applies to the undercurrent of humor that makes these kinds of movies meaningful. The humor is part of an understood "what if?"—what if this could really happen?—that touches our deeper selves. Our sense of humor—our ability to appreciate the uncanny and the inexplicable, to speculate on the impossible—creates an odd attraction to the characters and story at the same time we are filled with dread. It gives us the flexibility to enjoy the techniques with which the effects are foisted on us without feeling too threatened to consider the deeper meanings of these experiments with fear.

John Morreall[1] and Louis H. Palmer[2] believe that, to appreciate horror movies at all, we must have the kind of flexibility and openness to new angles of vision that humor provides. Both genres rely on shared characteristics: surprise, shock, and incongruity, but most importantly, the abrupt reversal of accepted beliefs and commonplace expectations (such as, "Dead men tell no tales"). The difference is that horror is violent, threatening, and scary, whereas comedy is usually relaxed, reassuring and, well, funny. Bela Lugosi's *Dracula* creates unexpected humor, enjoyed by many comedians among us who, unoriginally, smirk and repeat in sepulchral tones, "I bid you Velcome"—with its double meaning. What, after all, is he welcoming us to? The answers—Death and Immortality—point to the focal thesis, the meaningful center of the work. Dracula welcomes us to the vampire's world of Not Dying, the ultimate rebellion against God and the natural order.

Dracula brings excitement, the aura of the supernatural, and the awareness that there might be a power and knowledge beyond that described in our Sunday-school lessons. Moreover, he (and his fellow vampires) radiate a kind of exuberant energy—suggestive of freedom, of refusal, of the beyond—even when they are represented jokingly, as in the case of Mr. Potato Head Dracula or Count Chocula cereal. Humorous disturbances function in similar ways, rending wild portals in the dismal walls that enclose most horror stories and revealing the wild, unexpected world beyond. Humor has a way of focusing our attention; by "cracking us up," it "cracks up"—or conceptually "fractures"—situations (the impending apocalypse, for example, in several episodes of *Buffy the Vampire Slayer* [1997–2003]) that have become too heavy with solemnity, too oppressively serious, to convey any meaning or inspire speculation. For this reason, even "serious" vampire movies insert comic episodes, characters, or dialogue. Generally, a sudden awareness of the ridiculous occurs in a particular context where it will be most unexpected, yet also apropos: for example, the elegant vampire in the drawing room has—poof!—become a bat. Even puns or curiosities of language, like Bela Lugosi's Hungarian accent, may be funny in context. Humor may thus play a mitigating role in literature or film, as it does in life. Whereas horror purveys gloom or hopelessness and maintains dogmatic and inflexible positions (rigid opposition between good and evil, or us and them, for example), true humor is tolerant and open-minded toward new ideas, new people, new creatures—angels, giant spiders, superheroes—or toothy villains.

Early Films—Prewar

Effectively used humor occurs in two of the very serious early vampire films based on Bram Stoker's novel: the silent *Nosferatu* and *Dracula*. In these, the Dracula figure (Count Orlok in *Nosferatu*) can be taken as a kind of dangerous trickster; he is an outsider, malign and destructive, frightening in appearance, and casually murderous. Both these vampires have left their ancestral castles and sailed off, murdering the ship's crew on the way, to settle in other towns and to bring death and disease. Their exploits will have irreparable consequences, and their ruthless obsession with young girls will wreak havoc in the lives of the central characters. They introduce the innocent townspeople to the real meaning of intractable evil and to horrors that can infect and corrupt a whole community.

So what's funny? Nosferatu himself looks like a walking cutout on a stick as he scurries along with his coffin. A dismal procession of black coffins of the dead is followed by a frantic scene in which the villagers pursue the

Christopher Lee as the classic vampire (1958).

grinning and greedy real estate agent Knock—who brought the vampire and his disease to town—through the streets and into the surrounding fields. Funny as it is (Knock races up and down, onto rooftops, pelting his pursuers with buns), it adds a creepy and savage effect to the film. Here, the comic is horrifying. Sudden shifts to comedy within a solemn or tragic work are often said to momentarily ease the tension of suffering and sorrow. Years ago, however, Thomas De Quincy suggested that they achieve something more. Discussing the commotion at the castle gate that follows the murder of the king in Shakespeare's *Macbeth*, De Quincy argues that it pulls us back from the horror of the murdered king and returns us to the real world. "The reestablishment of the goings-on of the world in which we live," he concludes, "first makes us profoundly sensible of the awful parenthesis that had suspended them."[3] The chase through the peaceful town and countryside performs the same function in *Nosferatu*: It reasserts the context in which all the vampire-borne plague has occurred and holds Knock, an actor in the crime, up to ridicule as a lunatic.

In *Dracula*, Renfield (Dwight Frye) also plays an equally important role in our reaction to the film. His increasingly erratic behavior, like Knock's, draws our attention to the bizarre nature of the vampire story. Overhearing Dr. Van Helsing and Dr. Seward discussing the vampire, Renfield bursts into the room to demand: "Isn't this a *strange* subject for men who are *not* crazy?" His keeper, Martin, supplies a droll kind of chorus concerning belief in vampires and the question of who is "batty" and who is not. "He thinks they're talking to him," the baffled attendant says of the wolves that howl outside Renfield's asylum window each night. "He howls and howls back at them. He's crazy!" Professor Van Helsing, however, knows the truth—the "wolf" is Dracula in lupine form, calling to his minion, and Renfield is not insane, but trapped in the Count's evil schemes. If we "get" their humor, we partake in much more complex incongruities than are implied by the sight of Renfield eating spiders and howling in the night.

The vampires in these early films are, like the murderers in *Macbeth*, irredeemably evil. Nosferatu's stiffly awkward movements and Dracula's pause-filled speech ("I never drink . . . wine") remind us that they are only a few steps removed from being corpses. They are so far removed from day-to-day experience that acceptance of their existence seems tantamount to madness. Comedy and humor highlight the magnitude of the gulf between their world and the world of the mundane, and by counterpoint, the magnitude of the threat posed by these diabolical interlopers from the land of death.

The War and After

Humor largely disappeared from vampire films between the mid-1930s and
the mid-1940s. As the world darkened around them, Universal's direct
sequels to Dracula—Dracula's Daughter (1936) and Son of Dracula (1943)—
maintained a solemn and gloomy air, as did The Return of the Vampire (1943),
which retold the story of Dracula (an East European vampire wreaks havoc
in London), while transporting it from the Victorian era to the wartime
present. All three films maintain an atmosphere of unrelieved darkness;
even though few corpses are on display, the atmosphere of the charnel
house and the graveyard hangs over them. The gap between the vampires'
death-shadowed world and the everyday world outside the theaters had,
by 1943–1944, narrowed to the point that there was no need for humor or
comedy to bridge it. In The Return of the Vampire, the violence wrought by
vampires and the violence of the war intertwine. Vampire Armand Tesla is
accidentally disinterred from his tomb by a German bomb, and—disguising
himself as Dr. Hugo Bruckner, a scientist who has escaped from a German
concentration camp—wreaks havoc in London. In the end, Tesla is knocked
unconscious in another German air raid, allowing his much-abused werewolf
servant Andreas to drag him from the tomb where he has taken shelter so
that the morning sun cannot destroy him.

   Just as the war brought humorless vampire films, the end of the war
brought the first outright vampire comedies: Abbott and Costello Meet Frankenstein (1948) and Mother Riley Meets the Vampire (1952) parodied many of
the characters and plot devices of previous vampire horror films. The former
features Dracula (Lugosi), now in the role of mad scientist, trying to find just
the "right brain," stupid and controllable, to reanimate the stalled Frankenstein monster. Wilbur (Costello), a dim-witted freight handler at a shipping
company, seems like the answer to his problem, but—along with his coworker
Chick (Abbott)—throws Dracula's laboratory and plot into chaos. The latter
features a maniacal scientist named Von Housen (Lugosi again), who sleeps
in a coffin dressed in Dracula clothes because, he says cheerily, "I was buried
in them!" Dubbed "The Vampire" by the press, he has become notorious for
kidnapping young women, and whether he is a real vampire or not, he intends
to conquer the world—not with humans (since that didn't work), but with
50,000 robots, of which he has yet invented only one. He and his followers are
no match for the dotty Mother Riley (Arthur Lucan, in a drag performance he
created for the British music-hall stage), who trashes his plans through sheer
Irish pluck and incompetence (along with that of the British postal service,
which mistakenly delivers Von Housen's robot to her home).

The vampires in these films, whether presented as genuine threats (in *Abbott and Costello*) or deluded madmen (in *Mother Riley*) are defeated by ordinary, even bumbling, heroes. Bela Lugosi plays both as flamboyant parodies of the Dracula figure, displaying an unexpected depth of talent and rarely acknowledged degree of comic enjoyment as he exaggerates the character's most recognizable traits. The films, by inviting laughter first at the vampires' pretensions and then at their downfall, gave audiences a chance to enjoy a slapstick laugh at the expense of the death-dealers of the war years—earlier embodiments of evil brought down by ordinary folk.

The Hammer Films: Gothic Adventure

Fear of death remained vivid throughout the Cold War, intensified by news of dangers from the Eastern bloc and undiminished by the growing power of science to cure disease. Perhaps in reaction, the old gothic vampire was revived again, this time by London-based Hammer Film Productions, which inaugurated a series of stylish, atmospheric horror films with *The Curse of Frankenstein* (1957). *Dracula* (1958), which established "Hammer horror" as a cinematic brand, embraced the gothic melodrama that suffused Bram Stoker's 1897 novel and the 1924 stage adaptation by Hamilton Deane and, later, John Balderston, while adding copious doses of graphic violence and—taking full advantage of Technicolor film—bright red blood. It also added, here and there, scenes of comic relief like those used in the prewar Universal films. The humor in such scenes was derived from the exaggerated terror exhibited by the village peasants of Transylvania when confronted even by the *idea* of Dracula. The villagers' reactions seem comical in their extravagance until the imposing and deathlike figure of Dracula actually appears on-screen. Christopher Lee plays Dracula as a Byronic villain: a tall, handsome, arrogant, pleasure-seeking loner, who—as he bites the necks of young women, corrupting their innocence and transforming them into vampires—serves only Satan and himself. No matter how pure, joyous, and vivacious his victims may be, his look and his bite (even his very thoughts) are enough to quell them and bend them to his will. He is Death incarnate, and in every moment he is on screen, he conveys Death's inescapable, corrupting presence.

As befits a figure representing Death, Lee maintains a straight face and perfect dignity throughout the movie. Beneath the seriousness, however, the Byronic, pleasure-seeking side of the character is evident in an undertone of irony or cynicism—a kind of drollness, even amusement, that acknowledges the incongruity of it all. In this, Lee represents a transition from the horror-movie villainy of Bela Lugosi and Boris Karloff to later, more self-aware performances by Vincent Price, Peter Lorre, and Jack Nicholson (going mad in *The Shining*). Supremely, arrogantly confident of their power over those around them, they allow themselves a hint of a smile or a fleeting smirk over how *easy* it will all be. As Dracula, Lee burnishes the vampire image created by Stoker and brought to the screen by Lugosi, firmly establishing it as a cultural icon to be imitated and expanded in later films. It is Lugosi's and Lee's vampire that is revisited as a comic figure in *Love at First Bite* (1979) and a tragic hero in *Bram Stoker's Dracula* (1992), reimagined as a modern-day Western outlaw in *John Carpenter's Vampires* (1998), and then transformed into a brooding seeker of redemption in *Forever Knight* (1992–1996) and *Angel* (1999–2004).

These vampires are not comic figures, and the films in which they appear are not comic films, but we do not need to laugh out loud to find an experience humorous. We can (and do) laugh—briefly, nervously—at films like those that Lee made for Hammer, but it is laughter generated by specific, fleeting moments of incongruity: Dracula's persistent ignorance of the way he fails to "fit in" wearing his trademark evening clothes and satin-lined cloak, or the exaggerated gestures with which he brings young women under his hypnotic spell. It often seems that the vampires in these films are amused at the spectacle they are creating—that they are mocking themselves, and us, for believing in vampires at all.

Bela Lugosi as the quintessential vampire in *Dracula* (1931).

Tellingly, Lee's performance as Dracula lost its power to chill audiences only in later Hammer films like *Dracula A.D. 1972* and *Dracula Has Risen from the Grave* (1973). Set alongside the hippies and New Age cultists of "swinging London," his stern, Old World Dracula was so far out of place that he became an overt, laugh-out-loud comic.

Vampires in Modern Life

While monster horror films continued to be popular, vampires had mellowed by the 1980s. The self-consciously villainous Dracula played by Lee was aware of his solemn mission as a bearer of horror and evil, but the passage of 20 years turned the Count into a magical demon lover (as played by Frank Langella in *Dracula*) or a cheery, good-natured urbanite finding love and amusement in New York City (as played by George Hamilton in *Love at First Bite*). The reversal of roles by the vampire hunters—dour Laurence Olivier in *Dracula* and manic Richard Benjamin in *Love at First Bite*—in these films created opportunities for vampires to provide comic commentary on human wrongdoing. Lee's *Dracula*, like Lugosi's and Stoker's, derived its dark power from the ease with which he threatened to dissolve Puritan moral (and sexual) rigidity. In films like *My Best Friend Is a Vampire* (1988) and *Blood Ties* (1991), however, it is the religious fanatics and the self-righteous bigots who are truly dangerous, and the undead, not the living, who are innocent victims. *Sundown: The Vampire in Retreat* (1990) pushes the reversal of roles to its logical conclusion and takes it into the realm of comic absurdity. Vampire patriarch Jozek Mardulak (David Carradine)—the antithesis of smoldering, Byronic sexuality in his dark glasses, broad-brimmed hat, and pasty sun-blocking makeup—is not a transgressive figure, but a committed advocate of accommodation and assimilation who urges his followers to slake their thirst with synthetic blood. His nemesis, Robert Van Helsing (Bruce Campbell), is equally far removed from his famous ancestor's relentless single-mindedness and rigid, icy rationality: a wild-eyed lunatic bent on vampire genocide. We might, with reason, call these films comedies with horror elements, rather than the reverse.

Fright Night (1985), a successful horror-comedy film of the era, teeters on the edge between the two genres, turning the horror plot from *Salem's Lot* (a dismal 1979 television miniseries, based on Stephen King's 1975 update of *Dracula*) into a zany comedy of evil in the suburbs. One pleasant night, Charley Brewster (William Ragsdale) gets the creeps when he sees his dapper young neighbor, Jerry Dandridge (Chris Sarandon), and his assistant (Billy Cole) moving a coffin into their suburban basement. This, and other strange goings-on, convinces Charley that Jerry is a vampire, and he enlists the help of Peter Vincent (Roddy McDowall), a horror-film host at a local TV station whose on-screen persona is that of a "vampire killer." Initially skeptical, Vincent is thrilled when Charley (using a broken mirror as a prop) finally convinces him that Jerry is a vampire. "Just like it was in the movies!" he chortles, delighted that the fictional vampire lore he has mastered for his on-screen role has value in the real world. The separation between fiction and fact, already tenuous in Vincent's mind (and, given his perception of Vincent as an expert, in Charley's as well) dissolves entirely at this point. The mundane world that Charley and Vincent inhabit and the fantastic world in which vampires are real collapse into one.

As Jerry is stalked by Charley and Vincent, his smarmy charm gives way to fury and supernatural violence. The film's shocking moments swing between the comic and the horrific—Jerry's sudden, startling displays of impossibly large teeth are juxtaposed with the disintegration of his assistant into a pool of goo—until the vampire, too, meets his end in the traditional glare of sunlight. Lightness and humor are as central to film's meaning as its many dark elements; it combines the fearsome and the funny, sometimes in the same on-screen moments. The moral? Even if we cannot entirely defeat death, we can still laugh in the face of its big teeth. Horror is never far away, however, and it is horror—or, rather, foreboding—that prevails at the end of the film. Charley is back in his home, congratulating himself on his victory, when another dark car pulls in next door.

Killing vampires, once a deadly serious enterprise infused with religious symbolism, also became overtly comic in American vampire films of the 1980s and 1990s. Laughter and sardonic quips—designed to give the attackers confidence by framing vampires as silly, unthreatening, and therefore vulnerable—replaced traditional defensive weapons like garlic, prayer, or brandished crosses. Wooden stakes have remained potent, but while Van Helsing staked vampires as they lay in repose, latter-day slayers used trickery and supplemented their stakes with improvised weapons that (though often comical in appearance) were deadly in action. The heroes of *The Lost Boys* (1987) defeat a leather-jacketed gang of vampires using squirt guns filled with holy water, and the last-stand climax of *From Dusk till Dawn* (1996) features condoms used as holy-water balloons, a crossbow loaded with wooden bolts, and a sharpened stake strapped to the shaft of a reciprocating saw. Buffy, in the two-part inaugural episode of *Buffy the Vampire Slayer*, impales one vampire assailant with a pool cue and decapitates a second with a cymbal—thrown, Frisbee-style, across the room. She then, with a knowing grin, tells the vampire master that "there's something you forgot about: sunrise" and smashes the blacked-out window behind him with the cymbal stand. Light streams in, and he instinctively raises his arms to shield himself—realizing too late that that he has been tricked into mistaking the harmless beam of a streetlight for the deadly rays of the sun. "It's in about nine hours, moron," Buffy says, and drives her stake deep into his back. Even the deadliest and most powerful of vampires can be defeated by cleverness, and a sense of humor helps the heroes cope with the unimaginably high stakes of the battles they fight. Surveying the destruction, Buffy's friend Willow asks: "Did we win?" Buffy's response reflects the series' trademark blend of wit and horror: "Well, we averted the apocalypse. You gotta give us points for that."

Vampire films, even very serious ones, blur the line between life and death. They render the dead conscious and aware, and—in the process—humanize death and ease our fears of it by rendering it less threatening. "Death" at the hands of Dracula, even if it is framed in the film as unspeakable corruption, still comes across as less terrifying than death by more conventional means. The vampire's (un)dead victims still move, still speak, and are still at least a shadow of their living selves, which quells the fear we associate with death. Vampires themselves—articulate and charismatic even though they are undead—further blur this line. Jules Zanger notes that, as their popularity has increased, vampires have become increasingly humanized and "free spirited" and less and less a "Puritanical moral enormity," particularly in America.[4] Turning vampires into overtly comic figures intensifies the process. Their ability to climb walls and turn into bats, once terrifying signs of their association with Satan, are now treated as endearing parlor tricks or occasions for sight gags and puns.

Laughing at comical vampires further dissipates the trepidation that comes with thinking about death. When Gary Oldman's tragic romantic hero in *Bram Stoker's Dracula* dissolves into Leslie Nielsen's pompous aristocrat in *Dracula: Dead and Loving It* (1995), the enormity and finality of death—central themes in the former, intensely serious film—dissolve as well. Scenes of vampires trying to integrate themselves into modern life, the basis of the comedy in films ranging from *Love at First Bite* to *What We Do in the Shadows* (2014), emphasize the "living" side of their liminal undead state and further dissipate their association with death. Their awkward attempts at integration into our world—speaking in slightly off-key colloquial language, arguing over household responsibilities, dancing in discos, and drinking cocktails at parties—amuse us and soften our image of them. We expect them to have a "good side," in part, because they have a funny side.

Conceptual Shifts

Humor, John Morreall argues in *Taking Laughter Seriously*, requires a certain flexibility of mind to appreciate, but it also encourages such flexibility. Repeated exposure, therefore, has a broadening and liberating effect on our thinking. It loosens the constraints of logic and reason, involves at least the temporary suspension of rules, and gives us the distance and flexibility to examine our thoughts and emotions anew. Horror—which also depends on temporary suspension of the rules and also requires flexibility of mind—has a similar effect. To see the funny side of horror, therefore, is to consider new ideas about death and immortality and about our place in the cosmic experience. Horror-story monsters may provide us with a focus, but humor gives us the nerve and wit to follow the implications of their existence—to make reluctant adjustments in our understanding of the world, our ideas of right and wrong, and even our ideas about the nature of reality.

In *Innocent Blood* (1992)—an improbable mixture of vampire-horror film, crime drama, and comedy—the conceptual shift takes place at the individual level. The principal vampire character in the film, a young Frenchwoman named Marie (Anne Parillaud), tells her own story. The first-person narrative encourages viewers to sympathize with undead rather than the living, as do the mechanics of the plot. Marie, unwilling to harm the innocent, takes advantage of a war between organized-crime families to "go Italian" for her next meal. She successfully drains and dispatches her first victim—a gangster she picks up outside a mob-owned club—but her second feeding goes awry, transforming mob boss Sal "The Shark" Macelli (Robert Loggia) into a ruthless vampire himself. Joining forces with undercover policeman Joseph Gennaro (Anthony LaPaglia), who becomes her lover, Marie sets out to stop him before he (and the henchmen he has turned into vampires) can take over the city.

The collision between Marie's demure appearance and her vampire nature drives much of the film's comedy. She herself smiles about her supernatural strength, which allows her—despite her slender build—to rip heavy doors off their hinges. The audience, aware she is a vampire, is invited to laugh in anticipation when she gives her first victim's neck an experimental nip during a tryst in the back seat of his Cadillac, and he asks: "What are you—some kind of a freak?" A close-up of her face before she leans down to bite him in earnest (eyes glowing red, a demonic growl rising from her throat) reveals how fatally right he is. Later, having drained his blood and recovered her human visage along with her composure, she straightens her dress and calmly blows his head off with a shotgun—obliterating telltale fang marks and preventing his resurrection as a vampire.

Marie's capacity for violence also underscores the ways in which the film forces viewers to adjust their perspectives. She is far from innocent, but—by vampire standards—highly ethical: discriminating in her choice of victims and careful not to leave loose ends when she feeds. Having inadvertently turned Macelli into a vampire, she spends the rest of the film attempting to correct her error. *Innocent Blood* thus twists the traditional dualism of the vampire story. Marie may be a sweet young woman menaced by a satanic vampire, but she is far from helpless, and innocent only by the standards of her own kind, not ours.

From Dusk till Dawn, another film that finds humor amid exaggerated violence, executes a conceptual shift on a larger scale, playing an elaborate joke on the audience as it transforms, midway through its running time, from a crime drama to a vampire story. The film opens with two violent criminals—unstable psychopath Richie Gecko (Quentin Tarantino) and his somewhat more rational brother Seth (George Clooney)—fleeing across the barren plains of Texas after a bank robbery. Headed for Mexico, they hijack a motor home and bring its occupants (disillusioned ex-preacher Jacob Fuller [Harvey Keitel] and his two teenaged children) with them as hostages.

Despite eruptions of violence, the first half of the film seems to be a broad parody of a conventional outlaws-on-the-run story. The Gecko brothers' dialogue is comically elaborate; the police and FBI are mired in muddled, self-promoting pursuit; and a pretty, blonde reporter announces the rising death toll as if reading the football scores, underscoring the shallowness of American attitudes toward death and violence. The parodic atmosphere continues as the quintet arrives at the rendezvous site: a Mexican strip joint called the Titty Twister. The barker at the front door (Cheech Marin) delivers a deliriously lewd monologue cataloging the endless variety of "Pussy! Pussy! Pussy!" available inside, and the patrons include a biker named "Sex Machine" (Tom Savini) who carries a whip and has a pistol mounted in his codpiece.

Soon, however, the tone of the film abruptly shifts. Lead dancer Santanico Pandemonium is named for the legendary capital of Hell, and when she takes the stage, a writhing white snake draped around her scantily clad body, the interior of the Titty Twister becomes hell on earth. The dancers and staff transform into demonic vampires who feed on the human patrons, turning the club into crashing, exuberant, uncontrolled, blood-soaked chaos. The survivors fight for their lives in a melee filled with broad sight gags, unrelenting mayhem, and bizarre sights such as a decapitated vampire head, still alive, vomiting forth a sort of slime demon. Seth and the Fullers, the only survivors, retreat to a storeroom behind the bar, where they plot their last stand and Seth helps Jacob regain his lost faith in God. They emerge and, wielding their improvised weapons, hold off the demonic hordes until dawn, when the rays of the rising sun (reflecting off the club's disco ball) vaporize the remaining vampires.

The conceptual shifts through which *Dusk till Dawn* leads viewers are rooted in the same bizarre juxtapositions as its comedy. The vampires are supernatural horrors, demons of hell, presiding over a carnival of mayhem and cruelty. They draw in their prey—the gluttonous, the lecherous, and the greedy—by promising (and giving) them what they want. The patrons of the Titty Twister, like the sinners in Dante's *Inferno*, create hell for themselves and, once ensnared in it, can only continue to howl and fight, capering along in their violent dance of death. Even as it tells their story, however, the film itself gives its target audience what *they* want: comic-book clichés of psychopathic drifters, oddly charming murderers, vampire whorehouses, and grotesquely comic deaths. Humor lies in the recognition of our own fall into this grisly trap of rigidly choreographed, predetermined trash—both parody and satire of the apparently bottomless fantasies of the American public for entertainments such as true-crime stories, reality TV, and Internet porn.

The film ends with a final abrupt-but-effective cosmic joke. The camera pulls up and back to reveal what the Geckos and the Fullers all failed to see when they arrived at the Titty Twister. The club is the façade of a ruined Aztec pyramid, and we have, all along, been witness to a medieval moral tale.

Dancing with Death in Buffyland

In Canto IV of *Don Juan*, Byron writes: "And if I laugh at any mortal thing, /'Tis that I may not weep." The teenaged heroes of the series *Buffy the Vampire Slayer* take a similar approach to the world. Faced with a constant onslaught of demons and monsters, they respond to the ever-present threat of death with humor and use cleverness to keep awareness of their own mortality at bay. The comic dimension is apparent from the beginning when Buffy—an average California high school student—is told by Mr. Giles, the school librarian, that all is not as it seems. Sunnydale High, he explains, is located over a gateway to Hell; she is the "Chosen One" who must save the world from the demons that pour through it, and he is her "Watcher." Buffy reacts to these apocalyptic pronouncements with comic understatement. Giles lists the magical beings that gravitate to Sunnydale—vampires, werewolves, zombies, succubi, incubi—and pulls book after matching book from the library shelves to bolster his point. They are, he says, "everything you ever dreaded under your bed and told yourself couldn't be by the light of day." Buffy remains unimpressed. "What did you do," she asks, indicating the stack of books "send away for the Time-Life series?"

The series relies on zany, fast-paced plots that mix life-or-death battles with vampires and more typical teenage struggles. The inanities of Sunnydale High mirror, in comically exaggerated form, the high school experiences of those watching: the sneaky principal who declares "I hate young people," the locker rooms where strange deaths occur, the dingy and mysterious basement, and the sense of something sinister about the place. *Buffy* thus literalizes the idea of high school as hell, with vampires, demons, and other supernatural beings pouring forth from the Hellmouth beneath Sunnydale. The frequency with which Buffy and her friends are called to rescue the world from apocalyptic disaster becomes a running joke in the series. "When the apocalypse comes," she says, "beep me."

Buffy and her friends are unlikely heroes in this battle against cosmic evil. Xander is a bumbling joker, Willow is (at least initially) a naïve social outcast, and Spike (who joins the group midway through the series) is a centuries-old vampire who has been stripped of his powers. Buffy herself is regarded by school administrators as having a "behavior problem," since she was kicked out of her former high school for burning down the gym (which no one else believed was full of vampires). No matter how powerful the supernatural enemy or how grave the situation, however, they keep up a steady stream of quips aimed at the monsters they fight, the adults whose supervision they must endure (or sidestep), and each other. "I laugh in the face of danger," Xander declares, "then I . . . hide till it goes away." Another episode has Giles asking the group, as they face the threat of the week: "Well, aren't we going to discuss this? Save the world or go to the mall?"

The jokes are a necessary defense mechanism in a universe where magic is so pervasive, supernatural creatures so numerous, and alternate dimensions so densely layered that reality itself seems mutable. Almost everything and everyone in Sunnydale is capable of sudden and incongruous transformations—in one episode, the characters actually *become* what they have dressed up as for Halloween. In another, they find themselves trapped in a musical, unable to speak without singing. *Buffy*'s universe is, in this respect, like a carnival fun house through which the characters travel: a fantastic maze of mysterious tunnels, traps, past and future lives, deaths and revivals, ghosts and demons, dreams and fantasies, heavens and horrors. When the apocalyptic end finally approaches we can feel confident that the characters will not die, but find themselves in another dimension, or maybe just another town. Beyond their comic effect, however, these transformations of time, place, and being suggest that life and death may not be the fixed, immutable states that they are in our world, but merely facets of a complex, multidimensional existence. They may even be a dream, within which, with a little effort, we can find another life.

Conclusion

The modern vampire story is rooted in the gothic horror tradition, and Martin Tropp reminds us that the "final revelation" of gothic horror is "Death itself."[5] Horror literature fascinates, he argues, because it compels us to confront our "fear of our own mortality" and teaches us "to accept the certainty of death, to *laugh* at the madmen running the universe, to find *joy* in the midst of despair."[6] Vampire stories participate in this process by giving life and consciousness to the dead and human form to death itself. They allow us to confront, face to face, the thing we most fear, and help to dissolve its power over us. Even as our image of vampires (and the stories we tell about them) has changed, one thing remains constant: They are part of another world, and strangers in our own.

The comic elements in vampire stories mediate between the two worlds. Where the gulf is vast, humor calls attention to its magnitude, suggesting that the very fact of the vampire's existence—his dress, demeanor, and speech—can seem deeply strange, and a detailed recounting of his supernatural powers can sound like madness. Where the gulf is modest, but still visible, humor reminds us that the apparent similarities between our vampires and ourselves are still trumped by the differences—that vampires, however much they may seem like us, are among the undead, and thus forever separate from the living. Where the gulf has (seemingly) disappeared, and vampires (seemingly) become fully integrated into our society, the humor inherent in their collisions with our world reminds us of the differences between their worldview and ours.

The humor in vampire movies and television series also prepares us to come to grips with—to appreciate and understand—the vampire's world. It challenges ideas we take for granted, disrupts the bonds of cause and effect, and loosens the constraints that confine our thinking, freeing us to consider the possibility that familiar, seemingly solid boundaries—including that between life and death—can become fluid and mutable. It prepares us to watch as those boundaries are redrawn on the screen and to enter into a world where death has no finality, the physical body need not decay, and love can last beyond the grave.

Humor and horror work hand in hand, then, not just because both depend on our apprehension, and appreciation, of the unexpected, but because humor facilitates the cultural work that horror does. Flexible, open, tolerant, and curious, it breaks—or at least weakens—the paralyzing hold that death (and the fear of it) casts over us, the living. With humor, death is manageable; without humor, vampire films are, well, deadly.

Notes

1. Morreall, *Taking Laughter Seriously*, 96–98.
2. Palmer, *Vampires in the New World*, 133–34.
3. De Quincey, "On the Knocking at the Gate."
4. Zanger, "Metaphor into Metonymy," 17–26.
5. Tropp, *Images of Fear*.
6. Ibid., 291 (my italics).

Bibliography

De Quincey, Thomas. "On the Knocking at the Gate in *Macbeth*." [Originally published in *London Magazine*, October 1823] In *English Romantic Writers*, edited by David Perkins, 732–33. New York: Harcourt Brace Jovanovich, 1967.

Morreall, John. *Taking Laughter Seriously*. Albany: State University of New York Press, 1983.

Palmer, Louis H. *Vampires in the New World*. Santa Barbara, CA: Praeger, 2013.

Tropp, Martin. *Images of Fear: How Horror Stories Helped Shape Modern Culture (1818–1918)*. Jefferson, NC: McFarland, 1990.

Zanger, Jules. "Metaphor into Metonymy: The Vampire Next Door." In *Blood Read: The Vampire as Metaphor in Contemporary Culture*, edited by Joan Gordon and Veronica Hollinger, 17–26. Philadelphia: University of Pennsylvania Press, 1997.

CHAPTER TEN

~

Queerness and the Undead Female Monster

Lisa Cunningham

Movies like *Bordello of Blood* (1996), *Jennifer's Body* (2009), and *All Cheerleaders Die* (2013) engage directly with a long-standing trope of horror film: female queerness and difference as monstrosity. Comedy-horror films like these, however, do so in a different way than (for example) Bram Stoker's *Dracula*, in which Lucy is made an irretrievably monstrous child-killer. Because the "monsters" in these films are comically, hyperbolically portrayed and constructed, they force us to question their positioning as "monstrous" (and the ideas that they represent, in that position). The characters in these contemporary films are more complexly layered, and the films actively ask the audience (both narratively and using cinematic devices like lighting, editing, soundtrack, and shot composition) to reconsider the unequivocal mainstream cultural damnation of the queer woman.

Each of the central characters considered here revives from death early in the course of her film in order to show the ways in which supposedly "normal" laws and rules no longer apply to her. Indeed, *only* death can free each of them from the strictures that everyday social norms impose. Being dead is the epitome of being Othered—identified as "other than" (in this case) the optimal "normal" state of being human—and these women become impossible incarnations of the Other. Being undead also releases the stranglehold that heteronormative social expectations and structures can hold over these women. Each of the films I examine here revolves around a queer undead woman—in fact, each film is as concerned with her queerness as her violence or her undeadness—making the lines of monstrousness that converge in her more apparent by their juxtaposition with one another.

Bordello of Blood follows the convergent storylines of Lilith (Angie Everhart)—a centuries-old vampire—and Katherine (Erika Eleniak), a conservative Christian woman. Lilith runs a brothel where she and the other female vampires she has created feed on, and kill, the male customers. The two women's repeated encounters transform Katherine into a more fully-realized, alternatively sexual woman (and succubus). The titular Jennifer (Megan Fox) of *Jennifer's Body* is one of two girls—along with Needy (Amanda Seyfried)—in a deeply complicated relationship about which Needy comments, "sandbox love never dies." The depth of their physical and mental connection is constantly a concern of the film and is ultimately proved by Jennifer's death at the hands of her friend and Needy's resultant transformation into a being that, in a number of ways, more closely resembles her undead friend. *All Cheerleaders Die* follows Maddy (Caitlin Stasey) on her quest to exact revenge on an abusive group of cheerleaders and football players. Her plan, however, is thrown off-track when a psychopathic quarterback murders all of the cheerleaders; Maddy's ex-girlfriend Leena (Sianoa Smit-McPhee) resurrects all of the girls as vampiric succubi, and the war between the gendered factions rages until a final showdown, after which Leena re-resurrects Maddy and the two are more permanently and concretely connected. The consistency of certain narrative and thematic elements here points to the fact that these films (among others) are interested in the construction of the monstrous woman and the variety of ways in which women are "made monstrous"—physically, ideologically, aesthetically, socially, and sexually.

It is exactly because these comedic films play with conventional horror narratives and film design that they can question the heteronormative social structures that they draw out and caricature. Not much screen time needs to be devoted to establishing individual characters in *Bordello of Blood* or *All Cheerleaders Die*, for example, because doing so is made narratively superfluous by using stereotypes and tongue-in-cheek signals and standards of the genre. *Bordello*'s Katherine needs no significant development: She is called an uptight religious woman in the first scene in which she appears, and her skirt-suits and blonde bob, as well as the fact that she works blindly and devotedly for an ethically questionable preacher, underscore her innocent and naïve nature. Similarly, *Cheerleaders'* supporting football-player and cheerleader characters are not given much in the way of individual development, instead embodying hyperbolized performances of whatever their "place" is in the group through aesthetic and small (but recognizable) conversational or behavioral signifiers: the lieutenant, sniveling to her leader and abusive to those beneath her (Martha); the groveling, insecure social bottom rung (Hanna and Manny, in each camp); and the pot-smoking, unobservant fool

(Ben), to name a few. Because these films can invoke archetypal characters from traditional comedy and horror films instead of having to create original roles, time that would otherwise be narratively spent on these secondary expository scenes can be spent instead on over-the-top generic action, and on the development of more complexity in the nuances of characters' relationships. Specifically, the films develop the same-sex relationships of each of their female protagonists, as well as each woman's complex identity as simultaneously "undead" and "female."

The complexity with which these films examine female queerness and identity is similar to the troubled complexity of punk-rock girl bands' examination of the same concepts; as Karina Eileraas points out in her study of punk female body resistance, "Their surrealist juxtapositions create a visual economy that emphasizes the violence to and alienation from the body that obedient performances of 'pretty' femininity entail."[1] Their "monstrous" qualities, then, are visually hyperbolized or emphasized versions of real-life characteristics that are denied to "obedient" women in order to make a point about the very fact that these characteristics are identified as always already monstrous in females. Comic horror, however, stands at the intersection of the gothic, which has long-standing precedents regarding the constructions of monsters and of Otherness, and the carnivalesque, which revels in turning powers and structures on their heads. Whereas the "persistent scream/howl/ wail/moan/shriek of girl-band music signals an aggressive, antidecorum presence,"[2] undead women in comic horror are allowed to signal their violent presence with enthusiastic bloodshed and murderous anti-polite resistance. These moments are often immediately followed by puns or quips, designed to remind the viewer that they are allowed to enjoy what they just witnessed and to "laugh off" the serious implications of a given scene—a traditional cue of the comic horror genre, as in the Tales from the Crypt series or *Shaun of the Dead*. While the focus of each of the three films considered here is a monstrous woman, the different ways in which the women are narratively treated reveal a complex relationship between contemporary comic horror and queer femaleness—one that recognizes its troubled complexity.

Femininity, Tradition, and Monstrousness

In *The Monstrous-Feminine: Film, Feminism, Psychoanalysis*, Barbara Creed outlines the ways in which monstrousness is located—both in film studies and in psychoanalytic tradition—directly in the sexual difference of women. As Creed points out, "All human societies have a conception of the monstrous-feminine, of what it is about woman that is shocking, terrifying, horrific, abject."[3] By looking at the ways in which women are portrayed and understood as monstrous we can understand how a society defines undesirable (and thus, desirable) femininity. Typically, this monstrousness is rooted in women's "difference" from men—their reproductive capability and lack of a penis (as linked to castration anxiety, etc.)—casting it as nonnormative.

Horror narratives have a long-standing tradition of engaging with these types of psychoanalytic structures and concerns. More specifically, they have a history of linking certain types of monstrousness with certain archetypes of femininity—for example, the castrating mother, the hysterical and emasculatingly powerful witch, the alluring and deadly siren. As Creed suggests, the horror film is a necessary psychological exercise through which one can cathartically experience the expulsion of and purification from the abject—qualities that are designated (culturally or unconsciously) as disgusting and ultimately undesirable.[4] Horror narratives comment on specific structural dichotomies, such as heterosexual/homosexual, male/female, or privileged/oppressed, often by locating these binaries in characters who are placed in opposition to one another, with one quality and character clearly marked "good" and the other "bad." This is often accomplished in very visually straightforward ways. There is little doubt, for instance, that the pastel-clad and brightly lit Laurie Strode of *Halloween* (directed by John Carpenter, 1978) is the "good" character, and that both Michael Myers (who always stands in shadows and wears a dingy jumpsuit and mask) and the other teenagers (who also frequently appear in the dark and in darker colored, more revealing clothing) are various versions of the "bad" counterpart.

Comic horror films take great pride in caricaturing their parent genre, making similar commentary while simultaneously pointing to the ridiculousness of discussing such significant topics in this filmic format. Whereas female gothic monsters, like punk girl bands, "perform ugliness as a way of showcasing the self-hatred that cultural constructions of femininity produce and/or amplify," they are allowed, in the comic horror tradition, to explore alternative routes of femininity.[5] Courtney Love's band Hole "couples the strategic evocation of 'ugly' female self-image with incitements to corporeal violence" because 1) the "pretty" female self-image specifically denies violence, and 2) she is not able to perform the violence she wants without consequence.[6] The latter realization does not occur—or occurs in an altered form, as the ghouls' bodies are, themselves, a realization of physical alterity—for undead women. The comedy in *Bordello*, for instance, consciously couples sexuality with over-the-top bloody violence—screaming, lingerie-clad women erupt into flames and explosions of sparks minutes before the bloodthirsty Lilith reveals that she has "never killed a woman"—in order to highlight the ridiculousness of excluding even the possibility of violent behavior from definitions of womanhood. This carnivalesque disregard for established filmic structures allows for the kind of holistic questioning of social structures and values that comic horror can accomplish. The flaunting of structures and expectations pushes at the boundaries of the structures themselves, antagonizing the comfortable—often inherently binary and hierarchical—"balance" that the structures purport to maintain.

Jack Halberstam argues that the identity of a monster "always depends utterly upon the various lines of constructions that coalesce in his [or her] humanity."[7] If, indeed, monsters can be identified by examining the structures that condemn them, then examining the ways in which women are made monstrous in comic horror can give insight not only into the ways in which certain types and qualities of femininity are valued over others, but also into the shape and construction of the very structures that condemn them. Importantly, Halberstam also notes that it can be easy to read contemporary concerns into texts simply because those concerns are circulating so heavily in popular discourse. Comic horror, however, conveniently tends to reduce the margin for error by making many of the cultural narratives it addresses abundantly clear, through either direct narrative statement or filmic techniques like sound and editing. These monstrous bodies are like gothic monsters in that they are "open to numerous interpretations . . . precisely because monsters transform the fragments of otherness into one body."[8] These bodies are not women, but monsters, and so they are neither female nor homosexual, but bear the marks of femaleness and homosexuality. The monster's monstrousness always points to boundaries that are being unsettled, to qualities that have been deemed "undesirable" in the cultural imagination.

Structural Violence

One of the more notable ways in which horror films can challenge these assumptions is through violent disruption. Narratively, moments of intense violence often disrupt a linear storyline, literally "arrest[ing] the narrative as the viewer waits with tension and excitement for the outcome while immersed in the spectacle," as Hilary Neroni outlines.[9] She argues that violence is a moment, an occurrence, which we cannot rationally comprehend within the same reasoning structures that govern our understanding of narrative progression, of how things are "supposed" to happen. Violence, then, has an intrinsic capacity for subversion, for the upsetting of stable structures or assumptions. Filmic violence, specifically, "often appears to erupt when ideology fails: when the symbolic or narrative structure breaks down, we turn to violence."[10] Since films also house ideological values and characteristics in characters that clearly represent those qualities metaphorically, moments in which characters are involved in violence often suggest (sometimes by literally stating as much in a character's dialogue) a specific tension at the ideological boundaries that are at odds between those characters.

Neroni's historiography of violent women in cinema reveals a distinct trend in the representation of these characters. She notes that "the violent woman is most clearly related to social problems and contradictions—and to the ideological response to these contradictions. The violent woman appears at moments of ideological crisis, when the antagonisms present within the social order—antagonisms that ideology attempts to elide—become manifest."[11] The conflicts in which the violent woman finds herself are, literally or allegorically, social issues and paradoxes—structural conflicts of interest between the interests of the monstrous woman (and her ideological values) and those of the non-monstrous protagonist or foil character. As Mary Ann Doane suggests of the carnivalesque tradition of the masquerade (which certainly seems apropos when looking at comic horror, which often provides caricatures rather than particularly complex characters in the same way the masquerade presents or produces a character rather than a whole person): "Womanliness is a mask which can be worn or removed."[12] Moments in which monstrous women in comic horror are violent are moments when they are disturbing the mask of femininity, perhaps loosening it, if not removing it entirely.

What We Make Monstrous

Examining monsters allows us to see some of the various ways in which "humanity" is constructed, by clearly exposing the dichotomies or value systems in which the monster is defined as different, as less-than, and thus, as monstrous. As *Bordello of Blood*, *Jennifer's Body*, and *All Cheerleaders Die* each feature a protagonist who is some version of a succubus, and who electively enters significant sexual relationships with women, it is not difficult to identify that the socially "negative" values assigned to these female monsters are being sexual, being homosexual, and being violent (or even being able to fight back). All three films explore this theme differently, but they share several common narrative elements: an undead woman (resurrected during the film) who must feed on humans in order to survive, has categorically significant relationships with women, and violent or abusive relationships with men.

Lilith, the monster, and Katherine, the erstwhile protagonist, dominate *Bordello of Blood*, a Tales from the Crypt film. The film follows the two women for the majority of screen time, and they are the focus of conversation when not on-screen. Lilith is quite clearly posited as the reification of monstrous womanhood, and the particular ways in which this personification is achieved gesture openly to cultural norms regarding womanhood, power, and sexuality. Lilith's influence on Katherine is similarly interesting, as the latter's arc suggests her innate interest in the subversive version of womanhood Lilith provides.

As the vampiric madam of a brothel (i.e., the bordello of blood), Lilith must necessarily be a traditionally physically attractive woman. The ways in which she is aesthetically represented throughout the course of the film, however, ask revelatory questions about beauty standards and their value, as well as the monstrous threshold for these standards. Lilith's first on-screen appearance is as a skeletonized corpse who only regains her beauty after eating the hearts of the men who came to retrieve her; her first visual image is that of a monster, and the scenes depicting her as a desiccated, slimy animated corpse who kills the guards and slowly regrows layers of flesh are no more humanizing. When Lilith next appears, however, she is in charge of the brothel, dressed in a corset and flowing silk dressing gown; her long, thick red hair always down and framing her face; her dark eyeliner and red lipstick impeccably applied. She is, at this point, the redheaded seductress, a siren of sex from whom men cannot easily escape. In a scene in which she kills a male client, Lilith thrusts her preternaturally long tongue down his throat and uses it to shove his heart out through his chest. Even at her most traditionally desirable, the monstrousness of her body manifests itself, reminding the audience that she is different, neither human nor female, at least by conventional standards. For the climactic battle of the film, she transforms herself into a huge beast, a mucus-dripping monstrosity similar to a dinosaur. She both begins and ends the film as an obvious monster, one who can be identified as such by sight alone, and so her most productive theoretical end is to indicate which qualities of her "normative" or "desirable" bodily performance signify monstrosity.

Katherine, narratively positioned as Lilith's counterpart, is defined by an opposing, but equally vivid, set of signifiers. She first appears in a conservative white dressing gown, scolding her brother for playing his music too loudly. The obvious narrative move toward establishing her as a naïve, dramatically religious innocent is continued when she is next seen in an off-white skirt suit, mouthing along ecstatically with a charismatic preacher for whom she works. She suggests to the preacher that she would "like to make a documentary on lust" in order to "warn young people about all the things that inspire it." The clear connotation of the statement—that she does not understand lust in a personal way—is made more interesting by the goal itself, which is to chronicle things that inspire lust rather than the dangers of it. Clearly, her interest is not solely sex prevention in "young people," but also her own curiosity about sexuality, which she seems to have wholly repressed in her pursuit of religious purity.

Where Katherine is innocent and a nearly blank slate, Lilith has centuries of experience. A succubus who has made a cadre of female vampires with which to staff her brothel, she plainly references their sexual intimacy with each other on multiple occasions; they lure men to their brutal deaths using the appeal of compulsory (paid-for) heterosexuality. In a beautifully unsubtle narrative move, Lilith's queer sexuality is also the monstrous weapon with which she ensnares her prey, including Katherine, who ends the film by eating the male protagonist Rafe (Dennis Miller), whose romantic advances she had been rejecting over the course of the film.

There is no single positive heterosexual interaction in *Bordello of Blood*: The men are often abusive and always abused (either killed or turned into sniveling Renfield-esque toadies). The Reverend (Chris Sarandon) for whom Katherine works, finding a magical way to hold Lilith in his power, immediately commands her to run a brothel and "punish the sinners" who come in to purchase their services. He echoes this phrase later, while violently slaying the female vampires in a hyperbolically edited and literally explosive montage intercut with several long close-ups of his face, his satisfied and thrilled expression lingering on-screen for nearly as long as the violent moments themselves. The joy he takes in the slaughter of the women he deems unfit is a direct parallel to the joy that heteronormative ideology (for which he is the character surrogate) takes in quelling queerness. The women, their overt sexuality, their violent possibilities, and their "monstrous" bodies are all destroyed. The only survivor of the film is Katherine, who has been made into a vampire by Lilith.

Arguably, Katherine is the evolution of Lilith. She not only survives the film, but kills Lilith herself—breaking, in the process, the only apparent rule the succubus had regarding violence. This seems a clear reference to the end of Harry Kümel's *Daughters of Darkness* (1971), in which Elizabeth Bathory, the film's reigning female vampire, is succeeded by Valerie, a woman she also converted and enslaved. Katherine, however, is more aggressive than her counterpart—killing Lilith and assuming her role, rather than waiting, as did Valerie, for fate to intervene. In the climactic fight scene, Katherine stabs Lilith through the back with a prop devil's pitchfork, ripping out and destroying her heart, ostensibly to save Rafe. At the close of the film, Katherine allows Rafe to touch her without physically shying away and uncomfortably deflecting his sexual banter, as she has every other time he made an advance, but she allows this momentary physical intimacy only long enough to lure him into the car. She then becomes snider, more assertive, and more confident—all characteristics of Lilith at her most human-appearing—and kills Rafe.

Ultimately, Katherine not only survives the film, but ends it much stronger and more capable than she began it. Once naïve and painfully submissive, she emerges as a literal man-eater—a role no longer quite as monstrous, since this "predator" was formerly treated by men as easy prey. She survives the final outdoor scene because she had the forethought to apply sunscreen; she is a more fully functional person at the end of the film than the beginning. *Bordello* seems to suggest that her dalliance with lesbianism—and, not coincidentally, with physical power and violence—is directly to her benefit, and will continue to be so.

Jennifer's Body similarly has two female main characters, Jennifer and Needy, who are also ostensibly posited as monstrous/good analogues. The two girls have a prior friendship that extends to their childhood, far beyond the time-scope of the film, opening their portrayal to examine the ways in which culture narrativizes girl friendship, female sexuality, and the possibilities of women's bodies when they are given the physical means to fight (back).

When a small, unpopular rock band decides to sacrifice a virgin to the devil in exchange for fame and fortune, they make the mistake of choosing Jennifer, who is decidedly and proudly not a virgin (but who maintains that she is when the lie suits her purposes). Sacrificed and then returned to life (undeath) as a vampiric succubus, she tells Needy, her constant friend and sometime intimate companion, that she "woke up, and found my way back to you." The pair share a heart-shaped "BFF" necklace set, which metonymi-

Leena feeds Maddy from her hand.

cally stands in for their relationship for much of the film. During the pair's final fight, it is not until Needy rips her necklace off and throws it aside that Jennifer gives up. The camera looks down from Needy's perspective onto Jennifer's face, which dissolves into an expression of heartache as she spreads her arms and allows Needy to deliver the final blow. The girls' relationship is by far the most intimate in the movie, as they exhibit extreme honesty (a rarity in this film), and are featured in the only truly romantic scene in the film—shot in soft focus, close-up, with pale white lighting and subdued music. They even have a slight psychic bond, centered around violence, and it is in those moments that Needy is most connected to Jennifer. Needy is able to sense when something horrible happens to Jennifer, or when she does something particularly violent. The breaking of this bond, signified by the discarding of the heart necklace, is the most damaging blow that the characters could have been dealt.

Men are a source first of attention and then of food for Jennifer, and—in the case of Chip (Johnny Simmons)—a comfortable crutch and sense of stability for Needy. Chip enacts the traditional horror trope of failing to heed a warning from the protagonist, and so is killed. He chooses to not believe Needy, even though he has no particular reason to think her insane; the sudden string of brutal killings are evidently not enough to convince him that, perhaps, his girlfriend is worth listening to. In contrast, Needy does not question Jennifer's story about being sacrificed and revived as a succubus (though Jennifer has the luxury of being able to prove it by harming herself and healing immediately). Needy's horrified expression as Jennifer tells her story signals that their relationship does not allow space for such a lie, though heterosexual relationships do.

Homosexual relationships—friendship and sexuality alike—are portrayed as far more romanticized and full of intimate possibility than heterosexual relationships, which are either fumbling and horrifying (for example, while Needy and Chip have sex for the first time, she panics, utterly unnoticed by him, as she envisions Jennifer as a ghoul beside her kill) or bloody and violent (Jennifer's repeated seductions of boys, which end in their deaths). The final scenes of the film center around Needy, who is confined in a mental institution for stabbing Jennifer and who has also, after a bite to the shoulder during their final confrontation, absorbed some of the physical powers of the succubus.

The final credits of the film are initially intercut with footage of the band that killed Jennifer, arriving at a hotel after a successful concert, but partway through the scene a sudden change in music signals a change in the subjects of the photographs. The rest of the montage is styled as grisly crime-scene photographs of their dead bodies, and the film ends on security camera footage of an angry Needy on their floor of the hotel. Through her connection with Jennifer, Needy reaches a level of empowerment that is not only monstrous but disruptive of both filmic form (the credits are the film's first montage with still images) and narrative function (uncertainty over how many of Jennifer's abilities Needy inherited makes the end no longer the end). Needy's ability to avenge her "sandbox love," and the zeal with which she attends to the messy task of vengeance in a system that refuses to punish the villains, is her monstrousness.

In contrast to the preceding two films, *All Cheerleaders Die* has two main female characters who act as joint protagonists. After the death of a child-hood friend during a stunt gone awry, Maddy joins the cheerleading squad at her high school with the aim to "ruin senior year" for everyone who failed to mourn her friend's death properly. She makes good on her promise by convincing head cheerleader Tracy (Brooke Butler) to break up with the psychopathically violent Terry (Tom Williamson) and then having sex with her at a party in the woods. Terry attacks the cheerleaders and eventually (with the rest of the football team in his car) runs them all off the road and into a river, killing the entire squad. Maddy's ex-girlfriend Leena uses magic to bring all five girls in the group back to life, and the ensuing war between the football team and the cheerleaders eventually leaves Leena (an ostracized goth and member of neither group) as the only survivor. She again resurrects Maddy, and the two share a kiss.

Maddy and Leena are more complicated characters than any of the monstrous women discussed thus far. Both behave in ways that are clearly framed as monstrous, but the relationship between them is clearly meant to evoke the traditional heteronormative romantic relationship that films so often glorify. Leena is the knight, constantly questing to save or resurrect Maddy, but is clearly the less emotionally controlled and less physically powerful of the two. Maddy, though physically and emotionally stronger by far, dies twice in the course of the film and must be saved by Leena. By giving each girl narrative moments of "traditional" relationship role fulfillment, their story asks significant questions about heteronormative expectations of relationships and individuals' roles within them.

Aesthetically, Leena fits the high school "goth girl" profile. She is pale with long black hair and wears all-black clothing, dark red lipstick, and heavy black eyeliner (messily applied). She positions herself as submissive to Maddy (and almost everyone around them), constantly apologizing and averting her eyes when speaking to anyone. Maddy, on the other hand, begins the film as a quiet "artsy" type in baggy sweaters, but is transformed almost immediately into a perfectly coiffed cheerleader. Her ability to buy a new wardrobe and "paint [her] face up like those whores" is convincing enough that the cheerleaders trust and accept her—a notable achievement in that it shows she understands how to consciously adopt a masquerade of a particular brand of femininity—one that relies on makeup and external signifiers of wealth. This is Maddy's most conspicuous ability early in the film, whereas Leena is framed as the outcast who doesn't know how to "pass" as a popular girl. She is portrayed as the opposite of the emotionally calculating and vicious (monstrous) Maddy, and her inability to read aesthetic and behavioral signifiers places her in a distinctly weaker position at the beginning of the film.

Once she wields magic, however, Leena becomes the most consistently powerful character in the film. She is only overpowered once, by Terry, who systematically abuses every other female character in the movie: raping Maddy before the story begins, punching Tracy, killing all the cheerleaders, and eventually rekilling most of the undead girls and cannibalizing the source of their power. Leena sacrifices Maddy and injures herself in the process, but she completes the revenge plan that Maddy could not. Ultimately, she is the successful protagonist of the film. Given that her grief resurrects Maddy a second time, she is clearly in the winning position.

There are three instances in which Leena and Maddy are romantically entangled, all of which are thematically similar: when Leena feeds Maddy from her hand so she won't have to go hungry (or kill someone), when Leena clings to Maddy's back during a dramatic motorcycle chase, and when the two share a kiss after the climax. All three scenes—jarringly, given the nature and composition of the scenes around them—use a slightly soft focus, have lens flare and soft white background lighting, and are scored with sweeping, dramatic, romantic orchestral music. Clearly, the queer love story is the romantic plot of the film, and the construction of the scenes designates Leena and Maddy as the sanctioned couple: the relationship against which all other relationships in the film are judged. Homosexuality, intimacy, emotional bonding, personal sacrifice, and power are the film's valued qualities. Interestingly, power here is always violent power—resurrections are apparently a painful business for everyone involved—but it is necessary and useful, nonetheless. The girls are no less feminine for having power; Leena's power, in fact, seems inherent to her, rather than being rooted in her femininity.

The sources of the two women's physical monstrosity serve the fairly traditional romantic subplot, which is ultimately the most positive narrative thread in the film. Their queerness and their monstrosity work in conjunction, and neither is "punished" or abjected in this discursive space. The

Lilith—the first kill in the bordello.

gothic and horror traditions typically make the marginal monstrous—then kill or otherwise punish them—largely in order to identify and attempt to abject, or to symbolically remove and destroy, undesirable qualities. The comic bent of *All Cheerleaders Die*, however, allows for its subversion of this trope and, ultimately, its successful creation of a discursive space in which queerness is not monstrous—or, at least, where neither queerness nor monstrousness is seen as negative.

Conclusion

The queer, undead women of *Bordello of Blood*, *Jennifer's Body*, and *All Cheerleaders Die* represent an empowered and violent femininity—one that is able to defend itself—a subversive possibility that upsets familiar gender norms, undermines traditional social structures, and breaks the narrow bounds placed on women. The queer women in all three films are firmly situated within the horror genre, and their stories involve familiar horror-film tropes such as surreally exaggerated violence and supernatural revenge for personal injustices. All of them, however, actively participate in the horror stories that unfold around them: instigating violence, exacting revenge, and initiating the queer relationships that shape the films. In doing so, they challenge the genre's established narrative frameworks.

A traditional understanding of femininity—passive, conventionally pretty, and heteronormative—is woven through the structure of most horror films, which frame women as powerless victims and cooperative objects of (male) desire. Their heroines swoon into inert helplessness when faced with the (male) undead monster, only to be snatched from it at the last moment by a (male) lover/protector. The neo-traditional horror film appears to depart from this model—allowing, even obliging, the heroine to rescue herself after would-be male protectors are sidelined or proven unworthy. In practice, however, such films carefully constrain the heroine's power, limiting it to the defensive and reactive, and implicitly link it to her chastity—her self-denial in anticipation of a worthy (male) lover/protector to whom she will surrender in the off-screen future. Not so, however, for the characters discussed in this essay. Their undead nature, queer sexuality, and willingness to act—violently, if necessary—place them in opposition to, and thus undermine, the genre's rigidly traditional views of gender and sexuality.

That all three of the films discussed in this essay are horror-*comedies*—comic not just incidentally and intermittently, but comprehensively and structurally—is key to their subversive nature. The assumptions we construct surrounding femininity, violence, and queerness are so strongly coded as "normal" that they can be easily uprooted only after comedy has weakened the fabric of normality. These films, in other words, *must* be comic in order to alleviate the narrative stress they create by troubling deeply entrenched categories and assumptions. The topsy-turvy comic worlds they create through their marriage of the carnivalesque and the grotesque allows for the disassemblage of presumed structures and boundaries—in both bodily and personal possibilities—creating spaces in which radically new expressions of femininity can establish themselves.

Notes

1. Eileraas, "Witches, Bitches & Fluids," 124.
2. Ibid., 125.
3. Creed, *The Monstrous-Feminine*, 1.
4. Ibid., 14.
5. Eileraas, "Witches, Bitches & Fluids," 127.
6. Ibid., 128.
7. Halberstam, *Skin Shows*, 32.
8. Ibid., 92.
9. Neroni, *The Violent Woman*, 3.
10. Ibid., 7.
11. Ibid., 18.
12. Doane, *Femmes Fatales*, 25.

Bibliography

Creed, Barbara. *The Monstrous-Feminine: Film, Feminism, Psychoanalysis*. New York: Routledge, 2007.

Doane, Mary Ann. *Femmes Fatales: Feminism, Film Theory, Psychoanalysis*. New York: Routledge, 1991.

Eileraas, Karina. "Witches, Bitches & Fluids: Girl Bands Performing Ugliness as Resistance." *The Drama Review* 41, no. 3 (1997): 122–39.

Halberstam, Jack. *Skin Shows: Gothic Horror and the Technology of Monsters*. Durham, NC: Duke University Press, 1995.

Neroni, Hilary. *The Violent Woman: Femininity, Narrative, and Violence in Contemporary American Cinema*. New York: State University of New York Press Albany, 2005.

CHAPTER ELEVEN

~

Rules for Surviving a Horror Comedy

Satiric Genre Transformation from Scream *to* Zombieland

Chris Yogerst

Viewers who grow up with horror films often find that, by a certain age, laughter is a more common reaction than fear. What is terrifying to a child or shocking to an adolescent is met with ironic detachment by adult viewers steeped, by years of schlocky zombie adventures and absurd slasher films, in the conventions of particular subgenres.[1] Repetition of genre tropes breeds familiarity, robbing once-shocking images and plot twists of the impact they originally had. The more popular the trope, the more quickly it loses its power to shock. James Whale's *Frankenstein* (1931) began with a prologue in which a tuxedoed Edward Van Sloan explained to viewers, on behalf of producer Carl Laemmle Jr., that they were about to witness "one of the strangest tales ever told." Van Sloan declared of the film—billed on posters as "The Story of a Man Who Made a Monster"—that "I think it will thrill you. It may shock you. It may even . . . horrify you."[2] Two decades and a half-dozen film appearances later, both man and monster had lost their strangeness. Mad scientists, brain-transplant experiments, and monsters jolted to shambling life by electrical storms had become the stuff of Abbott and Costello comedies and Bugs Bunny cartoons.[3]

Horror films as a genre have gradually changed over the late twentieth and early twenty-first centuries in response their audiences' evolving reactions, with hybrid horror-comedies becoming as common as straightforward tales of terror. The shift took place especially quickly in undead horror films, as the uncanny beings at the center of their narratives—vampires, zombies, werewolves, and mummies—became familiar to audiences through repeated exposure. Mel Brooks's *Young Frankenstein* (1974), shot on the same sets and using the same laboratory props as the 1931 version, kept an utterly straight face while pushing the gothic horror tropes of both Whale's film and Mary Shelley's novel to comically absurd extremes. *Love at First Bite* (1979) transplanted Dracula to present-day New York, sublimating the menacing sexual undertones of the original into a disco-era romantic comedy. George Romero, who had virtually invented the modern zombie film in the relentlessly serious *Night of the Living Dead* (1968), added pitch-black, blood-spattered humor to its sequel, *Dawn of the Dead* (1978).

Films like these coexisted with repeated—and, in productions like the AMC television series *The Walking Dead*, ongoing—attempts to make the familiar staples of undead horror scary again by making them darker and bloodier, more realistic and more overtly sexual. The two approaches, however, were diametrically opposed. Where films like *The Curse of Frankenstein* (1957), *Dracula* (1979), and *The Mummy* (1999) strove to show audiences things that they had never seen on-screen, undead horror-comedies entertained audiences by inviting them to remember—and knowingly laugh about—what they *had* seen, time and time again, in earlier films. The mainstream success of films like *Young Frankenstein* and *Love at First Bite*, and the near-cult status accorded to *Dawn of the Dead* by horror fans, opened the way for undead horror filmmakers to incorporate broad comedy and satire, knowing that their target audience would not only "get," but quickly find, comfort and enjoyment in the result.

Filmmakers' willingness to recognize and reward audiences' familiarity with genre tropes has steadily grown in recent years, fueled by the success of horror films—beginning with *Scream* (1996)—that overtly acknowledged this form of genre play even as they engaged in it. Films such as *Shaun of the Dead* (2004) and *Baghead* (2008), among others, have applied the genre-awareness of *Scream* to the undead horror subgenre. *Zombieland* (2009), however, takes the genre-savvy undead horror film to new satirical extremes. It is simultaneously a zombie-apocalypse film in the tradition of George Romero (and his many imitators) and a satire of such films that depends, for its comic impact, on its core audience's comprehensive, intimate familiarity with horror film tropes. If *Scream* represents the beginning of the trend toward self-reflexive horror-comedy films that began in the last years of the twentieth century, then *Zombieland* represents that trend in its fully mature form, as assured and highly polished as the straightforward zombie horror films it winks at.

Genre Reflexivity and Audience Expectations

Film genres, with their stocks of increasingly familiar plot elements, characters, and images, cultivate audience expectations with each new film. Once established by repetition, however, those expectations allow filmmakers to engage with the genre in increasingly complex ways. Jean-Loup Bourget observes, for example, that genre conventions can be "used as an alibi (the implicit meaning is to be found in the film) or turned upside down (irony underlines the conventionality of the convention)."[4] John Cawelti goes further, arguing that a film genre can pass through multiple stages, ranging from burlesque and demythologization to the cultivation of nostalgia and the reaffirmation of myth.[5]

Horror-comedy films have the potential to work on each of these levels, depending on the individual viewer's frame of reference and level of genre-awareness. *Young Frankenstein*, for example, parodies the conventions of 1930s gothic horror films, but it does so by re-creating the look and feel of such films—their sets, props, and distinctive black-and-white cinematography—with such fidelity that it is still capable of affirming the myths of the subgenre, or even evoking in viewers a nostalgic desire to revisit the original films that it lampoons. At the same time, however, *Young Frankenstein* also has the power to demythologize. James Whale's scene of Fritz (Dwight Frye) stealing a disembodied brain for his master now brings inadvertent smiles from viewers for whom it is overwritten with memories of Igor (Marty Feldman) proudly presenting his master with the stolen brain of "Abby Normal." Boris Karloff's indelible performance as the Monster is—for those who have seen *Young Frankenstein*—a little less imposing because of Peter Boyle's interpretation of the Monster, deftly soft-shoeing to "Puttin' on the Ritz." Once demythologized, common genre conventions become impossible for audiences to view (and filmmakers to present) as seriously as they had done before.[6]

Whether the result is affirmation or deconstruction, however, horror-comedy films enter into dialogue with the subgenres they belong to, and audiences need a working familiarity with (sub)genre conventions in order to appreciate them. Andrew Tudor makes this point in his discussion of changes in the horror genre toward the end of the twentieth century.[7] The horror-comedy films (and horror films with comic elements) that proliferated in the 1970s and 1980s were, Tudor notes, aimed squarely at the youth market. Teenagers' reputation as enthusiastic, indiscriminate consumers of horror films—established in the 1950s, when low-budget horror films became staple programming at drive-in theaters—made them the ideal target audi-ence. Having already seen the same genre conventions play out in dozens of formulaic, low-budget horror films, they were well-prepared both to get the joke and to appreciate the mockery. The proliferation of home video systems between the mid-1980s and the mid-1990s reinforced the trend. Several decades' worth of low-budget films—including scores of limited-release and direct-to-video titles—crowded the "Horror" shelves of video stores, even in the self-proclaimed "family-friendly" Blockbuster chain. Independent video stores, then experiencing their golden age, offered even broader selections and more exotic titles.

Scream, released well into the home-video era, took full advantage of its youthful target audience's (presumed) immersion in horror films and famil-iarity with their conventions. *Zombieland*, which took the deliberately, defi-antly self-reflexive humor of *Scream* to a new level, took similar advantage of the still-deeper immersion permitted by the advent of DVD-by-mail and video-on-demand services. Both films, like their predecessors in the 1970s and 1980s, assume audience familiarity with horror-film conventions in general, and with the ways in which those conventions play out in particu-lar subgenres. *Scream*, however, assumes a greater *degree* of familiarity than earlier horror-comedy would have dared to, and plays with that familiarity in more sophisticated ways. *Zombieland* ups the ante further, making self-reflexive commentary on the genre not just a form of comic relief, but the entire point of the film.

"Do You Like Scary Movies?"—*Scream* and Self-Reflexivity

Scream, directed by horror film veteran Wes Craven (creator of the *Night-mare on Elm Street* franchise), highlights the conventions of the slasher film, using genre-conscious characters to make in-universe comments on them and thus point them out to viewers. It opens with a familiar slasher film situation: A teenage girl, alone in her house, answers the phone (expect-ing her boyfriend) but finds an anonymous stranger on the line instead. Rather than threaten her, however, the stranger engages her in a conversa-tion about horror films, which introduces the genre-conscious nature of the movie. *Scream* differs from previous horror movies in that at least some of its characters acknowledge the horror genre, as the opening scene makes clear. Characters having a conversation about horror films *within* in a horror film immediately draws attention to Craven's intention to play with genre and to the fact that "elements and conventions of a genre are always *in* play rather than simply being *replayed*" in the film.[8] The stranger calls again, declaring that he wants to "play a game" involving horror-movie trivia with the frightened girl, and—at her first wrong answer—breaks into the house and kills her. The film's central message is thus established: The penalty for a lack of genre-savvy is death.

Elaborate self-reflexivity is key to the film's narrative and an essential ingredient in its humor. Throughout *Scream*, "characters deliberately and repeatedly make reference to, mock, and model their behavior after parameters laid down in films familiar to the scriptwriter's target audience."[9] Peter Hutchings—who dubs the *Scream* trilogy and similar late-1990s horror films "postmodern slasher films"—notes that the characters in these films must "probe into the past" in order to uncover the secrets that will enable them to "make sense of the present and then be able to act decisively," in order to survive.[10] The characters in *Scream* are all formally aware that horror films exist as a genre and that the situation in which they find themselves—trapped in a house, stalked by a knife-wielding killer—is commonplace in such films. It falls to Randy (Jamie Kennedy), the most film-obsessed (and thus genre-aware) of them, to call their attention to the implications of this parallel, and the filmmakers use his encyclopedic knowledge of popular horror films to remind the other characters (and thus the audience) of the game being played.

The comedic backbone in *Scream* is reinforced by a scene in the video-rental store where Randy works. It opens with tight shot of a TV screen playing the classic *Frankenstein* (1931) and zooms out to show Randy riding a cart of cassette tapes through the store to restock the popular "mass murder" section. Asked by his friend Stu why Billy—a third friend, and a suspect in Sidney's death—has been released by the authorities, Randy quips: "Because obviously they don't watch enough movies." He goes on to explain that "this is standard horror movie stuff. *Prom Night* (1980) revisited." The scene is a perfect play on the horror genre and its structural base. Randy's analysis of the friend's real situation through the lens of popular culture shows how film can imitate life in the form of a cultural mirror.

Randy's knowledge is on display again near the climax of the film, as he—accompanied by Billy, Stu, and other friends—watches a series of horror movies, beginning with *Halloween* (1978). Referring to Jamie Lee Curtis, who plays the film's teenaged heroine Laurie Strode, Stu jokingly declares, "I wanna see breasts. I wanna see Jamie Lee's breasts. When do we see Jamie Lee's breasts?" Randy, ever-knowledgeable about film, responds: "Breasts? Not until *Trading Places* in 1983. Jamie Lee was always a virgin in horror movies. She didn't show her tits 'til she went legits. That's why she always outsmarted the killer in horror movies. Only virgins can do that. Don't you know the rules?" Randy then proceeds to explain "the rules" of horror films in the film's most famous, and most self-reflexive, scene. "There are certain *rules*," he declares, by which one must abide to survive a horror film:

> Number one: you can never have sex. BIG NO NO! BIG NO NO! Sex equals death, okay? Number two: you can never drink or do drugs. The sin factor! It's a sin. It's an extension of number one. And number three: never, ever, ever under any circumstances say, "I'll be right back." Because you won't be back.

The film's target audience, assumed to be as genre-savvy as Randy, is meant to grasp, immediately, that his rules summarize genre conventions and are thus—for characters in a horror film—"true." The scene thus performs several functions simultaneously: commenting on the characters' situation, displaying Randy's own genre-savvy, and rewarding viewers for theirs.

The apparent failure of Randy's friends to grasp that truth creates another, ironic level of humor in the film: All of the teens are drinking during the party, Billy and Sidney are having sex upstairs, and Stu has just said, "I'll be right back." Over the course of the film, the characters commit virtually all of the sins (and make all of the bad decisions) that genre convention proscribes for characters in a horror movie, and—in keeping with genre convention—some pay with their lives. The climax of the film, however, redoubles the irony. Stu and Billy are jointly revealed as the masked, knife-wielding killers, and they detail how their inspiration for murder came from watching horror movies. *Scream* thus immerses horror fans in a world where they, the killers, and the most astute of the would-be victims have all seen the same films and absorbed their genre conventions as "lessons." It remains self-reflexive to the final frame, using humor as a way of "inviting the audience to be complicit and self-aware."[11] Three sequels, and numerous other films in the tradition of self-reflexive horror-comedy established by *Scream*, would continue the invitation over the next decade.

Zombieland: From Self-Reflexivity to Genre-Savvy

Released more than a decade after *Scream*, *Zombieland* does for the zombie-apocalypse film what its predecessor does for the slasher film: It takes horror fans on self-reflexive tour of a familiar subgenre, in which knowing laughter is the reward for a deep familiarity with earlier films and genre conventions. While *Scream* was designed for an audience that (however genre-aware) had never seen a film quite like it, *Zombieland*, released after a decade's worth of similar films, had no need to explain itself.

Columbus (Jesse Eisenberg), *Zombieland*'s narrator-hero, acts as the audience's guide to a zombie-ridden, post-apocalyptic America. Like Randy, who plays the equivalent role in *Scream*, he articulates "rules for survival" that—because they reflect genre conventions—reward audiences' own genre-savvy. Columbus's rules for surviving the zombie apocalypse are so closely tied to horror-film conventions, in fact, that they might as well be titled "rules for surviving a horror movie."

Neither Columbus nor *Zombieland*, however, pauses to call attention to these ties. Whereas *Scream* constantly reminds the audience of the genre play it is engaged in, *Zombieland* simply assumes that its audience understands not only the conventions of the genre, but also the games that it is playing with them. None of its characters reference specific zombie-apocalypse films or acknowledge the existence of zombie films (or horror films generally) as a genre. *Zombieland* also assumes that zombie-horror conventions have become so ubiquitous, and thus so familiar, that its target audience does not need flashbacks or expository speeches to acquaint them with why the film's world is the way it is. It takes for granted that the audience—like the characters—knows that getting bitten by a zombie means becoming one; that zombies, despite their shambling and slow-witted appearance, are a mortal threat, particularly in large groups; and that carefully constructed, scrupulously observed rules are the key to survival.

All the conventions of "straight" zombie-apocalypse narratives, such as *Night of the Living Dead* and *The Walking Dead*, are present in *Zombieland*. There is a small group of survivors on a quest, once-familiar landscapes have been rendered uncanny and threatening, and the kill-or-be-killed nature of the post-apocalyptic moral universe often leads to epic violence carried out with improvised weapons. Unlike *Scream*, which briefly presents itself as a "straight" slasher film in the opening scenes, *Zombieland* begins its genre play immediately and without preamble, as Columbus laconically describes life in his post-apocalyptic world. His narration sets up a series of visual gags, which play on familiar zombie-apocalypse tropes and immediately place the film squarely in the tradition of comedy rather than horror. *Scream* is a horror film with consistent injections of comedy; *Zombieland* is a comedy film with a side of horror. *Scream* intends certain scenes to be startling, but *Zombieland* never truly sets itself up as a scary film.

Rules for Surviving the "United States of Zombieland"

The film's initial lines, delivered by Columbus in a narration, are: "Oh, America. I wish I could tell you that this was still America, but I've come to realize that you can't have a country without people. And there are no people here. No, my friends, this is now the United States of Zombieland." Familiar post-apocalyptic images accompany this lament: streets strewn with corpses and wrecked cars, smoke rising from the U.S. Capitol, and a zombie lurching toward the camera, its face smeared with gore. The zombie leaps onto an injured but conscious man lying helpless on the pavement, tears his throat out with a single bite, looks at the camera . . . and burps. The ascendancy of comedy continues as Columbus describes his rules for surviving in Zombieland, his coolly understated narration contrasting with images of people who died because of their inability to adapt to the zombie threat. "If the girls in your neighborhood are now . . . little monsters," he intones over a scene of a suburban mother fleeing from a horde of zombified grade-schoolers in princess costumes, "maybe it's time to stop driving carpool."

Rule number one is "cardio"—the film's shorthand for the ability to outrun zombies. "When the virus struck," Columbus explains, "the first ones to go, for obvious reasons, were the fatties." "Cardio" is not just the ability to run, however, but also endurance and agility—the ability to move quickly at a second's notice. An extension of the cardio rule, mentioned later in the film, is "limber up." No one wants to pull a hamstring when zombies are near. Rule number two is the double tap. During a scene in which a woman thought she had killed a zombie, Columbus explains: "In those moments when you are unsure that the undead are really dead-dead, don't get all stingy with your bullets. I mean one more clean shot to the head and this woman could avoid becoming a human happy meal." Rule number three, "beware of bathrooms," is illustrated by a man being attacked while sitting in a stall. Columbus's commentary is, again, sardonically humorous: "Don't let them catch you with your pants down." The on-screen illustration of this rule, while played for laughs, reflects a core convention of zombie-apocalypse films: The undead are everywhere and, as a result, nowhere is truly safe. Constant vigilance and careful attention to surroundings are essential to survival, and any place that encourages relaxation becomes dangerous as a result. In the United States of Zombieland it is wise to keep a loaded weapon within reach at all times, even—perhaps especially—in the bathroom. Rule number four, "seatbelts," is less intuitive, but the on-screen illustration immediately clarifies it: We see a woman in a minivan (the suburban mother, chased by literally monstrous children) hit a truck and become a human projectile. Launched through her windshield, she sails over the truck and into the street beyond. Unusual camera angles—first a midair view of her oncoming face, then an overhead shot of her body sliding across the pavement—render her death grotesquely comic, and Columbus chimes in, "Fasten your seatbelts. It's going to be a bumpy ride."

Once introduced to Columbus's rules (the list of which continues to grow throughout the film),[12] the audience is reminded—by a credit sequence full of slow-motion, over-the-top horror—precisely what kind of film *Zombieland* is satirizing. The stylish yet disturbing sequence is a montage of slow-motion zombie attacks set to a hard-rock soundtrack. The staging of the attacks reflects Dan Harries's contention that "film parody not only uses the genre's structure to create difference through processes of exaggeration, extraneous inclusion, inversion and misdirection, but also reiterates and reaffirms the conventions that constitute the genre's structure through these processes."[13] Most of the scenes that make up the montage are comically preposterous: A groom is attacked at the altar when his bride "turns" at precisely the wrong moment, firefighters intent on a blaze are blindsided by a flaming zombie, and a crowd of terrified middle-aged men flee an exotic dance club as a zombified stripper—her bare skin smeared with gore—closes on them from behind. Beneath the absurdity, however, there is genuine horror, as victim after living victim is wrestled to the ground to be devoured by the voracious undead. The rules, and Columbus's application of them, are funny, but the zombie apocalypse and the fight for survival in its aftermath are real.

"I survive because I play it safe and play by the rules. My rules," Columbus declares, but the sequence that follows the credits—the first in which he is visible on-screen—suggests that, even so, his survival is far from guaranteed. Pulling into a gas station parking lot, he is on the verge of cautiously entering its bathroom when a pair of zombies emerge and begin chasing him. As he continues to run, the word "Cardio" blinks on-screen, underscoring the message. He reaches the apparent safety of his car and drives away, only to have a zombie appear from the back seat. He crashes the car, ejecting the zombie through the windshield as "seatbelts" pops up on-screen, only to have the ghoul reappear and attempt to climb back into the car. Columbus fires his shotgun, blasting the zombie off the car, and then climbs out onto the pavement in order to shoot it a second time (evoking the "double tap" rule).[14] Throughout the sequence he is breathing hard, fumbling, cursing, and one step away from being eaten; "the rules," audiences are invited to assume, are all that stands between him and sudden death.

The story proper begins as Columbus, a self-described shut-in, sets out from his college dorm in Austin, Texas, to his eponymous hometown in Ohio, joining forces along the way with Tallahassee (Woody Harrelson)—a proud redneck and zealous zombie-killer with a fondness for Hostess Twinkies. Along the way, the pair meet Wichita (Emma Stone) and Little Rock (Abigail Breslin), sisters who—though initially rivals who trick them out of their vehicle and weapons—become wary allies and eventually friends. The sisters are

It's all about the rules!

headed for the Pacific Playland amusement park in Los Angeles, said to be a zombie-free sanctuary, and after learning that his hometown is in ruins and his family likely dead, Columbus elects to join them. The members of the group bond on the cross-country journey, learning to trust and rely on each other for survival. Columbus's cautious, introverted personality balances out Tallahassee's reckless bravado, and Wichita similarly complements Little Rock.

Columbus, his newfound friends, and *Zombieland* itself never explicitly reference specific horror films, or horror films as a genre. They have no need to. Whereas Randy, in *Scream*, distills his rules from the countless horror films he has watched, Columbus (the pre-credits and gas-station sequences imply) derives his from day-to-day experience in his post-apocalyptic world. Tallahassee, Wichita, and Little Rock—all veteran survivors—understand, before they meet Columbus, that discipline is the key to survival. There is no need for them to have the rules explained for their own benefit, and—after Columbus's brief summary of the rules at the start of the film—no need for them to explain the rules to one another for the benefit of the audience. They are all capable of surviving in the post-apocalyptic world, even though they all respond to the zombie situation differently (and none articulates "rules" as obsessively as Columbus). Unlike Stu in *Scream*, none of them needs to be educated.

The audience, too, understands the characters' world—from exposure to nearly identical worlds in other zombie-horror films—before the film even begins. Where *Scream*'s Randy speaks as a prophet who draws arcane wisdom from his movie-drenched brain, Columbus speaks to the audience (in his voice-overs) as an equal, matter-of-factly articulating truths that they already grasp. The film does not need to show us something; it is engaging in the genre *with* us. The filmmakers' assumption of shared knowledge allows the rules to frequently serve as punch lines, evoked by a simple note on the screen. For example, when Tallahassee pulls a muscle while vandalizing a minivan, the words "limber up" appear on the screen as a subtle reminder of another of Columbus's rules.[15] Harries notes that by "evoking the genre's codes and strategies of spectatorship, film parody also ends up being closely aligned to the genre it's spoofing to the point where the parody becomes a 'master map' of the genre."[16] In *Zombieland*, this alignment is so close that parody and straight zombie-apocalypse film merge and become indistinguishable. While *Scream* is sometimes a horror film and sometimes a self-aware comedy *about* horror films, *Zombieland*, for virtually its entire running time, is both simultaneously.

Comedy, Horror, Genre

Zombieland's consistent twinning of horror and comedy elements ultimately reinforces, rather than undermines, its status as a horror film. Discussing genre films, Thomas Schatz writes that "once we recognize the familiar cultural arena and the players, we can be fairly certain how the game will be played and how it will end."[17] Familiarity alone, however, is not enough to sustain a genre. As Schatz notes elsewhere: "The widespread exposure of genre films to the audience and the demand that filmmakers sustain audience interest in popular forms encourage continued manipulation of generic conventions if the genre is to maintain its vitality and cultural significance."[18] He concludes that, as critics, "we understand genre films because of their similarity with other films, but we appreciate them because of their difference."[19] *Zombieland* offers those differences in abundance, interweaving horror and comedy across its 90-minute running time, and provoking further humor by mixing in elements of still more genres.

The two principal male characters, for example, often seem to have come to the "United States of Zombieland" from entirely different corners of the cinematic universe. Columbus, with his unshakable nonchalance and constant stream of ironic commentary (he describes the zombie plague as "a fast-acting virus that leaves you with a swollen brain, a raging fever, makes you hateful and violent, and leaves you with a really bad case of the munchies") comes straight out of a slacker comedy. His backstory, however, is more in keeping with a coming-of-age film. His isolation from the world and lack of trust in his fellow humans was sparked—he explains in a flashback—when the attractive girl who lived down the hall showed up at his door. Having been bitten and turned into a zombie, the girl (who he knows only as 406, after her room number) attacks him. "You can't trust anyone. The first time I let a girl into my life and she tries to eat me," a frustrated Columbus explains over as the flashback shows him hitting 406 a second time with a toilet lid (a literal "double tap").

Tallahassee, on the other hand, has all the hallmarks of a classic Western hero: a loner with drawl, a cowboy hat, and a swaggering masculinity that expresses itself in unpredictable bursts of cathartic violence directed against the Other (in this case zombies) that menaces civilization. Seen in this context, his fondness for Twinkies—like Joe's affection for his mule in *A Fistful of Dollars*—is a quirk that he can afford to indulge because his masculinity (and lethality) is never in doubt. Tallahassee revels in his physicality and capacity for violence as completely as his erstwhile partner revels in detachment. "My momma always said I would be good at something," he marvels at one point. "Who knew that something would be zombie killin'?" Like many Western heroes, however, he stoically hides a tragic past: the death of his young son in the early stages of the zombie outbreak.

The climax of *Zombieland* brings all these genres into play at once. Wichita and Little Rock—consistent with *their* genre roots as free-spirited drifters from a road movie—have separated themselves from Columbus and Tallahassee and struck out on their own. Stranded on a ride at the Pacific

Tallahassee: Western hero meets zombie killer.

Playland amusement park, they are menaced by hungry zombies waiting on the ground below. Their rescue, involving chases and copious gunfire set to a heavy-metal soundtrack, evokes earlier zombie films like *Dawn of the Dead*, but also the climactic shootouts of Westerns like *High Noon* (1952), *Rio Bravo* (1959), and *The Magnificent Seven* (1960). Tallahassee, in his element, draws the zombies' attention with an air horn and, using the park's rides as cover and firing platforms, mows them down with his seemingly endless supply of ammunition. Columbus, meanwhile, uses his speed and agility to rescue the girls, killing an intimidating zombie clown along the way.

Columbus's victory over the clown (the focus of one of his numerous phobias) casts him in the classic Western role of the cocky young man who—like "Colorado" (Ricky Nelson) in *Rio Bravo*—proves himself through an act of selfless daring. His decision to act (in repudiation of rule number 17: "Don't be a hero") is motivated by his feelings for Wichita, and so echoes the last-act redemptions of cynical, wiseguy heroes from Rick Blaine in *Casablanca* to Han Solo in *Star Wars*. Together, the two actions complete his coming-of-age story by transforming him from a socially isolated slacker to a fully engaged member of what remains of human society. Tallahassee also finds redemption amid the violence of the climax: saving Little Rock, who he has come to see as a surrogate daughter, as he could not save his son. The girls, once rescued, reconsider their plan to strike out on their own, and the reunited quartet rides off into the sunset. This final image, evoking a trope shared by Westerns and road movies alike, is overlaid with a final, ironic voice-over by Columbus: "So until next time," he says, "remember: cardio, seat belts, and, this really has nothing to do with anything, but a little sunscreen never hurt anybody. I'm Columbus, Ohio, from Zombieland, saying good night."

Historically, "the law of genre is a norm of purity, a certificate of guarantee, and the occasional transgression of the law only serves to reinforce its validity."[20] What makes *Zombieland* stand out as a work of genre is the way in which—by a constant barrage of such transgressions—it critiques and subverts the zombie film. This subversion, which Ira Jaffe contends is inherent in all genre films, is brought to a natural climax in *Zombieland*.[21]

Conclusion

Zombieland serves as a perfect template for the latest stage of undead comedy films (and of horror-comedy in general). The "United States of Zombieland" is familiar to audiences because it is virtually the same post-apocalyptic setting used in dozens of earlier zombie films. The heroes in *Zombieland* flourish because they have discovered the principles by which their world operates in predictable ways and figured out how to use that knowledge to ensure their survival. Much of *Zombieland*'s humor, in fact, derives from the characters' absurd sense of confidence in their ability to survive, and the lightheartedness with which they kill zombies—to the point of comparing kills (i.e., "zombie kill of the week"). The main characters' mastery of their world comically deflates the zombie threat by underscoring how easily they can be defeated and comically underscores the ignorance of common-sense precautions and elementary tactics displayed by characters in traditional zombie films. The ultimate joke, however, is on the characters, who understand everything about their post-apocalyptic world . . . except for the fact that they are living in a formulaic genre movie. The viewer, who *does* understand, has the last laugh.

Celestino Deleyto notes that "film texts are meeting points in which various genres come into context with one another, vie for dominance, and are transformed."[22] *Zombieland*—equal parts horror film and comedy—engages, consciously and overtly, in genre transformation. Its climax—an epic battle between the living heroes and the undead hordes, staged at an amusement park where kids play and have fun—signals its nature as a "play" on the zombie-horror genre. Columbus's rules, which bookend the narrative, play a similar role: They are serious advice about matters of life and death, but delivered (unlike Randy's earnest exhortations in *Scream*) in a lighthearted, ironic tone. *Zombieland* thus begins and ends with a comedic grin that signals its intention to temper what would otherwise be a terrifying vision of a zombie apocalypse.

Such genre manipulation, as Andrew Tudor notes, depends on the audience, "as genre filmgoers, to know exactly what is happening" and to be "both willing victims of the technique and simultaneously self-aware parties to its construction."[23] The majority of the gags in *Zombieland* are designed to be funnier to audiences familiar with zombie-film conventions, and Columbus's rules for survival—the central comic conceit in the film—rely *entirely* on such narrative familiarity for their impact. Formulas, John Cawelti notes, "are important [because] they can serve as a sort of shorthand for speeding up the communication between writer [and, in this case, director] and reader,"[24] and a genre cannot attain the stage of complete satire until the audience members' familiarity with it is deep enough for them to connect with the humor. Horror films, including zombie films, now have a history deep enough to sustain such satire. Recent film parodies manage, as Harries argues, "to be both hip and staid guardians of Hollywood's genre-based past."[25] *Zombieland* simultaneously rehearses and lampoons the now-familiar conventions of the zombie film. Thanks to Columbus's rules of survival, they can live to be satirized another day.

Notes

1. My generation's introduction to horror was a series of half-serious, half-humorous films ranging from *Dawn of the Dead* (1978) and *Halloween* (1978) to the series based on *Friday the 13th* (1980) and *Nightmare on Elm Street* (1984). Joking about the unbelievable circumstances leading to each character's demise became commonplace.

2. Dirks, "Frankenstein (1931)," 1.

3. For example: *Hair-Raising Hare* (1946); *Abbott and Costello Meet Frankenstein* (1948); *Water, Water Every Hare* (1952).

4. Bourget, "Social Implications in the Hollywood Genres," 58.

5. Cawelti, "Chinatown and Generic Transformation."

6. Not all demythologizing is humorous. See, for example, Clint Eastwood's *Unforgiven* (1991).

7. Tudor, "From Paranoia to Postmodernism?" 107. This also invokes Rick Altman's "semantic/syntactic" approach to film genre; see Altman, *Film/Genre*.

8. Neale, "Question of Genre," 189.

9. Sanjek, "Same as It Ever Was," 113.

10. Hutchings, *The Horror Film*, 215.

11. Tudor, "From Paranoia to Postmodernism?" 113.

12. The final list, more than 30 rules long, includes: no attachments (number 5), travel light (number 7), don't be a hero (number 17), limber up (number 18), and know your way out (number 22).

13. Harries, "Film Parody and the Resuscitation of Genre," 283.

14. The fact that he uses a double-barreled shotgun—meaning that, if he follows his own rule, he *must* stop to reload after every kill—may itself be a subtle joke.

15. Other rules used in a similar manner are cardio, check the back seat, and double tap, among others.

16. Harries, "Film Parody and the Resuscitation of Genre," 286.

17. Schatz, "Film Genre and the Genre Film," 699.

18. Schatz, "Structural Influence," 99.

19. Schatz, "Film Genre and the Genre Film," 694.

20. Deleyto, "Film Genres at the Crossroads," 223.

21. Jaffe, *Hollywood Hybrids*, 6. See also Deleyto, "Film Genres at the Crossroads," 228.

22. Deleyto, "Film Genres at the Crossroads," 228.

23. Tudor, "From Paranoia to Postmodernism?" 111.

24. Cawelti, *Mystery, Violence, and Popular Culture*, 134.

25. Harries, "Film Parody and the Resuscitation of Genre," 291.

184 ~ Chris Yogerst

Bibliography

Altman, Rick. *Film/Genre*. 1999. London: British Film Institute, 2004.

Bourget, Jean-Loup. "Social Implications in the Hollywood Genres." In *Film Genre Reader III*, edited by Barry Keith Grant, 51–59. Austin: University of Texas Press, 2003.

Cawelti, John G. "Chinatown and Generic Transformation in Recent American Films." In *Film Genre Reader III*, edited by Barry Keith Grant, 243–60. Austin: University of Texas Press, 2003.

———. *Mystery, Violence, and Popular Culture*. Bowling Green, OH: Popular Press, 2004.

Deleyto, Celestino. "Film Genres at the Crossroads: What Genres and Films Do to Each Other." *Film Genre Reader IV*, edited by Barry Keith Grant, 218–36. Austin: University of Texas Press, 2012.

Dirks, Tim. "Frankenstein (1931)." *AMC Film Site*. http://www.filmsite.org/fran.html.

Harries, Dan. "Film Parody and the Resuscitation of Genre." In *Genre and Contemporary Hollywood*, edited by Steve Neale, 281–93. London: British Film Institute, 2002.

Hutchings, Peter. *The Horror Film*. New York: Pearson Education Ltd., 2004.

Jaffe, Ira. *Hollywood Hybrids: Mixing Genres in Contemporary Films*. Lanham, MD: Rowman & Littlefield, 2008.

Neale, Steve. "Question of Genre." *Film Genre Reader IV*, edited by Barry Keith Grant, 178–202. Austin: University of Texas Press, 2012.

Sanjek, David. "Same as It Ever Was: Innovation and Exhaustion in the Horror and Science Fiction Films of the 1990s." In *Film Genre 2000: New Critical Essays*, edited by Wheeler Winston Dixon, 111–23. Albany: State University of New York Press, 2000.

Schatz, Thomas. "Film Genre and the Genre Film." In *Film Theory and Criticism*, 6th ed., edited by Leo Brady and Marshall Cohen, 691–702. New York: Oxford University Press, 2004.

———. "The Structural Influence: New Directions in Film Genre Study." In *Film Genre Reader III*, edited by Barry Keith Grant, 92–101. Austin: University of Texas Press, 2003.

Tudor, Andrew. "From Paranoia to Postmodernism? The Horror Movie in Late Modern Society." *Genre and Contemporary Hollywood*, edited by Steve Neale, 105–16. London: British Film Institute, 2002.

~

PART III

THERE GOES THE NEIGHBORHOOD

CHAPTER TWELVE

~

Better Living through Zombies

Assessing the Allegory of Consumerism and Empowerment in Andrew Currie's Fido

Michael C. Reiff

Andrew Currie's *Fido*, a satirical zombie comedy released in 2006, reimagines America's 1950s utopian consumerist culture as a time when zombies have been defeated. But instead of decapitating or burning all of the shambling ghouls, a corporation called Zomcon has developed a method to turn the zombies into consumable products—commodities of leisure, servitude, and domesticity. The zombies are leashed by high-tech neck braces, "brain-washed" (so to speak), and marketed as the automated helpers of the future. They are bought and sold as servants, moving crews, and cooks. As pets. Sometimes, even as lovers.

Currie's reimagining of the zombie is absurd. It is strikingly funny. It is violent. But below its candy-colored and whimsically dark exterior is a satirical core that helps to reopen new avenues of critical thought on some already well-trod ground. Through Currie's lens, *Fido* provides an avenue for further exploration of complicated and troubling aspects of postwar America's interaction with consumerist society—its marketing and production models—as well as a twist on the evolution of feminist heroines in the genre and time period. While George Romero's 1978 *Dawn of the Dead* may have cracked open the door of critical thinking on consumerism and the active role of women in the zombie genre, *Fido* continues a contemporary trend toward reassessing the utility of the zombie, its place within a solely horror-centric genre, and the core societal issues the genre has dealt with in the past.

The Nostalgic Zombie

Fido is a strikingly revisionist zombie movie, but one that retains the core elements of the zombie genre. The dead are walking the earth, and their "nature" is to eat the living. It's just that they are no longer much of a threat. The utility of zombies has been discovered—or, rather, created. Zombies are now commodities. They are the hottest product to be consumed, compared, and deployed in keeping-up-with-the-neighbors rivalries on placid tree-lined streets. A society that uses the living dead in this way cannot be perfect, however, and therein lies the root of Currie's reinterpretation of the zombie film.

Fido tells the story of a Rockwellian American nuclear family—a mother, a father, and a son. The film is centered on Timmy Robinson (K'Sun Ray), a prototypical American youngster who, being weak and timid, is picked on by bullies and in need of fatherly guidance. But his father Bill (Dylan Baker) is a distant patriarch, disturbed by memories of the recently won zombie war and often meekly mewling in the presence of the tamed zombies now in his neighborhood. Rounding out the family is the mother, Helen Robinson (Carrie-Anne Moss), a restive housewife who is bemused by her lackluster life of leisure as well as her husband's growing emotional distance. This is exemplified by her frustration with Bill's increasing obsession with paying for the family's future burials (in Zomcon land, purchasing two caskets, one for the head, and one for the rest of the body, ensures no reanimation once six feet under), as well as his Sunday ritual of sneaking into funerals to see how the neighbors are being buried.

Thus, what at first is an act of compulsive and peer-pressured purchasing—the new neighbors across the street have a horde of zombie servants moving in their furniture—becomes an act of liberation. Helen purchases her own zombie (Billy Connolly), Timmy names it "Fido," and in the days that follow, the new product becomes a whimsical surrogate father figure to Timmy as well as a tool of expression and liberated domesticity for Helen.

The best elements of *Fido*, however, include not only the familiar, and divergent, family dynamics at the core of the story, but also Zomcon, the corporation that has enabled this bizarre and absurd consumerist society to flourish. Seemingly all things at once—corporation, police force, savior of humanity in the zombie war—Zomcon is presented throughout the film as a lodestar for understanding Currie's vision. Zomcon is the company that invented the collar that controls a zombie's flesh-eating urges and also compels the zombie to become an automated worker drone (illustrated in an early, and goofy, 1950s newsreel spoof, showing smiling children, affable scientists, and shambling zombies serving drinks to relaxing parents). Yet *Fido* quickly indicates that Zomcon is not simply a purveyor of products, but a designer of cultural mind-sets and patterns of behavior. Not content to simply market their zombie products to a yearning public, Zomcon has seemingly rearranged American society to accept its radical product as well as maintain a wartime mentality which is at times anxiety-ridden, while at others paradoxically prosaic as the public trusts the corporation to protect them.

The film opens with a fake newsreel montage—itself a work of marketing—explaining the recent history of the zombie war and the commoditization of the zombie. The newsreel—presented to children in grade school—emphasizes the violence of the previous zombie war, the perseverance of ingenious scientists, and the new, peaceful, societal norm that now exists, thanks to Zomcon. The peace that exists in the film's present depends on purchasing, not slaying, the zombies that once terrified the people. The worldview crafted in that opening sequence permeates the film, in scenes directly linked to the corporation itself as well as more tangentially. This carefully crafted consumerist mind-set—along with its real-world historical antecedents and references—is critical in understanding the full implications of the characters, the text as a whole, and most importantly, the zombie itself.

"I Can Throw Zombies in It!"

Taken broadly, the zombie genre has, in many ways, come full circle from George Romero's early films about the undead. Contemporary iterations of the zombie, along with the genre's overall resurgence in popularity, as Kyle Bishop notes, "fit post-9/11 cultural consciousness well," given the genre's "inescapable realities of unnatural death" and its presentation of "a modern apocalypse in which society's infrastructure breaks down."[1] Both today and in Romero's initial decades, these core elements—unnatural, inescapable death and the breakdown of conventional societal structures—are often maintained and provide avenues for social critiques. Indeed, as Romero himself noted during the release of his *Diary of the Dead* (2007), itself a zombie film critical of mass media, the zombies are often merely the marketable trappings of a film—the idea, the critical conceit, is the foundation of the zombie film, with the shambling ghouls the macabre pop-culture lure.[2]

Contemporary zombie films are often compared to the intellectual clarity found in Romero's *Dawn of the Dead*, his groundbreaking critique of consumerism, and a film from which *Fido* clearly draws both generic and critical allusions. Like *Fido*, *Dawn* features moments of ebullient consumerism as fleeing victims of the zombie outbreak find refuge in an abandoned shopping mall, and in which, as Stephen Harper notes, "the survivors indulge in a fantasy of purchase power."[3] The consumerist fantasy in *Dawn of the Dead* is played out in small vignettes: a man throwing wads of cash into the air; another fondling pristine firearms in a sporting goods store; and a woman lavishly wearing expensive makeup, mugging for the mirror, and waving a gun about. In *Fido*, this indulgent fantasy is society-wide, and many of the iconic materials (money, makeup, and firearms) are repeated, though often in heightened and comical ways. But Currie adds a twist, as the zombies in their midst are viewed more as the commoditized kindly helper inside the home and not the killer at the door.

For both Romero and Currie, the critique of consumerism also allows for critical thought on social dualities—the haves and have-nots, conformers and outliers, systemic supporters and anarchic disruptors. As Harper notes, "Romero's script emphasizes the economic exclusivity of consumerism,"[4] a sentiment reflected in the duality between the survivors and the zombies in the mall (shoppers who can take goods vs. those who can't) and between the survivors and the anarchic biker gang that destroys the mall at the end (individuals who conform to expectations of orderly consumerism vs. those who do not, and in the end disrupt and dismember the system). These fraught relationships are also presented, though more whimsically and subtly, in *Fido*. Helen feels the economic pressures of keeping up with her neighbor's purchasing habits and status, at one point asking her husband in deadpan dinner conversation, "Did you know that [the new neighbors] have six zombies?" and is therefore compelled to purchase her own zombie to keep up appearances. And while her husband is assiduously paying down the Zomcon headless burials for the family, his seemingly singular fear of zombies is, itself, an oddity in the community, a social stigma put to rest by the purchase of a key product.

More importantly, though, Helen and Timmy's relationship to the consumer society begins to diverge from those of their neighbors. Toward the end of the film, neither adheres to the rules of the system as they should. Through their evolving relationship with Fido, both Timmy and Helen eventually upend the Zomcon system, reflecting the actions of the anarchic biker gang in *Dawn of the Dead*. *Fido* diverges from *Dawn of the Dead*, however, in its portrayal of individuals'—especially women's—overall relationship to consumerism. Consumerism and feministic urges are bound up in Helen, who pushes toward liberation, disruption, and self-articulation through her purchases and products.

While the original *Night of the Living Dead* may have depicted femininity in a fragile state, Romero's 1990 remake of the film showcases a striking role reversal in female power within the zombie narrative, an element featured in *Fido* as well. As Barry Keith Grant notes in his analysis of the 1990 *Night of the Living Dead*, the film "attempts to reclaim the horror genre for feminism, for all those female victims in such movies who attempt to resist patriarchal containment."[5] In the remake, Romero reinvents Barbara as a "true professional," a character who is able to dispassionately "perform the unpleasant but necessary tasks"[6] required to survive, with dignity, in the zombie apocalypse. Her self-sufficient and confrontational identity also prevents the viewer "from delighting in the voyeuristic spectacle of a frightened and helpless woman"[7] as Barbara is consistently presented as a cool and collected, gun-toting heroine.

Many of these elements are also exemplified by Helen in *Fido*; she is consistently shown taking control of the situation, whether subtly (early on, purchasing Fido) or more assertively (wielding her own gun to save Timmy from zombies in the middle of the film, and racing to his rescue again, dragging Bill along for the ride, in the end). By dint of her behavior and choices, however, Helen also provides a humane (yet steely) contrast to Zomcon, which is governed, clearly, by a male-dominated mind-set. While she purchases the primary Zomcon product, she does not dehumanize it as the men do in *Fido*. Instead, she gradually subverts a male product into something better than its original form. And perhaps most important (and often the source of much of the humor in the film), Helen is not a "frightened and helpless woman" but a contrast to her pusillanimous husband throughout, as well as to the frightened masses that swarm around her at the film's climax. As the icons of the paternalist society, namely her own husband and the chief security officer of Zomcon, are destroyed, Helen appears in much the same light as Barbara in the 1990 *Night of the Living Dead*: calm, collected, and far more capable than her male counterparts of surviving in a zombie-infested world.

Helen's world, however, is a more complex and subtle dystopia than the Hobbesian world of zombies and men run amok that Barbara confronts. Like Americans after the 9/11 terrorist attacks and the residents of the fortified urban enclave in Romero's 2005 film, *Land of the Dead*, the suburbanites of *Fido* "are asked both to continue their lives as if no real threat existed and to behave in certain ways because of the threat that does exist."[8] Now that the zombie war is "over" the best thing to do is consume, and consume Zomcon products particularly. And because zombies, in this new equilibrium, are simultaneously a threat *and* a fixture of the characters' living rooms, the humor and the tension is heightened even further. As in *Land of the Dead*, the rupture in the status quo is brought about by the characters' materialist way of life, providing varying degrees of humorous irony.

Also like *Land of the Dead*, *Fido* features undead characters that defy the traditional image of zombies as mindless and, especially, as unable to create. *Fido*'s title character grunts with acknowledgment, acts nobly for those he "cares about," is seen at the end of the film as a surrogate father, and even restrains himself from eating Helen and Timmy when his collar malfunctions. This seeming rehumanization of the zombie is a bold step forward in the genre,[9] but also a troubling element in the world of the film. It has foundation-shaking implications for a society that simultaneously consumes zombies as products and villainizes them as unthinking enemies, controllable only through Zomcon tools.

Marketing Dehumanization

The histories, mythologies, and paradoxical normalization of the zombie that Zomcon compels in *Fido*'s society reflect the dehumanization, and then reintegration, of the Japanese that took place during and after World War II in the U.S. media. Indeed, there are striking overlaps between depictions of the Japanese in the 1940s and Zomcon's media blitzes designed to instill fear of the zombie, while encouraging their domination and domestication.

Depictions of the Japanese depended on dehumanizing images, language, and codes, designed to simultaneously vilify them and soothe fears of the threat they posed to the United States. This dual methodology was necessary to bolster wartime spirit as well as to ward off civil unrest. On the one hand, "racist images of a ferocious, subhuman enemy with whom there could be no compromise"[10] were propagated in the media to dehumanize the Japanese. As MacDougall explains, "Anti-Japanese sentiment was often expressed through subhuman or non-human imagery"[11] found in newsreels, comic books, and magazines for all ages. This "subhuman" imagery is, of course, on display throughout *Fido*, in media depiction of the zombie as well as in the creatures' actions. But this dehumanization of the other isn't Zomcon's only method of cultural control, and for that we must look at the other ways in which the Japanese were depicted.

The Japanese were presented as "subhuman" or "inhuman," but were also portrayed as animals to be subdued and domesticated. Phrases such as "mad dog," "yellow ape," "ape-men," and "monkey meat" were used to caricature, dehumanize, and "animize" the Japanese.[12] These terms—in particular phrases like "monkey meat" that connote a commodification of the Japanese soldier—are reflected consistently throughout *Fido*, as the zombies are commoditized themselves. In the opening "newsreel" montage, the Zomcon propaganda acts in much the same way, first presenting the zombie as an existential threat, and then with the advent of the collar, as a manageable pet—a leashed and trainable helper, like an organ grinder's monkey.

Indeed, while wartime hysteria is still milked for societal obedience and vigilance, the comical presentation of the zombie acts as much to pacify the denizens of Currie's village as it does to entertain, rather than horrify, the viewer. Postwar mentality is still evident in the training of gun-toting scouts (as eager to shoot a zombie as to spy on the soon-to-pass elderly) as well as in the omnipresent sense of Zomcon control, exemplified by the chief of security, Mr. Bottoms, who interrogates the townsfolk, including Timmy, from the driver's seat of his shiny sedan.

But the domestication of the zombie is far more potent in pacifying the populace. Early in the film, "newsreels" present smiling scientists patting now-placid zombies. Later, Currie provides whimsical moments, as when a milkman teaches his mindless zombie worker how to place (and not throw like a newspaper) a bottle of milk. In these illustrations, the threat of the "Other" is removed. The enemy has been domesticated to the level of a pet or mindless worker drone. And while the parallels are, of course, a bit skewed, in both cases we are presented with a similar script of reintegration of the "Other" in postwar America. In both cases, this reintegration is promoted through iconography deemed properly passive and manageable by both the government and the media. The zombie, like the Japanese, may have been a dangerous "mad dog," but, being dogs, or Fidos, they are still trainable and marketable.

The ways in which zombies and their interactions with humans are at first established in *Fido* help to clarity the vilification and domestication that is necessary for the setting's logic and the character shifts that occur later in the

A zombie milkman learns his trade.

film. Indeed, most individuals in *Fido* are naturalized to the enslavement of the Other. However, those most willing to embrace the Other as more than a villain, a pet, or a product—notably Timmy, his mother Helen, and their neighbor Mr. Theopolis—are also the ones most likely to not only break through the propagandistic mind-set, but also subvert the authority of Zomcon itself. One can put aside, for the moment, the rather lurid and ridiculous (yet still consumeristically subversive) relationship between Mr. Theopolis and "Tammy": a relationship between a living man and a very "young" domesticated zombie that not only seems sexually perverse (if she were alive), but also culturally transgressive, as this relationship is what ended Theopolis's work with Zomcon. Much more important is the quasi-father-and-son relationship between Fido and Timmy, as well as the woman-to-companion relationship between Helen and Fido. These relationships are the plot mechanisms that drive the infiltration of Zomcon's factory to liberate Fido from his corporate overlords in the film's hilariously wry and raucous conclusion. More importantly, these characters reject the media depictions of the Other so thoroughly that they actively undermine their own cultural system.

Purchasing Power

Breaking powerful cultural narratives requires a powerfully subversive character, like Helen in *Fido*. Her role in the film is centered on liberation—of herself, her son, and even a commoditized zombie—but her commercialism and relationship building, as well as her willingness to break social conventions, link her to key motifs of the zombie genre, both historical and recent. From cultural critiques of male-dominated society to the empowerment of "professional" and system-upending women, Helen's similarity to contemporary zombie-film heroines provides the progressive backbone of the film.

As Grant notes, *Dawn of the Dead* "self-consciously uses the zombie as a conceit for macho masculinism,"[13] a critique emulated in *Fido*, where it serves as the foundation for Helen's inner struggle as she continues to embrace some elements of the hegemony she seeks to subvert. Her dissatisfaction with her absurdly nebbish husband, and the Zomcon culture in general, epitomizes the cultural critique found in earlier zombie films. It does not, however, rise to an attack on what Robin Wood calls "the whole dead weight of patriarchal consumer capitalism."[14] Helen does not so much reject the "patriarchal consumer capitalism" that is the foundation of Zomcon's societal control, as subvert it and bend it to her will. This subversion reflects the obvious cracks in the system: Its major product is a dangerous, unpredictable one that frightens Helen's main oppressor, her husband, and disrupts the hegemon in the community itself, Zomcon.

Helen acts rebelliously, breaking with conventional norms, but she does so *within* the consumerist system. She breaks away from 1950s-style patriarchy of the suburbs, and from Zomcon's cultural control, but she does not wholly break from consumerism in general. Consumerism, indeed, is partly what empowers her. She succeeds by making a multiplicity of purchases and using them in ways singular to her own purposes. This consumerist/patriarchal distinction helps to differentiate Helen from, and advance her beyond, other zombie-movie heroines and lays the foundation for her wryly humorous character.

Also bound up in Helen's subversive purchasing power is the quasi-romantic relationship that forms between her and Fido—between living woman and undead man. Chera Kee writes in "Good Girls Don't Date Dead Boys" that the "pathological" urges being played out in these zombie/woman relationships reflect anxiety over "white heterosexual patriarchy's loss of control over"[15] women's sexual identity. There is no doubt that Fido's entry into Helen's life challenges her husband's control over both her and his own emotional state (from the first moment he sees Fido, Bill startles and squirms in the presence of the zombie). Fido is not, however, simply an element of the Robinsons' life, perhaps one purchased by Bill mistakenly. Helen herself purchases Fido, brings him into the family, and through various scenes instigates the relationship. In a car-wash sequence, she alluringly and humorously gazes at Fido as he scrubs her car, and later, after Bill refuses to dance with her, Helen kicks off her shoes and dances a seductive tango with a grunting Fido, sending Bill upstairs, apoplectic. In a brief scene, she even dresses the

Helen dances a tango with Fido.

zombie in Bill's clothing for a Sunday drive to a funeral. As she fixes his tie, Fido sniffs longingly at her perfume, a touching moment between woman and zombie. This is "patriarchy's loss of control" in a different sense—instigated by the woman using the Other, rather than vice versa.

Indeed, with the exception of Mr. Theopolis and his own zombie product, Helen is the only living person—and certainly the only woman—who has a relationship with a zombie; this unique pairing indicates a large amount of power wielded by the heroine, both for its exclusivity and for the agency it shows in the character. As Kee summarizes, "There is power in this sexuality" that arises from monster (zombie)/white female relationships, and "the look shared between the monster and the female may cast the female as victim, but it also shows that both the monster and the female exist outside of patriarchy."[16] *Fido* adds a further wrinkle to the woman/monster relationship: There is no victimization, only escape. When Helen gazes at Fido, dances with him, and fashions him as Timmy's guardian (if not also "father") by the end of the film, she is not doing so in the grip of horrified compulsion. She is certainly "outside of patriarchy," but by her own choice. Helen has created her own consumerist space because of her own purchase and because her unique linkage to the creature makes them "doubles," not in monstrosity but in independence, while still remaining firmly within the consumerist system.

For his part, Bill is presented as a troubled and neurotic man, clearly frightened by the zombies in his midst, a contrast made even more striking by Helen's self-assuredness. Bill mercilessly chains Fido in the backyard, less to demonstrate his dominance than to assuage his fears. He uses a handheld collar-buzzer to vindictively zap Fido, often when his masculinity has been challenged, giggling while he twiddles the knob. Bill is squeamish at the thought of fighting zombies. It's implied that he had to kill his zombified father during the war, but the malaise that has settled in him is punctured by Helen. In a late scene, on her way to rescue Timmy and Fido from a zombie outbreak at Zomcon, she reprimands Bill like a schoolboy with pitch-black humor: "Just because your father tried to eat you, does that mean we all have to be unhappy? Forever?" This key scene demonstrates Bill's powerlessness, as well as Helen's ability to confront previous fears and rationalize the current zombie-filled situation to her own benefit.

Bill's obsession over paying for future funerals is a final consumerist tweak. Early on, he explains his down payments on Timmy's future funeral by darkly noting that "the other kids hate him" at school. Later, when Helen tells him that she's pregnant, he simply worries that they "can't afford another funeral." This obsession with purchasing funeral paraphernalia is indicative of Bill's consumerist issues on a superficial level. But it also demarcates his relationship to his family and his deeper anxiety over a system that thrives from having the undead in its midst. Clearly, an adjustment in the patriarchal system is needed. Helen, of course, finds this in purchasing Fido.

The transference of patriarchal power from individual to product has some grounding in psychological thought from the 1950s. As Karal Ann Marling writes, "Motivational researchers [of the 1950s] told clients that 'in the minds of the consumers most . . . appliances have a definite masculine connotation"[17] and were typically purchased through patriarchal dollars. She suggests that "by that logic, housewives saw appliances as substitutes for men who did heavy work, or the man who paid for them."[18] This shift becomes a literal and satirical transference in Fido. Bill's money buys Fido (and Helen and Bill argue over her purchase of the zombie without his knowledge) and Fido does become, in more ways than one, a replacement for Bill. This transference is clean, precise, and often hilariously articulated. In the final scene of the film, Fido, wearing a Hawaiian shirt (presumably Bill's), plays catch with Timmy and even sweetly babbles with Helen's new baby, acting as the loving father Bill rarely was. But perhaps most strikingly, at Bill's funeral, Fido is in attendance, wearing Bill's suit, with Helen leaning on him and whispering into his ear—a true passing of the torch from living man to undead product. However, along with this animated product, Helen's other consumerist practices also provide outlets and replacements for Bill, showing the power of the product in her hands.

As the zombie outbreak is unleashed and then resolved at the climax of the film, Helen's dual modes of oppositional femininity and consumerist conformity revolve around her products and purchases. She acts quickly and assuredly to rescue Timmy from two zombie child scouts (a rescue instigated by Fido, acting in the mode of Lassie, signaling that there's trouble). Instead of asking Bill, Mr. Bottoms, or even Mr. Theopolis to aid her, Helen speeds to the rescue with a small but effective revolver in hand and dispatches the attackers. She doesn't need men to do this. She doesn't need the men's weapons either. She has her own. And this empowers her to do what few other people—especially men—are able to do in the film: thoroughly eliminate a zombie threat (albeit a limited one) and save her family.

By the end of the film, however, we see a return to domesticity, a seeming reversal of the violent sequences that depicted Helen gunning down the boy zombies in the forest. The final scenes show Helen serving drinks to happy guests, who recline on deck furniture, with Helen resplendent in a newly purchased dress. This scene provides resolution to the film: Helen is finally happy at home, Timmy is seen gallivanting around his father-figure zombie, and even Fido has been rescued from the clutches of Zomcon. This odd, hilarious, and vaguely perverse tableau also presents the zombie genre's ability to resolve feminist and traditionalist critiques of culture. The array of products—hallmarks of Helen's return to domesticity—also indicates a further triumph over the patriarchal model established at the beginning of the film. Bill isn't there—he's dead—and Mr. Bottoms, a social, physical, and corporate threat throughout the film, is now, ironically, a leashed and commoditized zombie himself, led by his own daughter to the backyard picnic ("I just call him Daddy," she says, nonchalantly). Fido, for all intents and purposes, is a surrogate father for Timmy and for Helen's new child, and a male companion for Helen—but exclusively on her terms. While this moment reflects a prevalent feminist undercurrent in zombie films, which often feature female victims "who attempt to resist patriarchal containment,"[19] Currie complicates this idea by using the zombie outbreak at the Zomcon factory to aid Helen in her resistance to "containment."

Grant notes that recognizing and grappling with "the failure of institutions" such as conventional "family, religion, even traditional humanism" is typically required, in zombie films, to "defeat the legions of the undead."[20] Fido's final shots do not necessarily indicate a defeat of the undead, but rather, their co-option by a new form of feminist capitalism. At the end of Fido, instead of a gritty determination in the face of never-ending zombie hordes, a new social and existential equilibrium is established in bright, broad, humorous strokes. The final shot of Fido is a familiar 1950s suburban tableau, but instead of a paterfamilias at the head of the table, the matriarch, Helen, is in complete control. She may be serving the drinks, but the products are serving her, and the men are merely guests, or products themselves, in her consumerist kingdom.

Conclusion: Consumerist Implications

Helen has, by the end of the film, liberated herself from a number of patriarchal controls, but Zomcon, with its dehumanization narratives and its omnipresent control over societal norms and behavior, remains. Indeed, while a zombie's infectious bite can be easily avoided with a deft bit of speed, the swing of an axe, or a Zomcon collar, the corporation's allure is much harder to shake. Helen may be liberated from both patriarchal forces and the undead, but as the absurdist final scene reveals, she is still ensnared by the candy-colored corporate haze.

Taking Currie's vision of Helen's consumer paradise to its logical conclusion yields two unnerving visions of the future. The first involves Zomcon and the total control and rapacious growth it aspires to achieve by using zombies—and, by extension, humans—for its own commercial and cultural ends.

It is one thing to have zombies consume people who then become zombies, but what about a corporation that profits off zombies in the first place—a corporation that preys upon not only the recently deceased (including one of its own), but also on the pocketbooks of the living? And what would happen if the supply of zombies ran out, but the demand did not? The chilling implications of Currie's satirical corporation—that consumerism's fuel is not only the living purchasing the dead, but also the living potentially becoming that product for purchase—is left lingering at the end of the film.

Also lingering is the danger of powerful automatons that Currie evokes in *Fido*. The havoc that products can wreak on a society is taken to absurdist and satirical lengths in *Fido*. The product literally rebels from inside the bowels of the factory in which it is made and emerges to consume the flesh of the consumer. In this climactic moment, the product must be destroyed in the place it was born, a savage feedback loop of anti-production. But while *Fido* ends on an upbeat note—Helen triumphant in her consumerist splendor—the implications still remain. The collars fail. Given time, and a series of inopportune technological failures, the product could overwhelm the consumer.

Currie's *Fido* gives us a hint of such disaster to come, and if we consider the zombie as a product, and not simply a monster, an even more disturbing dystopian vision emerges. Consider Ray Bradbury's 1950 short story "There Will Come Soft Rains," in which the plot consists solely of automated appliances in a suburban home lurching to life and acting as though the humans that once needed them are still around, though the reader understands they are irrevocably gone. Refract this image through Currie's undead lens, and we get another that is as chilling as it is absurd. Imagine zombies shuffling down sun-dappled streets, some walking dogs past white-picket fences, others vacuuming living rooms, or ironing shirts that will never be worn. With humanity gone, consumed by a few stray malfunctioning products, these automatons continue their lives, blissfully unaware of their redundancy, or their own culpability in society's destruction. They are instigators of their masters' destruction and their own obsolescence.

Notes

1. Bishop, "Dead Man Still Walking," 17–18.
2. Lee, "Vlogged to Death," n.p.
3. Harper, "Zombies, Malls and the Consumerism Debate," n.p.
4. Ibid.
5. Grant, "Taking Back the *Night of the Living Dead*," 210.

6. Ibid., 206.

7. Ibid., 209.

8. Bishop, "Dead Man Still Walking," 24.

9. Though Fido maintains his distinctly undead quality, unlike the literal rehumanization that takes place in 2013's *Warm Bodies*.

10. MacDougall, "Red, Brown and Yellow Perils," 61.

11. Ibid.

12. Blum, *V Was for Victory*, 47.

13. Grant, "Taking Back the *Night of the Living Dead*," 202.

14. Wood, *Hollywood from Vietnam to Reagan*, 118.

15. Kee, "Good Girls Don't Date Dead Boys," 180.

16. Ibid., 180.

17. Marling, *As Seen on TV*, 262.

18. Ibid.

19. Ibid.

20. Grant, "Taking Back the *Night of the Living Dead*," 205.

Bibliography

Bishop, Kyle. "Dead Man Still Walking: Explaining the Zombie Renaissance." *Journal of Popular Film and Television* 37, no. 1 (2009): 16–25.

Blum, John Morton. *V Was for Victory: Politics and American Culture during World War II*. New York: Harcourt Brace Jovanovich, 1976.

Fido. Directed by Andrew Currie. Burbank, CA: Lionsgate. 2007. DVD.

Grant, Barry Keith. "Taking Back the *Night of the Living Dead*: George Romero, Feminism, and the Horror Film." In *The Dread of Difference: Gender and the Horror Film*, edited by Barry Keith Grant, 200–212. Austin: University of Texas Press, 1996.

Harper, Stephen. "Zombies, Malls and the Consumerism Debate: George Romero's *Dawn of the Dead*." *Americana: The Journal of Popular Culture* 1, no. 2 (Fall 2002), n.p. http://www.americanpopularculture.com/journal/articles/fall_2002/harper.

Kee, Chera. "Good Girls Don't Date Dead Boys: Toying with Miscegenation in Zombie Films." *Journal of Popular Film and Television* 42, no. 4 (2014): 176–85.

Lee, Nathan. "Vlogged to Death: Romero and His Zombies Return to Lambast the Media." *Village Voice*, February 5, 2008. http://www.villagevoice.com/film/vlogged-to-death-6420423.

MacDougall, Robert. "Red, Brown and Yellow Perils: Images of the American Enemy in the 1940s and 1950s." *Journal of Popular Culture* 32, no. 4 (1999): 59–75.

Marling, Karal Ann. *As Seen on TV: The Visual Culture of Everyday Life in the 1950s*. Cambridge, MA: Harvard University Press, 1994.

Wood, Robin. *Hollywood from Vietnam to Reagan*. New York: Columbia University Press, 2003.

CHAPTER THIRTEEN

~

"Who You Gonna Call?"

The Supernatural and the Service Economy in the Ghostbusters Films

A. Bowdoin Van Riper

Horror films are intimate: They tell the story of an individual, a family, or a small group of friends and are set within tightly bounded spaces. Crowds represent potential allies, and open spaces the possibility of evasion or outright escape—both antithetical to the atmosphere of claustrophobia and helplessness on which horror depends. Even horror films that use the end of the world as a backdrop typically view it through the narrowest of lenses, focusing—as in *Night of the Living Dead* (1968) or *28 Days Later* (2002)—on a small isolated group of survivors amid a sea of monsters. The bias toward intimacy is, if anything, reinforced in films that blend horror with comedy. Rooted in the interactions of individual characters, observed at close range as they collide with the world around them and with one another, comedy is famously difficult to replicate on a broad canvas. Failed attempts at epic comedies—including the legendary flops *Paint Your Wagon* (1969) and *1941* (1979)—far outnumber successful ones like *It's a Mad, Mad, Mad, Mad World* (1963), and those that enjoyed box office success in their initial releases have, in many cases, not aged well.

Ghostbusters (1984) and its sequel *Ghostbusters II* (1989) are among the exceptions. They use one of the world's great cities as their canvas and are about threats to the city as a whole—first (in each case) from legions of ghosts that disrupt everyday life, and then from a single supernatural being from beyond the grave that seeks permanent dominion over the city. They work—often brilliantly—as comedies, however, because they focus on neither the undead nor their would-be victims, but on the small band of citizens who stand between their home and the armies of the undead.

The *Ghostbusters* films are among the most place-specific horror-comedies ever made. They are set not just in *a* major city, but specifically, concretely, in New York. Their plots, and their humor, are so location-specific that it is difficult to imagine them taking place elsewhere. The titular hero-experts are consummate New Yorkers—brash, confident, and fast-talking, distrustful of arbitrary authority but fiercely protective of their city—and their ghost-removal business fits seamlessly into the blue-collar service economy that keeps New York running smoothly. They are a far cry from Dracula's learned nemesis Dr. Van Helsing, or good-ol'-boy zombie hunter Daryl Dixon of *The Walking Dead*, but they are exactly the saviors that New York needs.

Ghosts, Gods, and Goo

Deep in the basement of the New York Public Library, strange things are happening: Books float from shelf to shelf in midair, cards spew from catalog drawers, and a librarian confronts a terrifying . . . something. Enter Drs. Venkman (Bill Murray), Spengler (Harold Ramis), and Stantz (Dan Aykroyd): "paranormal studies" researchers working in, but barely tolerated by, the psychology department of Columbia University. The film introduces them in a series of scenes that amply confirm their dean's withering characterization of them: "Your theories are the worst kind of popular tripe, your methods are sloppy, and your conclusions are highly questionable."[1] Leaving the university to investigate (haphazardly and ineffectually) the strange events at the library, they return to find their grant terminated, their laboratory space reassigned, and their equipment seized. Desperate, they develop a system for trapping and containing ghosts, set up shop in a decommissioned Manhattan firehouse, and advertise their services on late-night television as the Ghostbusters.

The balance of the first half of the film follows the trio up a steep learning curve as they handle a steadily increasing caseload, hire their first employees—receptionist Janine (Annie Potts) and fellow operative Winston Zeddemore (Ernie Hudson)—and gradually learn to do less property damage than the ghosts they are hired to eradicate. It also introduces their first customer: symphony orchestra cellist Dana Barrett (Sigourney Weaver), who calls them when she opens her fridge and discovers a ferocious entity that calls itself Zuul staring back at her. The Ghostbusters quickly discover that the growing frequency of paranormal activity in Manhattan is tied to the apparition in their client's kitchen. Zuul is the demonic familiar of an ancient being called Gozer the Gozerian, once worshiped as a god by the Sumerians, and the art deco apartment building where Dana lives was constructed by a latter-day cult of Gozer-worshippers as a portal through which he could someday enter the world of humans. Dana, possessed by Zuul, declares herself "the Gatekeeper" and goes in search of "the Key Master"—another of Gozer's minions, which has taken over the body of her nerdish neighbor (and would-be suitor), Louis Tully (Rick Moranis).

Recognizing that the second coming of Gozer would be catastrophic for humankind, the Ghostbusters struggle to keep the two apart but are temporarily thwarted by Walter Peck (William Atherton), an officious Environmental Protection Agency bureaucrat who forces them to shut down the ghost-containment system in the basement of their headquarters. The citywide chaos caused by dozens of escaping specters leads the Mayor to intervene on the Ghostbusters' behalf. He gives them carte blanche to solve the city's paranormal problems, but not before Dana and Louis have met, coupled, and opened an interdimensional gate atop the apartment building, letting Gozer loose in the city. The final showdown—which shifts from suspenseful to surreal when Gozer adopts the form of a hundred-foot-tall marshmallow man—ends with the deity vanquished, the Ghostbusters triumphant (if gooey), and the city elated.

Peter Venkman (left) confronts the Ghostbusters' other enemy—bureaucrats—in the form of EPA inspector Walter Peck.

Five years later (as the opening title card of *Ghostbusters II* declares), the elation has faded. Hamstrung by regulations and bankrupted by bills for damages, the Ghostbusters have shut down their operations and taken other jobs. Venkman hosts a daytime TV talk show about psychic phenomena, Spengler does research on human emotions (a subject with which he seemingly has no firsthand experience), and Stantz owns an occult bookstore. Dana, whose brief romance with Venkman and subsequent marriage to a fellow musician both ended unhappily, is raising an infant son on her own while working at a Manhattan art museum restoring a massive portrait of sixteenth-century Romanian tyrant Vigo the Carpathian.

The plot of the second film follows virtually the same arc as that of the first. The city is struck, once again, by a rapid increase in paranormal phenomena. The Ghostbusters (re)establish their business and struggle to rein the ghosts in, but are thwarted by a meddlesome bureaucrat (the Mayor's aide) and forced to the sidelines before the Mayor—recognizing that they are the best hope for restoring the city to normal—intervenes on their behalf. Once again the paranormal activity is linked to an ancient evil (the ghost of Vigo, voiced by Max von Sydow) determined to enter the city by way of a magical portal (the portrait) and take material form (by being "reborn" into the body of Dana's infant son, Oscar).

The most significant innovation in the plot of *Ghostbusters II* is a river of supernatural pink slime flowing through an abandoned subway tunnel beneath First Avenue—the physical manifestation of New Yorkers' negative emotions. The slime proves to be the connecting link between the ghost epidemic and Vigo's planned reincarnation, and the climax of the film has the Ghostbusters attempting to transform its malevolent negative energy to harmless positive energy by encouraging thousands of New Yorkers to spontaneously express warm and optimistic feelings. They accomplish this unlikely task with the aid of the Statue of Liberty—animated by a combination of positively charged pink slime and double-talk—a sound system that plays Jackie Wilson's "Higher and Higher," and a fortuitous accident of timing. Vigo's reincarnation is scheduled for the stroke of midnight on New Year's Eve, and when the crowds gathered outside the museum break into a heartfelt, if ragged, chorus of "Auld Lang Syne," the resulting surge of positive energy drives him back into the painting. The second film then ends, like the first, with the supernatural (once again) firmly in check and the Ghostbusters (once again) heroes.

New York State of Mind

Over the course of the long 1970s,[2] American filmmakers brilliantly, relentlessly portrayed New York City as an antechamber to Hell. The most admired products of the New American Cinema—including John Schlesinger's *Midnight Cowboy* (1969), Martin Scorsese's *Mean Streets* (1973), and Sidney Lumet's *Dog Day Afternoon* (1975)—portrayed the city as a cesspool of violence, corruption, and broken dreams, but so did gritty thrillers like *The Taking of Pelham 1-2-3* (1974) and fantasy adventures like *The Warriors* (1979). Exploitation films, whether aimed at black audiences (like *Shaft* and *Super Fly*) or white ones (like the *Death Wish* series) used the backdrop of an irredeemably broken city to justify their heroes' grimly righteous violence. Even *Saturday Night Fever* (1977), remembered today for the Bee Gees' music and John Travolta's dancing, is about the young hero's desperation to escape from his dead-end life in a working-class Brooklyn neighborhood. The trend reached its tongue-in-cheek climax in John Carpenter's *Escape from New York* (1981), set in a day-after-tomorrow future in which all of Manhattan has become a walled maximum-security prison.[3]

The cinematic resurrection of New York began with *Manhattan* (1979), Woody Allen's black-and-white love letter to the city, and gained momentum in *Fame* (1980), *Tootsie* (1982), and Allen's *Hannah and Her Sisters* (1983). It was in full stride by mid-decade, and the *Ghostbusters* films were fully and consciously part of it. *Ghostbusters* begins in the New York Public Library (at the corner of Fifth Avenue and 42nd Street) and *Ghostbusters II* ends at the base of the Statue of Liberty underneath a bright blue sky worthy of a picture postcard. Across the intervening 213 minutes, they feature dozens of iconic New York locations, from Rockefeller Center and the Empire State Building to Columbia University and the Tavern on the Green restaurant in Central Park. Dana Barrett's art-deco apartment building from the first film is "played" by 55 Central Park West, and the Ghostbusters' headquarters by the home of Ladder Company #8, off West Broadway in Tribeca. One key scene involving Stantz and Zeddemore ends with a long shot of them driving across the Manhattan Bridge as sunrise washes the skyscrapers beyond in pink and orange.[4]

Beyond making New York beautiful, however, *Ghostbusters* and its sequel depict a city that—far from being irreparably broken—works for most of its residents, most of the time. The streets are clean and well-lit, neatly bagged trash awaits pickup at the curb, police are abundant, and street crime is rare. Utilities, public transport, and other city services function smoothly, and the Mayor, played in both films by David Margulies, is a quick-thinking pragmatist who values practicality over politics. Public- and private-sector service workers figure prominently in both films: cops, utility workers, building superintendents, and hotel managers among others. Uniformly capable and efficient, they are—both films imply—the reason *why* the city works.

Both films go to elaborate lengths to establish the titular heroes as part of that vast, vital service economy. "What are you guys, exterminators?" asks a bystander who encounters them in the elevator lobby of the Sedgewick Hotel, the site of their first major job, and the comparison is apt. The Ghostbusters wear coveralls, boots, and heavy gloves on the job and carry their equipment strapped to their backs. They operate out of a scruffy, down-market neighborhood (Spengler compares it to "a demilitarized zone"), and their two most expensive pieces of equipment—the firehouse-turned-headquarters and a converted ambulance-turned-work-truck—are the worn-out castoffs of *other* service workers. Their television ad, glimpsed over Dana's shoulder early in *Ghostbusters*, imitates the awkwardly earnest pitches that ambitious plumbers and carpet-cleaning services air on local stations in the hours when screen time comes cheap.

Both of the Ghostbusters' employees are blue-collar New Yorkers who gripe (mostly) good-naturedly about wages and working conditions. "I've quit better jobs than this!" Janine the receptionist tells Venkman in a moment of frustration, to which he retorts that "someone with your qualifications would have no problem finding a top-flight job in either the food-service or housekeeping industries." Zeddemore, though he declared in his job interview that he'd "believe in anything if there was a steady paycheck in it," mutters during a particularly difficult assignment that "this is *not* worth eleven-five a year!" The central trio, despite their advanced degrees, find themselves living a distinctly blue-collar life once they take up ghostbusting as a profession. They work unpredictable schedules defined by other people's convenience rather than their own and frequently return from jobs sleep-starved, physically exhausted, and dirty.

One telling scene in *Ghostbusters* shows a visibly drained Stantz returning to headquarters, a cigarette dangling from his lips, and immediately being handed the next day's call sheet by Janine. They could, equally well, be a beat cop and his desk sergeant, a cabbie and his dispatcher, or a transit worker and his foreman—the weariness, and the sense that the work must be done even so, feels universal. Another, midway through *Ghostbusters II*, has the trio—posing as utility workers and wearing coveralls and hard hats not all that different from the gear they wear while chasing ghosts—encountering skeptical cops as they try to open a manhole cover on First Avenue.

Cop: What are you doing?

Venkman: What's it look like we're doing here? Why don't you let us work? We let you work!

Stantz [to Venkman]: Hey, take it easy. [to cop]: He's been working overtime. I'll tell you why we're here. We're here because some diaper bag downtown is being a jerk and making us work on a Friday night!

Venkman and Stantz are improvising—a point that becomes embarrassingly clear when they reveal their ignorance of exactly *where* the utility lines run under First Avenue—but both Venkman's feigned irritation and Stantz's fictitious excuse for it *feel* entirely plausible. Five years after stepping from the ivory towers of Columbia into the workforce that makes the city work, they have absorbed its mannerisms and its worldview.

Bulletproof Optimism, World-Class *Chutzpah*

Ghostbusters is filled with inspired comic performances. Harold Ramis, as Spengler, pushes the mad-scientist earnestness of Drs. Jekyll and Frankenstein into the realm of absurdity, insisting that an experiment to drill a hole through his own head "would have worked, too, if you hadn't stopped me." Dan Aykroyd, as Stantz, blends the wide-eyed naïveté of a sheltered child ("I've worked in the private sector," he tells the others, his awestruck tone suggesting a place as distant as Mars, "they expect *results*") with the equally wide-eyed credulity of a true believer in the occult. Rick Moranis, in only his third big-screen role, perfects the manic nebbish character on which he would spend the rest of the decade ringing changes. Sigourney Weaver, in the handful of scenes where Dana Barrett is possessed by Zuul, suggests the character's transformation into ravenous, hypersexual succubus-demon using only body language and a smoldering contralto voice. The moment that sets up her off-screen coupling with Louis Tully ("Take me now, subcreature," she intones, eyeing him like a cat contemplating a mouse) is among the film's most inspired visual gags.

Comedy is woven so effortlessly through these four performances that it is easy to overlook the fact that all four actors—along with the entire supporting cast—play their roles absolutely straight. Spengler explains the team's ghost-trapping equipment with the deadpan intensity of Scotty telling Captain Kirk about the dilithium crystals in the *Enterprise*'s warp drive. When Stantz and Zeddemore discuss the signs of the impending apocalypse, trading quotes from the Book of Revelations, their quiet seriousness makes the implied threat chilling:

Zeddemore: Hey, Ray. Do you remember something in the Bible about the last days when the dead would rise from their graves?

Stantz: I remember Revelations 7:12. "And I looked, and he opened the sixth seal, and behold there was a great earthquake. And the sun became as black as sackcloth, and the moon became as blood."

Zeddemore: "And the seas boiled, and the skies fell . . ."

The Mayor's interactions with Stantz and Spengler, or with other city officials, are reminiscent of similar scenes in natural-disaster films like *Earthquake* (1974) or *Volcano* (1997). The overall tone is brisk, focused, and businesslike. Individual lines within the scenes are funny—the Mayor, in *Ghostbusters II*, tells his staff that it is time to get serious, because "I spent an hour in my room last night talking to Fiorello LaGuardia, and he's been *dead* for forty years"—but it is the humor of a Howard Hawks movie: the banter of competent men doing a serious job. This underlying seriousness sells the atmosphere of danger and makes the supernatural threat seem real, even after the special effects used to render it have lost their original power to astound.

Peter Venkman, the fourth member and de facto leader of the Ghostbusters, arcs across this background of seriousness like Groucho Marx at one of Margaret Dumont's high-society parties. He is the only character in either film who is consistently, deliberately comic, and who takes neither the other characters nor the situation seriously. Venkman spends virtually all of the first film, and much of the second, in constant, comic motion. He plays pranks on students, friends, and total strangers alike; pulls faces and rolls his eyes in conversations with authority figures; and keeps up a steady stream of exaggerations, asides, and outright jokes that—although seemingly part of whatever conversation he is in—invariably ricochet in unexpected directions.

The pivotal scene in the original film where Walter Peck and the Ghostbusters confront one another in the Mayor's office shows Venkman at his anarchic best and captures the rhythms of virtually every conversation he has with Stantz and Spengler.

> Stantz: Everything was fine with our system until the power grid was shut off by dickless here [indicates Peck].
>
> Peck: They caused an explosion!
>
> Mayor [to the Ghostbusters]: Is this true?
>
> Venkman: Yes, it's true. [pause] This man has no dick.

Later in the same scene, while Stantz and Spengler earnestly try to impress the Mayor with the gravity of the situation, Venkman shifts the focus of his comic deflation to them.

> Stantz: Fire and brimstone coming down from the skies! Rivers and seas boiling!
>
> Spengler: Forty years of darkness! Earthquakes, volcanoes . . .

Zeddemore: The dead rising from the grave!

Venkman: Human sacrifice . . . dogs and cats, living together . . . mass hysteria!

Ghostbusters II has Venkman, though sadder and wiser by five years, still bobbing and weaving his way through serious conversations, unable to resist deflating others' serious pronouncements. "Vigo the Carpathian," Spengler muses, standing before the tyrant's life-sized portrait. "Also known as Vigo the Cruel, Vigo the Torturer, Vigo the Despised, and Vigo the Unholy." Venkman chimes in: "Wasn't he also Vigo the Butch?"

This consistent (almost compulsive) *lack* of seriousness defines not only the comic rhythms of the films, but also Venkman's character. He is a hustler and a con man by nature, skeptical of authority, convinced that no situation is beyond saving so long as he keeps moving and, above all, keeps talking. *Ghostbusters* opens with him seated across a lab table from two undergraduate research subjects, conducting an ESP experiment that he has rigged and is using as a pretext to seduce the (awestruck and clearly willing) female student. The sequel opens with him on the set of his TV talk show, feigning earnest interest as he interviews a pair of guests—both of whom he clearly believes to be deluded—about their prophecies regarding the impending end of the world. When his producer explains, after the show, that "no respected psychic will come on the show. They all think you're a fraud," Venkman cheerfully responds: "I *am* a fraud!" In the original trio of Ghostbusters, it is Spengler who provides technical expertise and Stantz who contributes an encyclopedic knowledge of the paranormal. Venkman—to whom the equipment is a mystery and the occult is a con game—contributes bulletproof optimism and world-class *chutzpah*.

Venkman is such a relentlessly comic figure that, on the rare (and thus highly significant) occasions when he *does* turn serious, the change is signaled not by a sudden absence of jokes but by a change in their tenor. The relentless barrage of quips and comically exaggerated come-ons that he directs at Dana Barrett throughout *Ghostbusters* (and, the sequel implies, the failed relationship that followed) gives way to quieter, more self-deprecating humor as he tries to win her back in *Ghostbusters II*. The comic patter he directs at baby Oscar, gently teasing him ("Named after a hot dog? Oh, you poor man . . . you poor, poor man") or warning him, in a mock-serious tone, not to soil a prized New York Jets jersey pressed into service as a substitute diaper, reveal the depths of his affection for both mother and child.[5]

At the climax of *Ghostbusters*, a different shift in the tone of Venkman's humor signals his transition from being the team's designated Fool to being its first-among-equals hero, and his emergence as the leader of

The Ghostbusters (left to right: Spengler, Stantz, Venkman, and Zeddemore) prepare to confront an ancient evil on the roof of 55 Central Park West.

New York's resistance to Gozer. Early in the battle, his jokes remain arch and ironic, aimed—as they have been throughout the movie—at deflating others' self-importance. When Stantz orders Gozer—now in the form of a woman with a form-fitting garment, growling voice, and glowing red eyes—to "cease any and all supernatural activity and return forthwith to your place of origin or to the nearest convenient parallel dimension," Venkman sarcastically retorts: "That oughta do it; thanks very much, Ray." Venkman is right—Gozer responds by blasting the Ghostbusters off their feet, snarling "Die!"—but in that moment he also reaches a turning point, taking the supernatural threat seriously for the first time in the film. Regaining his feet, he abandons irony and exaggeration for 007-level double entendre. "Okay, this bitch is *toast!*" he declares, and leads the Ghostbusters, call-and-response style, in powering up the phallic, beam-emitting "wands" of their proton packs: "Grab your stick! (Holdin'!) . . . Heat 'em up! (Smokin'!) . . . Make 'em hard! (Ready!)"[6] As they stand shoulder to shoulder, weapons charged and faces grim, Venkman's humor shifts to swaggering action-hero mode: "Lets show this prehistoric bitch how we do things downtown!"

Who You Gonna Call?

The *Ghostbusters* films are classic "high concept" comedies, their shared premise easily summed up in a sentence: What if supernatural beings from beyond the grave invaded New York City? It could have been the basis for a straightforward apocalyptic horror film—*Godzilla*, with ghosts—and screenwriters Dan Aykroyd (Stantz) and Harold Ramis (Spengler) conceived of *Ghostbusters* in just those terms. The first film's structure (carried over, unaltered, into the second) reflects its serious roots: Its supernatural beings, beginning with the ghoul in the library basement, are genuinely terrifying, and Gozer the Gozerian (like Vigo the Carpathian in the sequel) is a mortal threat to the city and citizens of New York. The comedy, in both films, comes from the ways that New Yorkers—personified by the Ghostbusters, and particularly by Venkman—react to them.

Mild weirdness would, the films suggest, simply pass unnoticed on the streets of New York. Louis Tully, running from Sumerian hell-hounds in *Ghostbusters*, presses himself against the windows of the famous Tavern on the Green restaurant in Central Park without even drawing an inquisitive glance from the diners inside. Had he stumbled into the restaurant he would—like a slime-covered Spengler and Stantz in a similar scene from *Ghostbusters II*—have crossed the line from curiosity to nuisance, triggering a phone call to the police. Outside, rendered mute by the glass, he is an unremarkable part of New York's chaotic street life, functionally invisible to diners determined to "mind their own business." Minutes later, back at Central Park West, a cop investigating the ruins of Dana's apartment unwittingly doubles down on the joke when Venkman asks him what happened. "Some moron brought a cougar to a party," he explains (his nonchalant tone adding an implied *again* to the seemingly improbable event) "and it went berserk."

The film's by-now running gag—New Yorkers' penchant for taking seemingly inexplicable events in stride—reaches a climax a few scenes later when Louis—now possessed by a minion of Gozer—encounters a Central Park carriage driver.

Louis [to the horse]: I am Vinz—Vinz Clortho, Keymaster of Gozer. Volgus Zildrohar, Lord of the Sebouillia. Are you the Gatekeeper?

Carriage driver: Hey! He pulls the wagon. I make the deals. You want a ride?

Louis looks at the driver and emits a low, animal growl, eyes glowing red.

Louis: [still to the horse]: Wait for the sign. Then all prisoners will be released!

As the crazed Louis scurries into the night, startling passersby and shouting, "You will perish in flames! You and all your kind!" the driver is unmoved. Shaking his head, he delivers a New Yorker's three-word benediction: "What an asshole!"

Willingness to simply shrug off weirdness has its limits, however, even in New York. It ends, in the *Ghostbusters* universe, at the front door. A ghost encountered on the street might be local color—like subway-platform musicians, sidewalk mimes, and dealers in cut-rate watches—but a ghost in the home or workplace is a nuisance. Both films use ghosts (or ghostly activity) as an excuse for visual gags that are complete in themselves: Cards erupt from the catalog drawers of the New York Public Library in the opening scene of *Ghostbusters*, eggs pop from their cartons and fry themselves on the countertop in the equivalent scene of *Ghostbusters II*, and a corpulent green poltergeist that the heroes nickname "Slimer" wreaks havoc in both films. Those gags, however, also lay the groundwork for a meta-joke that runs through both films: If ghosts actually *did* exist in New York, they would become just another nuisance of urban life—inconvenient, but hardly apocalyptic—and dealing with them would become someone's job. No heat from the radiator? Call the building superintendent. Hungry? Call for delivery. Haunted? Call the Ghostbusters.

The Ghostbusters flourish—and, as a montage in *Ghostbusters* reveals, become media icons—because New Yorkers are, in both films, dedicated to the all-important business of getting on with their lives. Ghosts are a problem only to the extent that they get in the way of that goal, and the Ghostbusters are local heroes only to the extent that they are perceived to solve more problems than they create. The director of the New York Public Library tolerates their intrusion, the manager of the Sedgewick Hotel pays their $5,000 bill (after initially refusing), and the municipal court judge in *Ghostbusters II* drops all charges against them because they all see the alternative—uncontained ghosts, loose in their workplace—as much worse. The Mayor, though impatient with Venkman's smart-ass commentary ("But if I'm *right*, and we *can* stop this thing . . . Lenny, you will have saved the lives of millions of registered voters"), gives them free rein to confront Gozer (and later Vigo) for the same reason. A supernatural threat, however ridiculous it sounds, is still a threat, and he has a city to run.

Other public servants, with narrower responsibilities and fewer political burdens, accept the Ghostbusters' presence even more readily, grateful for the opportunity to hand off a problem they don't know how to solve. The chief of the New York Fire Department and the cardinal who heads the Archdiocese of New York (both present in the Mayor's office in *Ghostbusters*) follow this pattern, but it finds its purest expression in a nameless cop who pulls up to Ghostbusters headquarters in the middle of the night. Opening the door of a paddy wagon to reveal a straitjacketed, possessed Louis Tully, he explains: "Bellevue doesn't want him, and we were afraid to put him in the lock-up, and I knew you guys were into this stuff." Spengler agrees to take custody of the "Key Master of Gozer," turning the cop's intractable problem into the Ghostbusters' soluble one and allowing both to fulfill their obligation to keep the city running.

The Ghostbusters are, in multiple ways, ideally situated to deal with undead threats to the city: Spengler's improbable gadgetry, Stantz's encyclopedic knowledge of the supernatural, and Venkman's genius for improvisation under pressure all prove to be potent weapons, as does their ability to function as a team. Their greatest advantage over the undead, however, is that they are driven not just by their need for a paycheck or their desire to do their job well, but by a deep and abiding love for the city that translates into fierce opposition to anyone who would threaten it. It is no accident that the last words of *Ghostbusters* are: "I love this town!"

"This Is *Our* City!"

Stories in which New York City is threatened, or partially destroyed, by malevolent intruders play differently, now, than they once did. Scenes of the Empire State Building and White House being vaporized by aliens in *Independence Day* (1996), or of the upper floors of the Chrysler Building toppling into the streets of Manhattan in *Armageddon* (1998) have, since the September 11 terrorist attacks, taken on resonances that twentieth-century filmmakers never imagined or intended. The "Auld Lang Syne" chorus that vanquishes Vigo in *Ghostbusters II* plays differently as well. What once seemed hokey and false, now—after similar gatherings in the wake of attacks on Madrid (2004), London (2005), Boston (2013), and Paris (2015)—seems touchingly real.

Addressing the crowd at Fenway Park on the afternoon of the first Red Sox home game following the 2013 Boston Marathon bombing, first baseman David Ortiz declared: "This is *our* fucking city, and nobody is going to dictate our freedom. Stay strong!" His declaration of solidarity and defiance—an implicit rebuke to the terrorists—drew long and appreciative cheers from the crowd and quickly entered into local culture as a rougher, sharper-edged counterpart to the quasi-official slogan, "Boston Strong." Peter Venkman's defiant warning to the Stay-Puft Marshmallow Man as it lumbers through the Upper West Side—"Nobody steps on a church in *my* town!"—lacks the profane eloquence of Ortiz's famous statement, but anticipates its spirit: "This is *our* city . . . threaten it at your peril."

Notes

1. All quoted dialogue is taken from *Ghostbusters*, directed by Ivan Reitman (1984; Culver City, CA: Sony Pictures Home Entertainment, 2006, DVD) and *Ghostbusters II*, directed by Ivan Reitman (1989; Culver City, CA: Sony Pictures Home Entertainment, 2006, DVD).

2. By analogy with historian Eric Hobsbawm's "long nineteenth century" (1789–1914), the "long 1970s" could be said to begin with the inauguration of Richard Nixon in January 1969 and end with that of Ronald Reagan (and the end of the Iranian hostage crisis) in January 1981.

3. *Fort Apache: The Bronx* and the "Harry Canyon" segment of the science fiction anthology film *Heavy Metal*, also released in 1981, covered similar territory.

4. "Ghostbusters Film Locations," *On the Set of New York*, http://onthesetofnew york.com/ghostbusters.html.

5. Venkman is *completely* serious only twice: Once in *Ghostbusters* when he believes that Dana was killed in the final battle with Gozer, and once in *Ghostbusters II* as he tries to rescue Oscar from Vigo.

6. At the last command all four men perform an action that, though clearly meant to suggest racking the slide on a pump-action shotgun, is equally evocative of masturbation.

CHAPTER FOURTEEN

∽

The Queer and the Dead

Transgressive Sexuality in Shaun of the Dead

Shelley S. Rees

Edgar Wright's cult darling "RomZomCom," *Shaun of the Dead* (2004), appears at first glance to be anything but a sex comedy. The film is rated R for "zombie violence, gore, and language," with no mention of sexual content or "adult situations," and certainly no nudity. The two young couples at the center of the film exhibit no sexual energy; indeed, the most explicit reference to any character's sex life is Shaun's (Simon Pegg) scandalized reference to his stepfather as a "motherfucker." For an R-rated romantic comedy, *Shaun* is oddly sexless.

With overt sexual content so absent, it is no surprise that critics tend to focus on other prominent qualities of the film, such as its references to its politically charged namesake, George A. Romero's *Dawn of the Dead* (1978). Like Romero's living dead, whose mindless cannibalistic consumption stands in for thoughtless capitalist consumption, *Shaun*'s witty juxtaposition of the mechanized working class with shambling corpses invites Marxist criticism: "*Shaun* should be examined in terms of the postindustrial, service-oriented workforce the film portrays,"[1] Lynn Pifer explains and, as Marty Mapes notes, "*Shaun* also makes the point that many of the lower-paid workers in Western cities are practically zombies anyway. Demeaning, unimportant jobs leave them numb, and all some employers want is a body without a soul or a brain to get in the way of work, work, work."[2] The eponymous Shaun, transported dead-eyed to his dead-end job, may share his daily bus ride with literal zombies or merely workers so alienated from labor and life they are bereft of all concept of self, and the fact that Shaun cannot tell the difference appears at once comic and tragic. By the film's end, the zombie version of a young man retrieving grocery trolleys performs the work with exactly the same proficiency as his earlier "living" self, because the job neither requires nor nurtures an engaged worker.

But the sexual is of course also the political: Marxist analyses that identify zombies with alienated labor and mindless consumption also inform readings of social laboring and sexual appetite. As Eve Sedgwick explains, sexuality in culture is "a sensitive register precisely for delineating relationships of power and meaning, and for making graphically intelligible the play of desire and identification by which individuals negotiate with their societies for empowerment."[3] Viewed through the lens of heteronormative ideology, the lack of literal sex in *Shaun* becomes a meaningful lack, a present absence that points to the film's commentary on that ideology. With this in mind, I examine the ways in which *Shaun* uses dynamics of desire and empowerment to queer and critique sexual hegemony. I approach the concepts of queerness and homosociality as markers of structural relations and power imbalances, and desire as "the affective or social force, the glue . . . that shapes an important relationship."[4] In this context, "queer" does not have to mean homosexual or bisexual, but can indicate any relational dynamics that challenge or stand outside of the master narrative of heteronormativity.

Zombie Sex

In our post–Anne Rice world, we take for granted sexualized, and even queer vampires. But what about zombies? Do rotting corpses retain enough bodily integrity to claim gender? Can such bodies be sexualized? Does anyone really want them to be? Scholars who study zombie fiction and the metaphoric functions of these ambulatory corpses argue that zombie bodies do in fact carry sexual content. One way in which they do so is by embodying uncontrolled appetite, especially in that, like vampires, their penetration and consumption of the bodies of the living both feeds their hunger and performs a reproductive function. Mel Chen identifies zombie eating habits themselves as "queered," pointing to the incongruity of insatiable appetite and nonfunctioning digestion: "They cannot digest what they eat, for their own viscera are often disordered or nonoperational (they neither urinate nor defecate); and their apprehension by the uninfected or uninjured involves a mixture of fear and disgust. That zombies' voracious appetites cannot be satisfied is only confirmed by disarrayed and clearly nonoperational organs."[5] In essence, though zombies cannot digest what they eat, they are still driven on a primal level to consume; similarly, though they do not possess operational reproductive organs, they continue to experience a version of the reproductive drive, also accomplished through feeding. Zombie reproduction is therefore a form of queered horror focusing on bodily functions that deviate violently from cultural norms:

> Zombie films often center on the interrelated fears and desires wrought of reproduction. Zombie reproduction is threatening to heteronormativity; it is a queered reproduction that exists outside the ability of dominant structures to regulate. Zombies aren't produced through sexual relations: in some of the early films, they are produced through knowledge of (black) religion and magic; in others, they are produced through bastardizations of science or alien control, yet in either case, dominant structures have been subverted.[6]

Approaching the problem of zombie desire as contradictory and transgressive—that is, as desire that does not have as its object the reproductive results deemed appropriate by the dominant heteronormative culture—goes some distance toward illuminating the ways in which *Shaun*'s zombie narrative underscores its sex narrative. In *Shaun*, though the "living" characters do not have sex, zombies and zombie reproductive behavior are associated continually with sexuality. During Shaun and Ed's initial face-to-face encounter with a zombie—Mary the checkout girl, who appears in their garden—Ed (Nick Frost) teases Shaun that "she likes you," and when Mary lunges at Shaun, he stammers "I've just come out of a relationship" as if to deter her advances. When he pushes her away, she is impaled through the midriff by a metal pole and then lifts herself from it, pushing up from a grotesquely sexual backbend position in the foreground of the shot as Shaun and Ed watch, transfixed, in the background. Another scene, outside the pub, shows a couple who appear to be making out in the alley but are revealed, behind Shaun and Ed's backs, to be a zombie tearing out the throat of her victim. A pub patron whom Ed identifies as "Snake Hips," described as a man of infamous sexual prowess always "surrounded by women," is later shown stretched out on his back on the ground and surrounded by female zombies who consume his entrails in a gruesome mockery of fellatio. Later in the film, post-crisis, we also discover that at least one woman has decided to keep and continue to sleep with her zombie husband, to the morbid fascination of tabloid television viewers.

Indeed, from the film's start, the zombie crisis is a sexual crisis, and Shaun's psychosexual issues are at its center. Horror that dramatizes repressed sexual anxiety and sexual transgression dates back at least to the gothic fiction of the nineteenth century. According to George Haggerty:

> Transgressive social-sexual relations are the most basic common denominator of gothic writing, and from the moment in the early pages of Walpole's *The*

Castle of Otranto when the anti-hero Manfred presses his suit on the fiancée of his deceased son (and she flees into the "long labyrinth of darkness" in the "subterraneous" regions of the castle), a gothic trope is fixed: terror is almost always sexual terror, and fear, and flight, and incarceration, and escape are almost always colored by the exoticism of transgressive sexual aggression.[7]

Though *Shaun of the Dead* cannot boast the elevated gothic hysteria of Otranto, the example serves well to remind us of how psychosexual anxiety, including taboo fears such as incest and necrophilia, informs horror traditions. Haggerty goes on to argue that gothic texts "occur in a period that had yet to construct the elaborate superstructure of sexuality that emerged in the age of sexology at the end of the nineteenth and beginning of the twentieth centuries" and thus "gothic fiction offered the one semi-respectable area of literary endeavor in which modes of sexual and social transgression were discursively addressed on a regular basis."[8] Part of *Shaun of the Dead*'s genius lies in the way it conflates this psychosexual gothic tradition with comedy, another genre that engages and transgresses dominant narratives, including sexuality. The resulting chimerical subgenre of comedic horror becomes a uniquely penetrative tool for exposing and examining literary, filmic, and psychosexual archetypes and anxieties.

The Incredible Oedipal Ed

One way *Shaun* invokes the gothic horror tradition is through its Oedipal subplot, developed in the film to reveal the depth of Shaun's sexual immaturity. Throughout the film, Ed embodies Shaun's desire/aversion dissonance; he is the force to which Shaun is most drawn yet also the one that gets him into the most trouble. Indeed, when Shaun has problems with his girlfriend and his roommate, representatives of relational and economic maturity, respectively, both identify Ed as the problem. Like the id (and the Oedipus) his name so resembles, Ed externalizes Shaun's unmitigated desires, and the film's writers establish this relationship through Freud's most recognizable narrative of sexual pathology, the "Oedipal complex." The Oedipal son wishes to depose his father from his position of power and reserve his mother's affections for himself; thus, Ed makes sex jokes about Shaun's mother ("I love his mum too. She's like butter!") and cheerily reminds Shaun, "Don't forget to kill Philip!" when Shaun goes home to rescue his mother from his zombie-bitten stepfather. In fact, after discovering that his stepfather has been bitten, Shaun engages in a series of hilariously childish Oedipal fantasies in which he kills Philip (Bill Nighy) with his phallic cricket bat and then he and Ed carry Shaun's ex-girlfriend Liz (Kate Ashfield) and mother Barbara (Penelope Wilton) to zombieless safety. Ed's articulation of the plan to kill Philip with such cavalier unconcern causes Shaun to stumble with a startled "What?" as he heads toward his mother's house, indicating his discomfort with having his interior fantasy life exposed in this way. Moreover, it is clear that for Shaun/Ed, Liz and Barbara are conflated: Shaun buys flowers for Barbara that he later tries to give Liz, and answers his phone "Liz!" only to switch to "Mum!" when it turns out to be Barbara on the line. Ed emphasizes the sexual element of this connection when he relays Shaun's phone messages: "Your mum rang about tomorrow night. Liz rang about the two of you eating out tonight. Then your mum rang back to see if I wanted to eat her out tonight."

At his mother's house, Shaun, like a much less articulate Hamlet, attempts to convince Barbara that her marriage to his stepfather is a mistake, obviously a conversation they have had many times since Philip's arrival seventeen years earlier, when Shaun was twelve. (Intriguingly, the film never reveals what happened to Shaun's biological father, referring to Shaun having "lost" him without providing detail.) Shaun holds a knife throughout this scene, his mum having asked him to slice bread, another joke on Shaun's ineffective attempts to wield phallic power with his mother. The sandwiches that Barbara insists they make recalls Ed's earlier teasing about Barbara being "like butter," as well as Barbara's tendency to call Shaun by the nickname "Pickle," a moniker that relegates Shaun's phallic potency to the nonthreatening status of condiment. The Oedipal undercurrent of Shaun's resentment is exposed further by his labeling of Philip as "motherfucker" and his obsession with Philip's phallic dominance, represented by Philip's fancy Jaguar, which Shaun is not allowed to touch, and the "bit of wood" with which Philip chased Shaun around the garden as a child for violating the Jaguar's purity with a melted candy bar. Viewers see Philip from Shaun's perspective in most of his scenes, with a stiff posture and stern unsmiling stare that Shaun has trouble meeting. Clearly he makes Shaun feel like a powerless child. Even as Shaun threatens the wounded Philip with his cricket bat, Philip need only turn and ask what he's got there for Shaun to drop the bat in shame, prompting Barbara to further emasculate him by asking if Shaun plans to donate his bat to the "jumble," or rummage sale. She continues by telling Shaun she has given away his old toys, at which point the façade of manly competence with which he entered the house falls completely as he pouts over their loss. Meanwhile, as Shaun attempts to distance himself from Philip—repeatedly, petulantly insisting that "he's not my dad"—Ed, Shaun's truth teller, acknowledges the appeal of Philip's shiny masculinity by whistling at the Jaguar and crooning, "Who's a pretty boy?"

Shaun's ineffective attempts to wield phallic power with his mother.

"He's Not My Boyfriend"

Shaun's anxiety, in part, lies in his struggle to affirm an adult masculine identity. In the face of other characters' demands that he grow up and be "a man," Shaun feels exposed and humiliated—reflected by the repeated line, "you've got red on you"—in his inability to satisfy them. In contrast with the zombie hordes moving in mindless unison, Shaun stumbles and stammers, disappointing the social expectations of friends, family, and romantic partner and failing to affirm the unequivocally heterosexual life defined as meaningful by the dominant cultural paradigm. Jokes about his phallic impotence continue past the scene with Barbara and Philip: One scene involves Liz and her flatmate Dianne (Lucy Davis) pantomiming thrusting motions to show Shaun how to run a zombie through with a metal tetherball pole instead of swinging the soft tetherball ineffectually at its head, and he proves equally incompetent with a rifle. The film also hints at Shaun's gender fluidity in several scenes. When another (male) zombie arrives to join Mary during the battle in the garden, Shaun and Ed line up to confront them with phallic cricket bat and shovel, respectively, and as they prepare to do battle, Ed asks Shaun, "Girl or bloke?" Shaun hesitates, "Uhhh . . . first one," and they switch sides. Later, as Shaun pilots his group toward the hoped-for safety (and snacks) of their local pub, the Winchester, they run into another group of survivors, led by a woman named Yvonne (Jessica Hynes). Shaun and Yvonne (note the rhyming names) speak of their plans for a moment and then, in a delicious sight gag, we watch the two groups pass in opposite directions and realize that they mirror each other. Behind Shaun are Liz, David and Dianne, Shaun's mother, and Ed; behind Yvonne are her boyfriend, another couple dressed similarly to David and Dianne, Yvonne's mother, and Yvonne's Ed-like cousin, staring at a mobile phone just as Ed does. In this mirroring dynamic, Shaun's Other self is a woman—a capable one, as we find out later that she also survives the zombie outbreak. Perhaps by aligning Shaun with Yvonne, the writers suggest that a version of Shaun unconcerned with masculine gender performance could be confident and empowered as opposed to beleaguered and anxious. Further, Ed, who voices sexual truths in so many instances, labels all talk of love as "gay" whether it be heterosexual or homosexual, at least where Shaun is concerned. When Shaun tells Ed that he must check on Liz's safety even though she has dumped him, he explains this need by saying, "I love her." Shaun himself looks surprised at this admission, but Ed's response is "Okay, gaayy." And, again, when Liz and Shaun ascend from the cellar of the Winchester, leaving the bitten Ed behind to die, Liz says "love you" to Ed (to which Ed replies "cheers"). When Shaun says he loves him as well, Ed responds with the same "gaayy."

Both of the young heterosexual couples in the film are sexually inert, partly because they are triangulated—each has a third party keeping the relationship from progressing—and triangulated desire is queered desire in that it deviates from heteronormativity. In the case of Dianne and David (Dylan Moran), the triangulation takes a conventional, even conventionally comedic form: David is in love with Liz but has settled for her roommate, Dianne, as a substitute. Shaun and Liz's problem presents a more intriguing and potentially transgressive triangle, however, as the third position of their triad is occupied by Ed.

In noting the centrality of these relationships to the film, critics tend to focus on their narrative function, not their erotic function. James Rose sees them as another way in which *Shaun* mirrors Romero's work structurally, as both *Shaun* and *Dawn* "are about a set of couples coming together to form a larger group who then travel to an assumed safe haven" and "both films deal with the concept of relationships and how specific situations can be used to critique that dynamic."[9] Rose also recognizes that the movie presents Shaun and Ed as a couple of sorts, in that, "as long term friends, Shaun and Ed understand each other, sympathize with each other and, ultimately, care for each other," but stops short of painting Ed and Shaun's connection as erotic.[10] However, by orienting Ed as the externalized embodiment of desires that Shaun cannot express himself, *Shaun* moves this homosocial relationship beyond the typical buddy comedy or "bromance" into the realm of desire. Nothing illustrates this connection more than the film's opening scene, in which Liz, on their three-year anniversary, tries to talk to Shaun about their relationship—particularly the fact that they never go out without

Ed—while Shaun's eyes wander from Liz toward his friend. Liz and Shaun confront each other across a table with Ed positioned between them in the background, playing an arcade game and facing Shaun's side of the table: framing that reinforces the triangulated dynamic. As Liz leans toward Shaun and says, "It would just be nice if we could . . . " Ed completes her thought by yelling "Fuck!" at the game he is playing. Indeed, the film presents Shaun and Liz's relationship as friendly but lacking sexual charge; Ed remains the only character who makes sexual references, often while wearing his "I GOT WOOD" t-shirt. As Liz and Shaun do not discuss sex openly, it is Ed who has to vocalize the sexual content of Liz's timid suggestion that she and Shaun spend some time alone. In this way Ed is not merely the stereotypical vulgar best friend; he is Shaun's sexuality.

Though Shaun assures Liz that he is committed to improving their relationship, he undermines it immediately by neglecting to make promised dinner reservations and attempting to give Liz his mother's flowers in apology. This results in Shaun being "spectacularly binned" by Liz, so instead of spending that time alone with her on their anniversary, he ends up drunk with Ed, who asserts, "You don't need Liz to have a good time." Shaun and Ed spend the night singing Grandmaster Flash's "White Lines" to each other—"(Ooh White Lines) Vision dreams of passion / (Blowin' through my mind) And all the while I think of you"—followed by more dancing and singing back at Shaun's flat while wearing identical hats. Shaun's integration of Ed into his life is so complete and so unconscious by this point that when his flatmate Pete complains about the noise, Shaun explains it by saying,

Shaun and Liz: No sparks here.

"*We* split up with Liz tonight." Later, after Shaun and Ed have collected the others and taken them to the Winchester to wait out the zombie crisis, David calls Ed Shaun's boyfriend, followed by this revealing exchange:

Shaun: "He's not my boyfriend!"

Ed: [handing beer to Shaun] "It might be a bit warm, the cooler's off."

Shaun: "Thanks, babe." [winks]

"Why Is Queen Still Playing?"

If we acknowledge zombie sexuality as inherently transgressive, or queered, we can also read the film's use of a zombie outbreak to reflect Shaun's sexual confusion as suggestive of his queer status, with Ed as the queering influence both in life and "death." Rose, like most critics, reads Shaun's connection to Ed as a negative influence, since "in the end it is actually this relationship that forms part of Shaun's biggest problem—his inability to grow up and assume adult responsibilities."[11] Continuing this assertion that Ed and Shaun's relationship functions as something Shaun must overcome, Rose concludes that:

> In the end it is only Ed's infection and consequent transformation into a zombie that finally allow Shaun to be free of this ultimately repressive relationship. As Ed sits bleeding to death, he suggests to Shaun that he should make a go of it with Liz. As Shaun starts to answer, Ed interrupts by saying "I only hold you back." In their final (human) moments together both friends are honest with each other. Nothing more needs to be said. Shaun smiles and puts a cigarette into Ed's mouth and lights it.[12]

This unequivocal privileging of Shaun's (heterosexual) relationship with Liz as a sign of maturity pervades *Shaun* criticism. Pifer, not quite so down on poor Ed, at least credits Shaun with successfully integrating Ed's admirable qualities of individuality and rebelliousness: "Shaun pops out to the shed, joins in the game, and smiles at Ed as Queen's 'You're My Best Friend' plays and the credits roll. Ironically, the opening line of the song is 'Ooo, you make me live.' In this scene, Shaun smiles sincerely for the first time in the entire film; he finally gets to sit and play with his best friend."[13] Pifer goes on, however, to describe Shaun's new situation as evidence that his immaturity has not been improved:

> Shaun may have appeared to have matured and entered domestic life in the earlier shot of the redecorated flat with Liz, but we now learn that he has managed to preserve the part of his life he treasures most: he has kept the

friend who was "hold[ing] him back," and, having eliminated the voices of the socially responsible and upwardly mobile characters who used to surround him, he can remain in his regressive state.[14]

Of course, clinging to Ed still counts as "regressive" behavior in this analysis, so that even while acknowledging Ed's beneficial contributions to Shaun's life, Pifer concludes that Shaun's heroic victory depends upon his newfound dominance over Ed: "Shaun holds in check the friend who formerly had held him back. The shed and the video games beckon, but the rest of Shaun's life is Ed-free. By compartmentalizing the monster, Shaun is able to regain his relationship with Liz. He also manages to deconstruct the loser/hero binary."[15]

Though neither Pifer nor Rose identifies Shaun's desire for Ed as erotic, the implication remains that the relationship that Ed embodies stunts Shaun's heterosexual destiny. To grow as a mature person, coded as relinquishing his resistance to heterosexual domestication, Shaun must confine Ed to the shed. He must closet him—in S/M chains, no less—and use him judiciously and only on his terms. He must stop letting Ed drive the Jaguar.

I am not convinced, however, that Shaun's character trajectory necessarily moves from static/homo/loser to active/hetero/hero. In fact, Shaun hardly seems changed at all at the film's end, aside from being happy. He still wants the same things at the end of his story as at the beginning: Liz, Ed, a pint, and tea—now with two sugars, after having scoffed earlier that "I haven't had sugar in my tea since 1982." The difference is that now he has them all and he no longer has to hide any of those desires from anyone. He has Liz, preparing tea and perfectly willing to go round to the pub later, and Ed, waiting to play video games. Far from dismantling the relational triangle, Shaun has stopped viewing it as deviant and accepted his desire for both Liz and Ed: for two sugars, a doubly sweet life. Our final moments with Shaun show us a man who has suffered and finally escaped the primal horror of mediated desires. Relaxing with Liz, telling her unself-consciously, without shame, that he likes sugar in tea and wishes to play with Ed in the garden, with the framed photos of passed loved ones watching over but no longer oppressing him, one might read Shaun as the embodiment of René Girard's description of a man victorious over mediated desire: "Every level of his existence is inverted, all the effects of metaphysical desire are replaced by contrary effects. Deception gives way to truth, anguish to remembrance, agitation to repose, hatred to love, humiliation to humility, mediated desire to autonomy, deviated transcendency to vertical transcendency."[16] Viewed thus, the desire for Ed that others in the film label as indicative of Shaun's immaturity may, in fact, be more of a problem for them because it represents a threat to their normative strictures. Chera Kee argues that zombies represent a threat to normative hegemony because "bodies that are living and dead embody not only the desires of immortality associated with life after death but also nod to the attractive qualities of death itself." In that way, zombies also "stand as evidence not only that supposedly fixed boundaries can be transgressed but also that there might be pleasure gained from doing so."[17] Shaun's contentment with his living female partner and his dead male partner suggests avenues to happiness outside sanctioned heteronormative coupling. The talk show Shaun watches on television just before visiting Ed in the shed reminds viewers of the continued erotic potential of Ed and Shaun's relationship:

> Woman still married to zombie husband: I don't see nothing wrong with it but I know that some people would. But he's my husband, you know. I still love him and I got the ring.
>
> Talk-show host: You go to bed with it?
>
> Woman: Course I do.

Though Ed is relegated to chains in the shed and is, of course, no longer technically alive, Shaun's relationship with Liz is only marginally privileged. Shaun and Liz have more freedom, but they do not do anything more important. The plan for the day, as relayed by Liz, is: "Right . . . a cup of tea . . . then we get the Sundays. Head down the Phoenix for a roast, veg out in the pub for a bit, then wander home, watch a bit of telly, go to bed." Nothing about this itinerary suggests that heterosexual time is better spent than queer time. Again, the most striking change lies in how comfortable and contented all three characters now appear. Ultimately, Shaun cleanses his psychosexual trauma and achieves happiness for himself and his loved ones not by purging his desire to have it all and declaring for a prescribed team, but by claiming that desire and its queerness.

Notes

1. Pifer, "Slacker Bites Back," 168.
2. Mapes, "Shaun of the Dead."
3. Sedgwick, *Between Men*, 27.
4. Ibid., 2.
5. Chen, "Lurching for the Cure?" 26.
6. Kee, "Good Girls Don't Date Dead Boys," 179.
7. Haggerty, *Queer Gothic*, 2.
8. Ibid., 3.
9. Rose, *Beyond Hammer*, 129.
10. Ibid.

11. Ibid.
12. Ibid., 133.
13. Pifer, "Slacker Bites Back," 173.
14. Ibid., 174.
15. Ibid.
16. Girard, *Deceit, Desire, and the Novel*, 48.
17. Kee, "Good Girls Don't Date Dead Boys," 178–79.

Bibliography

Chen, Mel Y. "Lurching for the Cure? On Zombies and the Reproduction of Disability." *GLQ: A Journal of Lesbian and Gay Studies* 21, no. 1 (January 2015): 24–31.

Girard, René. *Deceit, Desire, and the Novel: Self and Other in Literary Structure*. 1961. Translated by Yvonne Freccero. Baltimore: Johns Hopkins University Press, 1965.

Haggerty, George E. *Queer Gothic*. Chicago: University of Illinois Press, 2006.

Kee, Chera. "Good Girls Don't Date Dead Boys: Toying with Miscegenation in Zombie Films." *Journal of Popular Film and Television* 42, no. 4 (2014): 176–85.

Mapes, Marty. "Shaun of the Dead." *Movie Habit*, September 23, 2004. http://www.moviehabit.com/review.php?story=sha_iw04.

Pifer, Lynn. "Slacker Bites Back: *Shaun of the Dead* Finds New Life for Deadbeats." In *Better Off Dead: The Evolution of the Zombie as Post-Human*, edited by Deborah Christie and Sarah Juliet Lauro, 163–74. New York: Fordham University Press, 2011.

Rose, James. *Beyond Hammer: British Horror Cinema since 1970*. Leighton Buzzard, UK: Auteur Press, 2009.

Sedgwick, Eve Kosofsky. *Between Men: English Literature and Male Homosocial Desire*. New York: Columbia University Press, 1985.

Shaun of the Dead. Directed by Edgar Wright. Universal City, CA: Universal Studios Home Video. 2004. DVD.

~

CHAPTER FIFTEEN

Undead in Suburbia

Teaching Children to Love Thy Neighbor, Fangs and All

Leila Estes and Katherine Kelp-Stebbins

Zombie movies are coming for your children's brains! At least, that's the assertion we make in this chapter, where we delve into a range of comedies about the undead in suburbia to show the subversive messages these films convey to younger audiences. Children don't have to understand these films' subtexts of racism, classism, homophobia, and ageism in order to be affected by their messages regarding tolerance and the value of difference. The humor with which these messages are conveyed enhances their appeal, as does the use of the undead as surrogates for different types of people. Undead characters like zombies, ghosts, and vampires create the possibility for diversity and also serve as ironic reflections of staid suburbanites.

These movies show young viewers that fear of difference and inability to accept change is its own form of living death. In the films, death itself often seems less threatening than the fearful and joyless lives of the uptight suburban dwellers. Through collaborations, friendships, and even romance between suburbanites and the undead, these films encourage children to think beyond the complacency and sterility of suburban conformity. The paradoxes of "undead" and "suburban" guide our examination of how a variety of films directed at children and young adults use undead characters in suburban settings to teach the value of difference.

Peculiar Definitions: Dead or Alive and Cities near Cities

Part of the "joke" of the undead in suburbia rests on the curious constructions of each term. While they may initially seem unrelated, a closer look at their etymologies reveals unexpected commonalities. Both *suburb* and *undead* date back to pre-sixteenth century English usage and both feature prefixes that distinguish them from, and yet implicate them with, the nouns the prefixes modify. That is, a suburb is specifically not an *urbs*—Latin for city—but yet it is not the opposite of a city; that would be *rus*, Latin for "the country."[1] Thus, a suburb is at once not a city and yet dependent on the city for its very definition. So too, undead does not mean the opposite of dead—that is, "alive."[2] Rather, in the somewhat confusing *Oxford English Dictionary* entry, it means "not dead; alive. Also, not quite dead but not fully alive, dead-and-alive." In both cases we see a clear semblance of distinctions or boundaries, accompanied by the confusion of these boundaries. A suburb is *near* (sub-) a city and yet may also denote "the parts *of* a city outside the commercial and civic center." The un- before dead leads to the expectation that it distinguishes dead from not dead; instead, it means some combination of the two. The boundaries between dead and undead and urban and suburban are revealed to be far from stable, creating the possibility for humor in the crossing of these boundaries. In the films that we discuss below, suburbanites doggedly try to establish a space of order and safety apart from the chaos of the city or the country. Yet, as the undead characters who inhabit or invade these spaces with a torrent of blood, sweat, and suburban tears show, there is no order without chaos, just as there is no life without death.

Taking into account the shared sense of negation in both "undead" and "suburbia," the subsequent films will showcase the irony that such negative definitions entail. Because both terms depend on the idea of negative definitions, many movies introduce comedy through the failure of exclusions: What if the undead seem more alive than living people? What if the suburb fails to keep out those elements (violence, danger, difference) that it is designed to exclude?

Suburban Terror and Zombification

Suburbia's potent imagery is imbedded in our American consciousness. Characterized by iconic white picket fences, perfectly manicured hedges, and (supposedly) happy families, suburbia is visually recognizable as a safe haven for middle-class morals, values, and traditions—the ideal place to raise children, cradled in the reassurance of predictability and sameness. This life-affirming space separates itself from the urban, which is linked to danger, sin, and decay. Although allegedly a safe space, suburbia is often positioned cinematically not only as vulnerable, but also as a place that stifles individuality. Instead of granting life-affirming safety, the suburbs in such films as *All That*

Heaven Allows (1955) and *Peyton Place* (1957) manifest unhappiness, dehumanizing their inhabitants and fostering a sterile, stringent environment. As Bernice Murphy states in *The Suburban Gothic in American Popular Culture*, "The suburbs became symbolic of what they perceived to be the most oppressive aspects of 1950s life—sameness, blandness and materialism."[3] The trope of suburban conformity has appeared continuously in films since the 1950s: sometimes inflected with horror, as in *The Stepford Wives* (1975), *Disturbia* (2007), and *It Follows* (2014); sometimes played for humor, as in *The 'Burbs* (1989), *Parents* (1989), *I'll Be Home for Christmas* (1998), and a number of other movies and television series.[4] Occasionally, however, films use suburban conformity to combine horror and comedy.

The movies that we examine in this essay explore the confusing and polarizing nature of suburban space. Frequently the suburban inhabitants of these films treat the undead characters, or those connected to them, as social pariahs because of their abnormal behavior. In *ParaNorman* (2012) the entire town labels young protagonist Norman a "freak" because he can see ghosts; Tony, the hero of *The Little Vampire* (2000), is called a "creep" because he dreams of vampires. Neighbors mock and fear the Addamses in *The Addams Family* (1991) and *Addams Family Values* (1993), and a "normal" family goes to great lengths to exorcise the ghost couple that shares their home in *Beetlejuice* (1988). Suburban characters are perplexed and disgusted by the undead, because to exist within suburbia's confines means an acute commitment to conformity.

The films suggest that these humans are suffering in a purgatory that does not allow them to express themselves or their latent desires. "Zombification," already a part of the suburban experience, is exacerbated when undead characters are introduced into the narrative. As the undead characters are freer in nature, they ironically are more "vivacious" than the humans in the films. The alleged difference between suburbanites and the undead highlight suburbia's beautiful façade, leading to the nagging question: Which is truly horrifying—the presence of the undead, or the confines in which the suburbanites live?

As instructive works directed at younger audiences, but also films that the whole family can enjoy, these films demonstrate the vivifying effects of exposure to difference and miscegenation. Marketed toward children and all rated PG or PG-13, they intervene in suburban economies as films for familial consumption. By compelling audiences to identify with characters who do not fit in, the movies teach viewers of all ages, but particularly children and younger teens, to exercise tolerance for different types of people. Ultimately, undead films introduce suburbia as a site of tension, but through the narrative arc of necessary and inevitable exposure to difference, reveal suburbia to be a site of cross-cultural possibility.

American Dream, Suburban Nightmare: *ParaNorman*

In many ways *ParaNorman*, the stop-motion animated film from the Laika animation studio and directors Sam Fell and Chris Butler, seems too clichéd to be subversive. The plot follows outcast kid Norman Babcock (voiced by Kodi Smit-McPhee) as he negotiates the hazards of school (where he is friendless and bullied), small-town life (where his neighbors stare at him hatefully), and a wary family (his cheerleader sister wants nothing to do with him). Norman's situation is explained by his ability to—in an overt nod to *The Sixth Sense* (1999)—see dead people. But because *ParaNorman* is a comedy, unlike *The Sixth Sense*, his ability simultaneously makes him an outcast *and* the only person capable of saving his town from a witch's curse.

In the quest to overcome the curse, every character follows a well-worn path to redemption. The bully who has tormented Norman for most of the film becomes his respectful friend. The cheerleader sister (voiced by Anna Kendrick) eventually defends Norman against the raging townsfolk, who are so blinded by their fear of difference that they attack defenseless zombies (and Norman) without cause or logic. The "terrifying" zombies unleashed by the curse are shown to be frightened victims of supernatural violence and the targets of mob violence by the modern-day townsfolk. In reaction to the

Norman learns the witch's identity in *ParaNorman*.

town's rampage, Norman's new friend and fellow outcast Neil (voiced by Tucker Albrizzi) and Neil's jock brother Mitch (voiced by Casey Affleck) chastise the townspeople:

> Neil: All night long, [Norman's] been trying to save you guys.
>
> Mitch: Yeah but all you want to do is burn and murder stuff, burn and murder stuff, just burning and murdering.

Having stopped their violent frenzy, the town, in turn, learns a lesson about the dangers of bullying and fearing difference. Ultimately they (and we) are taught the necessity of understanding and acceptance—rather than fear—in the face of strangeness.

Beyond its clichés, however, *ParaNorman* delivers a series of messages, rooted in history, regarding difference and acceptance. The town's curse is explained by Norman's drama teacher (voiced by Alex Borstein), who chides the children for their ignorance of the town's past. She tells them that Blithe Hollow was founded by Puritans, "strict and devout settlers who came here to build a home, a place without sin." The town in *ParaNorman* is its own kind of suburban space, founded on a puritanical desire to escape the evils offered both by the wilds of urban and rural environments.

When the Puritans discovered a witch in their midst they put her on trial and sentenced her to death by hanging. In turn, according to the legend, the witch cursed her accusers to die horrible deaths and to "rise from their graves as the living dead, their souls doomed to an eternity of damnation." Thus, the town's founders are turned into the undead through their puritanical (pre-suburban) desire to separate themselves from sin. Paradoxically, in attempting to keep sin out they commit sins themselves, as Norman discovers when he realizes that the "witch" who had been hanged in Blithe Hollow's early history was actually a young girl who seemed strange to the town's fearful adults.

In the light of the historical violence it represents, the town's amusingly punny motto, "Blithe Hollow: A Great Place to Hang," becomes a commentary on the suburban commodification of historical trauma. It also indicates, in its ironic meaning, how humorous suburban simulations of trauma can quickly shift in meaning from blithely hollow to murderous and terrifying in the event of historical irruption. Central to *ParaNorman* is the problem of what happens when simulations of violence turn real, and the question of whether or not this process—the "blithe" repetition of past violence—is inevitable. As the modern townspeople "burn and murder stuff" (in Mitch's words) in their attempt to kill Norman, they implicitly echo their Puritan forebears' murder of a little girl out of fear.

Although the film rationalizes this process when Neil states, early in the plot, "You can't stop bullying, it's part of human nature," the historical context of the movie suggests that it might not be so much *human* nature as America's fearful and judgmental *Puritan* nature that, reduced to the empty humor—the Blithe Hollow—of suburban life, emerges in unfunny ways. Norman's sensitive nature and his habit of joking and laughing *with*, not about, the undead is established in the film's opening scenes. Watching a comically inept zombie movie with his (dead) grandmother, he listens to her running commentary—"What's he [eating her brains] for? That's not very nice!" and "I'm sure if they bothered to just sit down and talk it through, it'd be a different story!"—with an indulgent smile that signals his obvious affection for her. He saves his exasperation for his parents, retorting (when they insist that Grandma is dead and "in a better place"): "No she's not—she's in the living room!" His inability to be blithe about the town's ghosts, and his empathetic (rather than fearful) reaction to the undead suggest a method for living amid histories of suburbia without hollowing them out, or purifying them.

Although Norman can have a melancholy aura at times, other characters act as foils and provide comic relief. Neil, a chubby redhead, is intrigued by Norman and inquires about the veracity of the claims that Norman can "see ghosts like everywhere all the time." Norman hesitantly says "Yes" to which Neil replies with enthusiasm, "Awwessommmme!" Neil, whose dog Bub was killed by an animal rescue van (both "tragic and ironic," he observes), desperately wants to communicate with his lost pet. Norman is easily able to locate Bub in Neil's backyard but when Neil attempts to talk to his old playmate, he can only guess where Bub's face is. When he leans in to talk to his beloved pet, Norman has to tell him that he is actually addressing the dog's rear end.

If *ParaNorman* highlights the American roots of suburban fearfulness, other films, such as *The Little Vampire* and *Addams Family Values*, illustrate that the suburban mind-set can be transported to other sites as well. Whether a Scottish town or summer camp, similar values, and similar fears of difference, are exposed and confronted by the films' humorous storylines.

The Little Vampire: Suburbia Can Be a "Pain in the Neck"

In *The Little Vampire*, directed by Uli Edel, Tony (Jonathan Lipnicki) has moved across the world from urban San Diego to suburban Scotland so that his father (Tommy Hinkley) can design a luxurious golf course for a member of the Scottish aristocracy, Lord McAshton (John Wood). Tony's adjustment to life in Scotland's sumptuous green landscapes is quite difficult. Much like Norman in *ParaNorman*, Tony is bullied daily by two of his fellow class-mates (who are sons of Lord McAshton). On the first day of school, Tony is tormented (verbally and physically) by these young descendants. "This is for being a little creep," they tell him; "This is for coming here in the first place." The children's expression of xenophobia toward another child is mirrored in the adult characters' reactions to Tony's parents, and later in their behavior toward vampires.

To the chagrin of his family and teachers, Tony is fascinated by vampires and regularly has dreams about them. An outcast, his only friend is a young vampire named Rudolph (Rollo Weeks). Rudolph and his family aren't typical vampires. They drink cow's blood (so as not to harm humans) and their greatest desire is to be human again. Like the zombies in *ParaNorman*, they have become undead through a curse—not that the distinction keeps townspeople from harboring fear and hatred of them because they are differ-ent. The boys are drawn to one another because each wishes for the life the other seems to have—Tony fantasizes about being a vampire rather than a human, and Rudolph wants nothing more than to be a normal little boy— and become as close as brothers. Through Rudolph, Tony learns that not all stereotypes about vampires are true—that they are more than just undead creatures who crave blood and fear crosses and daylight—and similarly, Tony teaches Rudolph that not all humans are fear-driven persecutors of creatures of the night. The camaraderie between the two boys continues to be a space of mutual understanding and teaching, as when Tony teaches Rudolph the word "Duh." Both speak English fluently, but their misunderstandings comi-cally highlight the language barrier that separates speakers of British and American dialects.

When Tony and Rudolph first meet there is an amusing case of mistaken identity. Rudolph is not in a vampiric state, but rather is flying around as a bat. While flying past an open window that looks into Tony's bedroom, Rudolph thinks that he sees a vampire. Tony is convincingly dressed like one, with fake fangs, a "bloody" (actually ketchup-smeared) face, and a cape. Rudolph, still in bat form, flies into Tony's bedroom and slams into the fireplace. After regaining his bearings and turning back into a vampire, Rudolph realizes his eyes have deceived him. Tony was essentially "passing" as a vampire, at least for a brief few moments.

One of the most hilarious characters in the film is Tony's middle-aged babysitter, Lorna (Georgie Glen). Lorna's character brings into question one of the major themes of the film: Do we become more or less frightened as we age? Unbeknownst to Lorna, who has been downstairs, Tony has made paper cutouts of vampire teeth. When she enters the room, he hisses at her and she recoils in terror, exclaiming, in a comically thick Scottish brogue: "Sorry! What a fright you gave me! I didn't see you there . . . you nearly stopped my heart and it's nearly stopped enough as it is." The scene is one of many in *The Little Vampire* that finds comic irony in the fears of particular characters. A middle-aged woman should not be terrified of a little boy, but in the same vein, Tony is more afraid of the human bullies who torment him than he is of the supposedly dangerous vampires.

Tony's plight is directly compared, in numerous scenes, to that of the persecuted vampires. When Rudolph tells him, "You don't know what it's like for us vampires to be so tormented," he replies, "Oh yeah, I do—it happens to me every day at school." Both characters are ostracized and oppressed in their respective stifling environments. While Tony is bullied at school on a daily basis by Lord McAshton's young sons, Rudolph and his family are persecuted by Rookery (Jim Carter), a vampire exterminator. Both young characters suffer from suburbia's rejection of difference. Tony, however, gets his long-awaited revenge on the McAshton boys when, with Rudolph's help, he flies into the McAshton mansion and terrorizes them in their sleep, ensuring that they will sleep with one eye open for a long time to come. Now convinced that he is a vampire, they shrink from him in fear when they encounter him on the estate's vast lawn, and Tony commands them to crawl on hands and knees all the way to the mansion. Later, Rudolph saves Tony from Rookery's clutches by blocking the path of his truck with a herd of flying, red-eyed vampire-cows. Terrified, Rookery drives over a nearby cliff and into the loch below, just as Rudolph lifts Tony free.

Ultimately, the film has a happy ending, with a chance for transcendence of suburbia's myopic view of what is acceptable and tolerated. The curse on Rudolph's family is lifted, thanks to Tony's timely intervention and his mother's equally timely clobbering of Rookery with his own neon-lit cross, granting the vampires the chance to become human. Rudolph's family moves into the village, and the boys are able to restart their friendship as equals. The film teaches viewers, particularly children, that bullying and feelings of culture shock are unfortunately quite common.

Films such as these encourage children not merely to accept difference, but rather to embrace it. They illustrate that the erasure of boundaries and barriers can open up endless opportunities for friendship and adventure. While both *ParaNorman* and *The Little Vampire* are told from the perspective of the young, mortal protagonist, *Beetlejuice* and *The Addams Family* frame their narratives from the perspective of inhuman or undead characters, positioning the viewer to identify, at least in part, with those bizarre protagonists.

Beetlejuice: Embracing the "Strange and Unusual"

In *Beetlejuice*, directed by Tim Burton, Barbara and Adam Maitland (Geena Davis and Alec Baldwin) are the ideal suburban couple. They are young, attractive, and great supporters of their small community of Winter River, Connecticut. They know everyone in the town and everyone knows them. Despite visible displays of happiness, everything seems a little too perfect. The film begins with a long overhead shot weaving through their idyllic Connecticut town.[5] The camera weaves over the forest and the mostly white houses of the town. Yet there is a moment of visual trickery as a shot of the real Connecticut town morphs into a shot of the model town that Adam has created in the Maitlands' attic. The seamless transition between the suburban landscape and Adam's model town highlights how the real and fake suburban spaces are inextricably linked. The highly traditional setting—the story is set in 1988, but the town could easily be mistaken for Connecticut in the 1950s—similarly underscores the stagnancy of suburbia. While the urban environment is rapidly changing, the Maitlands' suburban environment seems frozen in time. At the end of the opening credits, however, the camera lingers on the small model house as a spider creeps up to the roof—an omen that the house will soon be "contaminated."

Beetlejuice's plot revolves around the Maitlands' furtive attempts to retain their suburban existence, even after their untimely deaths. They are condemned to live in a form of purgatory: still in their own house, but now cohabiting with its new owners, the Deetzes, and with Betelgeuse (pronounced "Beetlejuice"), a poltergeist who has become a squatter in Adam's model town. For Barbara and Adam, the situation is a double "home invasion": Betelgeuse invades their model home, while the Deetzes invade their real home and transform it, with the help of their interior decorator, Otho, into a modernist nightmare the Maitlands barely recognize. Appalled, the Maitlands pit the intruders against each other, teaming up with the boorish and conniving Betelgeuse—who bills himself as a "bioexorcist"—to drive the Deetzes out.

While the Maitlands may seem to represent typically fearful and disapproving suburban characters, their death throws a twist (and a lot of humor) into the scenario. In order to rid themselves of the Deetzes, the Maitlands must become freakish, embracing their newfound ghostly powers. They quickly graduate from appearing with sheets draped over themselves to possessing the Deetzes and their stuffy dinner-party guests and forcing them into an exuberant, body-shaking dance as they sing the calypso hit "Day-O." They even transgress the cardinal rules of the undead bureaucracy that governs the afterlife: revealing themselves to the living, allowing photographs to be taken of themselves, and defying the instructions of their caseworker Juno (Sylvia Sidney). Just like the Puritans in *ParaNorman*, who became sinners to eradicate sin, the Maitlands give up all vestiges of their humanity in their attempt to retain their normal (pre-death) human lives.

Betelgeuse is the comedic center of the film. Though undead for eons and physically repugnant, he has a *je ne sais quoi* that renders him bizarrely charming. He is a trickster, able to throw his voice, instantly mimic others' attire (as he does with Adam's plaid shirt and khakis), and alter his body at will: spinning his head like a top, unrolling his suddenly flattened arms like fire hoses, and transforming his face into a Medusa-like nest of writhing snakes. He also claims to have seen *The Exorcist* 176 times, which he sees as a definite boost to his credentials. He does all this while flirting shamelessly with Barbara, whom he calls "Babs," declaring himself "the Ghost with the Most" and taunting listeners to "Make my millennium!"

The Maitlands, disgusted by Betelgeuse's crudeness and concerned that he will harm the Deetzes rather than simply scaring them away, dismiss him, but their situation soon goes from bad to worse. Charles Deetz (Jeffrey Jones), intrigued by the escalating weirdness, contacts his former boss with a proposal to develop Winter River into a supernatural-themed tourist mecca. Betelgeuse, meanwhile, attempts to trick Lydia (Winona Ryder)—the

Beetlejuice: The Maitlands embrace the horror of their undead-ness.

Deetzes' adolescent daughter, who can see the Maitlands and has befriended them—into summoning him back into the world of the living.

The Maitlands, realizing the damage that their failure to accept the new residents has caused, resolve to peacefully share the house with them. Events, however, quickly spin out of control. A séance staged by Charles in order to summon the Maitlands goes awry, causing their ghostly bodies to begin disintegrating. This leads Lydia to deliberately call on Betelgeuse to help save them, which he agrees to do only if she will marry him. Adam and Barbara are saved, but must then save Lydia from her ghoulish suitor.

Betelgeuse is the film's most vivid character and the source of its most spectacular comic set pieces, but the Maitlands' dual transformation—from rejection to embrace of their undead nature, and from intolerance to acceptance of the "outsider" Deetzes—remains the narrative core of the story. Compelled to view events from their perspective, audiences are encouraged to share first their annoyance with the Deetzes and then their growing affection for them. Both transformations, however, are rooted in Maitlands' shedding of the conformist personalities they had in life and their embrace (in undeath) of anarchy, absurdity, and wild improvisation.

Death Becomes Them:
The Addams Family, at Home and at Camp

In *The Addams Family*, the Addamses are an anomalous familial unit in an otherwise idyllic suburban neighborhood. All the other houses in the neighborhood are interchangeable cookie-cutter American homes, with manicured lawns and well-tended gardens that are cluttered only with children's toys, but the Addamses' "surreal estate" is a dark, looming mansion on a grassless plot, complete with a cemetery where all of their relatives are buried. The Addamses themselves are considered equally macabre and abnormal. They embrace death, introducing it into the quotidian experience, thus placing themselves at (or beyond) the fringes of "normal" suburban society. Their unfiltered approach to death petrifies their suburban neighbors who deal with death in ways more typical of middle-class America—with veiled references and varied forms of deflection.

The Addams family engages in "typical" suburban activities, but in ways that comically violate suburban norms. The kids are sent off to school with bagged lunches filled with strange live creatures, and Wednesday's eyes widen with delight when she receives her moving lunch from the family's hulking butler, Lurch. Morticia (Anjelica Huston) "gardens," in a greenhouse with blackened windows, by cutting the flower buds off the stems. Gomez (Raúl

Juliá) practices his golf game by driving balls off the roof of the house, heedless of the fact that they sometimes fly into the home of their next-door neighbor, a prominent judge who, in one scene, has his otherwise-peaceful breakfast interrupted by one of Gomez's errant golf balls splashing into his cereal bowl. To the judge, and the rest of their neighbors, the Addamses are social pariahs, whose subversions of day-to-day suburban life terrify and trouble those around them.

Suburbia, in popular culture, is routinely associated with marriage and children, but rarely with sex—let alone between married couples.[6] Here, too, however, Morticia and Gomez are the exceptions to suburban norms. They are thoroughly monogamous, openly passionate with one another, and very vocal about their sexual desires. The film picks up a running joke from the television series—Gomez's uncontrollable reactions to Morticia speaking to him in French—and makes explicit what the series could only hint at: that the couple uses it as a form of foreplay.

Gomez: [Morticia wakes up] Unhappy, darling?

Morticia: Oh, yes. Yes completely.

[Gomez sits]

Morticia: Gomez . . . Sun. *Il me perce comme un poignard.*

Gomez: Oh, Tish, That's French.

Morticia: *Oui.*

Gomez: *Cara mia.*

[he kisses Morticia's hand]

Gomez: *En garde, Monsieur Soleil!*

Morticia: Gomez . . .

Gomez: *Querida?*

Morticia: Last night, you were unhinged. You were like some desperate howling demon. You frightened me. Do it again.

This amorous banter sets up their relationship as a foil to that of their lawyer, Tully (Dan Hedaya), whose wife Margaret (Dana Ivey) is disgusted with his failures in business and is clearly on the brink of divorcing him.

Margaret and Tully are constantly squabbling. At first, Margaret's character appears one-dimensional. She simply seems to be the shrill wife of a corrupt lawyer, but later the viewer sees that she possesses a softer side as she falls in love with the Addamses' Cousin It[7] (John Franklin)—an ambulatory mop of long, silken hair, sporting a derby and sunglasses—at a party for Fester, who has returned from the grave.[8] Although It's warblings are undecipherable to the audience, Margaret is able to communicate with him and confesses that she is unhappy in her marriage of two decades. She later divorces Tully and finds marital bliss with Cousin It. In the sequel, *Addams Family Values*, they are still married, and the proud parents of a new baby, named "What,"[9] who takes after It, with long brown hair and seemingly no facial structure. Margaret, in casting her lot with the outcast Addamses, has thrown off suburban conformity, indulged her sexual and romantic desires, and seemingly found her authentic self.

Addams Family Values picks up soon after the previous film. The plot focuses on the experiences of the children Wednesday (Christina Ricci) and Pugsley (Jimmy Workman) as they are sent off to camp by their duplicitous nanny, Debbie (Joan Cusack). The same prejudices and values that give rise to the conformity and fear of the suburban setting permeate the camp and its inhabitants. Thus, the film suggests that the notion of suburbia is bigger than any particular zip code, and it has the potential to seep into other aspects of life.

Camp Chippewa is run by a married couple, Gary Granger (Peter Mac-Nicol) and Becky Martin-Granger (Christine Baranski), whose cheerful

Addams Family Values: Margaret finds a new lease on life with the Addams Family.

smiles cover up their vindictive personalities. The Grangers embody suburban prejudices and values, making it their personal mission to fundamentally
change Pugsley, Wednesday, and their friend Joel (David Krumholtz), along
with other campers who (for reasons of race, religion, or disability) do not
fit the Grangers' ideal of what suburban children should look like. Summer
camp turns into a "conversion camp" designed to change the trio by forcing
the children to watch Disney movies that reflect suburban values.

In fact, however, the film encourages *Addams Family Values* of revolt,
death, and decay. The outcast protagonists appear to have been converted
by the Disney films (stoic Wednesday even cracks a smile), and they agree
to participate in the camp pageant, which re-creates the first Thanksgiving,
with the outcast children playing compliant, adoring Native Americans.
Once onstage, however, Wednesday goes radically off-script, declaring that
the Native Americans "cannot break bread with" the Pilgrims, because:

> You have taken the land which is rightfully ours. Years from now my people
> will be forced to live in mobile homes on reservations. Your people will wear
> cardigans, and drink highballs. We will sell our bracelets by the roadsides, you
> will play golf, and enjoy hot hors d'oeuvres. My people will have pain and
> degradation. Your people will have stick shifts.

Under Wednesday's direction, the outcast children revolt and burn down the
camp, using ziplines, suction-cup arrows, and torches to exact revenge on the
campers who shunned them. The climax of the scene occurs when a camper
in a wheelchair uses it to run rings around the Grangers, rope in hand, tying
them tightly to a pole and holding them captive. Unlike the unsuccessful
brainwashing by Disney films, *Addams Family Values* successfully idealizes
difference and resistance to conformity.

In the final scenes, Wednesday and Joel come to represent a new generation, as he dresses up like Gomez and they discuss their future together. The
two function as a future re-creation of Morticia and Gomez, showing that
such "mysterious and spooky, altogether ooky" people will persist in generations to come. In spite of, or perhaps *because* of, their obsession with death,
the Addamses offer far more possibilities for life and love than their suburban
contemporaries.

How I Learned to Stop Worrying and Love the Undead

In a scene that epitomizes *The Addams Family*'s reframing of tolerance for
the persecuted Other, Morticia reinterprets "Hansel and Gretel" for a group

of toddlers in a way that makes them weep for the poor, victimized witch. While the children in the movie cry at the witch's fate, it can be assumed that the children who are watching the movie are laughing, thanks to the switch in values that allows them to empathize with the witch, and to condemn the supposedly heroic Hansel and Gretel. Morticia's reframing of the story exemplifies the didactic potential of the films in this chapter, all of which invite children to laugh at, and sympathize with, the monsters that they have been trained to fear.

The movies depend on the suburban worldview for both their social message and their comedy, framing the drive to keep out potential threats as a force even more threatening than the dangers it seeks to exclude. They present fear of difference as a force that can threaten the happiness (even the lives) of children like Norman, Tony, Lydia, Wednesday, and Pugsley, who do not fit into the narrow suburban ideal. By reframing suburban intolerance as the object of fear, and featuring protagonists whose difference ultimately allows them to transcend and reshape suburban order, these films give children the agency to exercise tolerance, and to live, laugh, and even love with everyone.

Notes

1. Charlton T. Lewis and Charles Short, *A Latin Dictionary*, s.vv. "rus," "urbs." http://www.perseus.tufts.edu.
2. *Oxford English Dictionary*, s.v. "undead."
3. Murphy, *The Suburban Gothic*, 7.
4. The prevalence of suburban conformity as a thematic imperative can also be seen on television, as in popular programs like *Desperate Housewives* (2004–2012) and *Weeds* (2005–2012).
5. Although the film is set in Connecticut, the actual shooting location was East Corinth, Vermont.
6. Countless dramas, such as *The Ice Storm* (1997), *American Beauty* (1999), *Far from Heaven* (2002), and *Revolutionary Road* (2008), all depend on the lovelessness of suburban marriages for their narrative arcs.
7. While the character from *The Addams Family* TV series (1964–1966) was written as "Cousin Itt," the name is written as "Cousin It" in the script and credits of the 1991 film.
8. It appears that the character Gordon is actually Fester, whom Abigail (Gordon's "mother") found in the Bermuda Triangle with amnesia. Abigail also poses as Gordon/Fester's psychologist, Dr. Greta Pinder-Schloss.
9. The baby is named after the obstetrician's reaction to seeing the baby.

Bibliography

The Addams Family. Directed by Barry Sonnenfeld. 1991. Hollywood, CA: Paramount Pictures. 2015. *Netflix* streaming.

Addams Family Values. Directed by Barry Sonnenfeld. 1993. Hollywood, CA: Paramount Pictures. 2015. *Netflix* streaming.

Beetlejuice. Directed by Tim Burton. 1988. Burbank, CA: Warner Home Video. 2008. DVD.

The Little Vampire. Directed by Uli Edel. 2000. Los Angeles, CA: New Line Home Video. 2001. DVD.

Murphy, Bernice M. *The Suburban Gothic in American Popular Culture*. Basingstoke, Hampshire, UK: Palgrave Macmillan, 2009.

ParaNorman. Directed by Chris Butler and Sam Fell. 2012. Universal City, CA: Universal Studios. 2012. DVD.

CHAPTER SIXTEEN

~

Some Assembly Required

The Do-It-Yourself Undead

Cynthia J. Miller

The story of Frankenstein's monster teaches us that there is a reason why humans should never know "what it is like to be God." The dangers of pride, shortsightedness, violating the boundaries between this world and the next, and using powerful knowledge for personal gain are overwhelmingly apparent.

And yet, we never seem to learn.

Time and again the tale repeats itself, and it seldom ends well: Life is created from the midst of death, with devastating results. The Frankenstein allegory has been borrowed, mirrored, and adapted in numerous films, but a small cluster of these from the late twentieth century is of particular interest. Beginning in 1984, films such as *Frankenweenie* (1984), *Weird Science* (1985), *Frankenhooker* (1990), and *Rock 'n' Roll Frankenstein* (1999) all revisit the theme of creation, taking their basic plotlines from the original Frankenstein story. In each case, science—albeit bizarre, unfettered, shortsighted science—is used to create life, and the results form a cautionary tale about the limits of human agency.

Taken together, however, these contemporary adaptations of Mary Shelley's classic tale do much more than lend new twists to a well-known plot. They wrest science from the hands of the specialist—the learned professional whose obsession has led him down a path of darkness—and place it in the hands of the "everyman," claiming a power for the masses that is ordinarily reserved for a mere few. Manipulating the boundary between life and death is no longer the domain of scientific gatekeepers, but of grieving children, stricken lovers, ambitious students, and grasping promoters.

Laden with comic mishaps, each of these forays into do-it-yourself un-death democratizes reanimation, suggesting that the process is more dependent on creativity than technical expertise, and offering an anarchic look at the outcomes of scientific power and privilege in the hands of everyday individuals. This essay, then, takes a look at these freewheeling revisions of the Frankenstein story, considering both the urge to "create" and the comedy that ensues when fallible amateurs take life into their own hands.

Thinking about Frankenstein and the Doctor

In the introduction to her novel, Mary Shelley confessed her terror at the "effect of any human endeavour to mock the stupendous mechanism of the Creator of the world," and the disaster that would ensue when man "aspires to become greater than his nature will allow."[1] At its heart, Shelley's *Frankenstein* is a cautionary tale about knowledge and power—one of the most controversial intellectual debates of its day, between instrumental science that sought to harness, control, and manipulate nature, and Romantic science, which held that the mysteries of nature could not be reduced to processes and mechanisms—that natural forces were far more than the sum of their parts.[2] As M. K. Joseph observed:

> Mary Shelley wrote in the infancy of modern science, when its enormous possibilities were just beginning to be foreseen by imaginative writers like Byron and Shelley and by speculative scientists like Davy and Erasmus Darwin. At the age of nineteen, she achieved the quietly astonishing feat of looking beyond them.[3]

Shelley cast Frankenstein and his monster at the pivot point of that controversy, pitting "good" science—as Anne Mellor suggests, "the detailed and reverent description of the workings of nature"—against "bad" science, "the hubristic manipulation of the forces of nature to serve man's private ends."[4]

"Good" science, for Shelley's contemporaries, took the form, on the one hand, of Enlightenment science's detached, rational observation and deductive reasoning, and on the other, of Romantic science's sense of poetic wonder. Romantic chemist Sir Humphry Davy argued that understanding nature required "an attitude of admiration, love, and worship . . . a personal response."[5] Davy and his like-minded colleagues in Europe—such as Friedrich Schelling and Alexander von Humboldt of Germany and Hans Christian Ørsted (Oersted) of Denmark—contended that dogmatic categorization of the natural world and its processes was merely an attempt to impose order.

They emphasized the elements of mystery and inspiration interwoven in understandings of nature and, as Schelling elaborated in his works on *Naturphilosophie*, the elegant simplicity of the inner "soul" of nature.

Generations earlier, natural philosophers sought control over nature in a manner that echoed the colonialist urge, articulated in Francis Bacon's oft-cited claim: "I am come in very truth leading to you Nature with all her children to bind her to your service and make her your slave."[6] Almost two centuries later, these sentiments pressed forward, reflected in the writing of Nicolas de Condorcet, who affirmed: "Long since persuaded that the human species is infinitely perfectable . . . I considered the task of hastening progress to be one of my sweetest occupations, one of the first duties of a man who has strengthened his reason by study and meditation."[7] These scientific idealists pitted their drive for knowledge against nature as an adversary; it was "interrogated everywhere" . . . "attacked simultaneously by a variety of methods and instruments capable of tearing away its secrets" . . . and "[e]very discovery [was] a conquest."[8]

A product of his era, Shelley's young scientist Victor Frankenstein learns similarly from his tutors about the heroes of modern science:

> They penetrate into the recesses of nature and show how she works in her hiding places . . . they have discovered how the blood circulates and the nature of the air we breathe. They have acquired new and almost unlimited powers; they can command the thunders of heaven, mimic the earthquake, and even mock the invisible world with its own shadows.[9]

The young Frankenstein's obsessive pursuits echo these perspectives, framed in the language of pursuit and conquest:

> Life and death appeared to me ideal bounds, which I should first break through, and pour a torrent of light into our dark world. A new species would bless me as its creator and source; many happy and excellent natures would owe their being to me.[10]

"Frankensteinian knowledge," as Elaine Graham writes, is thus *dangerous* knowledge, born of an "obsessive, alienated pursuit of certainty and controlling power."[11] Wendy Lesser concurs, arguing that:

> The desire to control nature through science . . . is part of a larger desire for control and mastery . . . Mary Shelley . . . was concerned with this sort of ruthless mastery—the sort exhibited not only by fanatical scientists, but also by all-powerful rulers toward the native inhabitants of colonized territories.[12]

The dual themes of power and control would, going forward, be the hallmark of the scientist in his role as gatekeeper—standing at the threshold between society and the unknown, proprietor of what lies beyond—divulging only as much information as he believes those lacking his expertise can handle and retaining the rest, in secret, for himself. Those who fail in this role invite disaster; those who invest their work with too much secrecy invite accusations of madness.

Victor Frankenstein embarks down the winding path into darkness when he first suggests that "to examine the cause of life, we must have recourse to Death."[13] As he begins his quest to create life, he is motivated by grief, anger, and frustration at the frailty of the human form and the inability of the nascent field of medical science to mediate between life and death, but his descent into madness soon follows. In Frankenstein, Shelley crafts a character that increasingly warps and frays in the single-minded pursuit of knowledge beyond the boundaries of convention. He embodies what Richard Holmes calls "the dazzling idea of the solitary scientific 'genius,' thirsting and reckless for knowledge, *for its own sake and perhaps at any cost*," and is characterized as "one of the great, ambiguous creations of Romantic science that we have all inherited."[14] Brilliant but arrogant; visionary but shortsighted, Frankenstein embodies all the fears that plagued Shelley's contemporaries about the dangers of a scientific world void of compassion and humility.

The tale draws its life from London, a city which, as Roseanne Montillo observes, was on the verge of a medical revolution in the early 1800s, creating a fertile context for Shelley's story. Hospitals were abuzz with doctors and their students, testing and experimenting to find cures for the disease and decay that threatened to engulf them.[15] As research by Giovanni Aldini and others advanced, electric shock, based on Luigi Galvani's famous experiments with frogs, seemed to offer hope for bridging the gap between health and disease, life and death. Trailblazers and charlatans alike sought to win support for their "miracles"—if not in the medical community, then at least in the public sphere—and the moral boundaries between what science could create and *should* create blurred.

Some, like James Graham, relied on the public as patrons of his scientific Temple of Health, which featured the mysterious "Celestial Bed"—an apparatus designed to expose its users to a continuous electrical charge, "filling the air with magnetic fluid calculated to give the necessary degree of strength and exaction to the nerves."[16] According to Graham's promotion, the bolts of electricity administered by the Celestial Bed would cure everything from headaches to gout, and those who made use of it would be "blessed with progeny" and cured of both sterility and impotence.[17] Other scientists, legitimate and illegitimate alike, advanced their knowledge and careers through grave robbing, public autopsies, dissections, and even attempts at reanimation—unsavory acts that shocked the general public and appalled the Church—the building blocks on which contemporary medical science was built.

Following in the Doctor's Footsteps

The tale inspired by these characters and controversies has given rise to an array of cinematic retellings, revisions, and adaptations, from the 1910 silent *Frankenstein* to twenty-first century television films, miniseries, and straight-to-video releases. Even more numerous, as Caroline Joan Picart has demonstrated, are those motion pictures inspired by the novel's characters or key themes, both in and out of the horror genre.[18] The story is, as she observes, "an enduring cinemyth" that speaks to "recurring themes of humanity, creation, and society" in ways that shift and evolve to reflect their historical moment.[19] Not only has the monster become a kind of cultural mascot, the doctor himself has gone on to spawn a range of demented scientists, both within and outside the horror canon.[20]

The four films considered here include an animated children's short (*Frankenweenie*), a risqué teen comedy (*Weird Science*), and a pair of bizarre, low-budget exploitation films (*Frankenhooker* and *Rock 'n' Roll Frankenstein*). Each is a comic romp through the Frankenstein cinemyth for which Picart's "reflection" functions more like a rearview mirror than a looking glass. Objects, or in this case, cultural commentaries, are larger than they appear.

Each of these films breathes new life into the monster maker's tale, with one very significant change: None of the "mad scientists" featured in the films are, in fact, scientists. And while it may not be apparent at first glance, that shift changes everything. *Frankenweenie*'s Victor Frankenstein is a lonely young boy whose best friend and confidant is his dog Sparky; *Weird Science*'s Gary and Wyatt are a pair of perpetually bullied suburban high school nerds—outsiders who just can't score; *Frankenhooker*'s Jeffrey Franken is an electrician and medical school dropout; and *Rock 'n' Roll Frankenstein*'s Bernie Stein is a sleazy music agent who recruits his ne'er-do-well necrophiliac nephew Frankie (Stein) and a roadie named Iggy to form a slapstick trio of reanimators. All of these characters take on the role of "creator," not for knowledge or power, but rather for love or money—for social, cultural, and economic "capital," if you will. While other *Frankenstein*-inspired films of the era (notably, cult classic *Re-animator* [1985] and Troma Entertainment's *Dr. Hackenstein* [1988]) also complicate the title character's motives with romance and greed, they still retain the source novel's casting of a scientist in that role, and the transition away from that role is key, not only to the films' significance as a cluster, but to the merging of horror and comedy in them as well.

As nonspecialists, each of the characters' motivations for attempting to create life out of death is highly personal. Some are driven by loss: When Sparky is hit by a car and killed, young Victor Frankenstein grieves the loss of his companion. Remembering how his biology teacher amazed the class by electrically reanimating a dead frog's leg, he sets out on a mission to bring his beloved pet back from the grave. In a desperate experiment that pays homage to Universal's 1931 rendition of the tale, Victor achieves success and brings a grateful, patchworked Sparky back to life in a makeshift attic laboratory. Soon, he is resurrecting deceased pets for all of the children in the neighborhood. A similar grief leads Jeffrey Franken to push the boundaries of both knowledge and common sense when his fiancée Elizabeth is killed—cut to ribbons in a freak accident with a remote control lawnmower. Jeffrey keeps her head in a freezer and hatches a plan to reassemble her, harvesting body parts from New York City prostitutes. Once he has everything he needs, he brings his creature to life with the help of an iconic electrical storm. The new Elizabeth, however, is the sum of her parts and emerges as the titular Frankenhooker. Rather than living "happily ever after" with Jeffrey, her only desire is to turn tricks and kill.

The wayward teen reanimators of *Weird Science* and the self-serving promoter of *Rock 'n' Roll Frankenstein*, however, seek far more mundane forms of "capital" as they try their hands at creating life. Typical awkward teens, Wyatt and Gary delve into the mysteries of science in order to attain the two things desired by most boys their age: acceptance and sex. Continually mocked by their peers for their ineptitude, the two boys are on the fast track to a socially doomed adolescence. Inspired by the Universal Pictures classic *Frankenstein* (1931), they conspire to "build" the perfect girl, whom they name "Lisa," on their computer. After programming their desired specifications ("Should we give her a brain?"), they connect the computer to a doll via electrodes and, wearing "ceremonial" brassieres on their heads, hack into a government computer system on a stormy night for more power. When lightning engulfs the house, their teenaged fantasies miraculously become real.

For Bernie and Frankie Stein, and their sidekick Iggy, it's all about fame and fortune. Tired of representing unsuccessful and ungrateful talent, Bernie hires his nephew, who has an unhealthy attraction to dead things, to create the ultimate rock-and-roll superstar. The trio's grave robbing and organ stealing results in a bizarre, conflicted creature, cobbled together from the

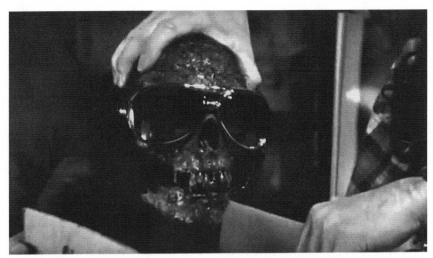

Elvis's head: A key component of DIY monster making in *Rock 'n' Roll Frankenstein.*

parts of deceased icons: Elvis's head, Jimi Hendrix's hands, Sid Vicious's buttocks, and—as the result of a slapstick screwup—Liberace's penis.

Amateurs all, these characters take Shelley's Frankenstein tale down the rabbit hole, providing countless comic misadventures. Theirs is a science of imitation, with none of the higher-order goals that inspired the philosophers of nature or the revolutionaries of science. They represent ordinary individuals attempting to redirect the courses of their lives through reanimation—comic versions of "better living through chemistry." They are not chemists, or biologists, or physicists, or physicians; and none are great thinkers—but they *are* Makers.

From Dreamers to Makers

Social philosophers have, for thousands of years, pondered the relationship between being in the world, knowing the world, and acting in (and on) the world. Aristotle, in fact, began his *Metaphysics* by observing that "all men by nature desire to know."[21] He continues with "science and art come to man through experience; for 'experience made art' as Polus says 'but inexperience luck.'"[22] As we struggle to understand our worlds, an important—maybe *the* important—way of knowing is, as Martin Heidegger argues, doing: "The less we just stare at the hammer-thing, and the more we seize hold of it and use it, the more primordial does our relationship to it become."[23] In other words, if thinking is interlinked with action, then truly comprehending the world depends on experiencing it—*doing* things—creating.

These sentiments are also echoed in a far more contemporary text: the Maker Movement manifesto, which affirms:

> Making is fundamental to what it means to be human. We must make, create, and express ourselves to feel whole. There is something unique about making physical things. These things are like little pieces of us and seem to embody portions of our souls.[24]

Tinkering and experimenting are the beating heart of the Maker Movement—the classic, and often comic, "Let's see what happens if I do *this!*" Contemporary Maker culture emphasizes learning by doing, encouraging innovation, and working at the intersections of traditionally separate domains. The premise of this culture is that "[w]e are on the cusp of an opportunity to more fully tap into our creative potential, driven by significant technological innovation that is democratizing the means of production . . . harnessing the power of the machine to unleash and amplify our creative energies."[25] Through individual creativity, Makers contend, we develop agency—control over the conditions of our lives, our relationships with institutions of knowledge and power, and our fates.

Philosopher Matthew Crawford contends that the struggle for individual agency is at the very center of modern life.[26] He observes that we have come to live in a world that "does not elicit our instrumentality. . . . We have too few occasions to *do* anything, because of a certain predetermination of things from afar."[27] Thus, making—creating—is essential for reclaiming one's place in the world.

The attempt to gain—or regain—agency is at the center of each of the four "reanimation" films discussed here. In *The Rise of the Creative Class*, Richard Florida paints a picture of creative individuals as "bizarre mavericks operating at the bohemian fringe." These free thinkers are, as he observes, "at the very heart of the process of innovation," forming a creative class in science, engineering, and the arts.[28] "Bizarre mavericks" is, in one sense, an apt description of the range of everyday reanimators we see here. Each transgresses the laws (or at least, taboos) of man and nature in their attempts to bring forth life. Young Victor Frankenstein retrieves the body of his beloved Sparky from the grave under the cover of darkness, stitching it back together like a ragdoll before hoisting it skyward into the iconic lightning storm; Jeffrey Franken devises a formula for crack cocaine that causes its users to explode in order to acquire body parts for his creation, and despite relenting at the last moment, succeeds in blowing up half-a-dozen naked prostitutes, resulting in a giddy overabundance of parts from which to choose. Gary and Wyatt hack a high-security government computer to pirate the power they need to bring their custom-made woman to life; Iggy, following Bernie's orders, steals body parts of famous rock stars, not only from graves but from private collections as well.

In usurping the role of the (mad) scientist, each of the protagonists here is certainly insane by all the usual standards, but they are also laying claim to the ability to create—to control their destinies through the act of *making* life. According to Dale Dougherty, founder of *MAKE* magazine, fledgling Makers such as these all evidence a common trait: a spark that causes a shift in the individual from purely consuming products to having a hand in making them. All that is needed are the requisite skills and access to the means of production.[29] Our creators of reanimated life have all, by hook or by crook, cobbled together the knowledge, skill, means, and body parts necessary to become Makers, and with a bolt of lighting and a bit of cinematic good fortune, they achieve success. And that success, at least for a moment, allows each of them to experience the power and control jealously guarded by specialists—physicians, chemists, biologists— whose professional status allows them to experiment on both the living and the dead in the name of science. As in professional science, however, experiments often fail, and unlike sanctioned, regulated experiments, our characters' failures can neither be controlled nor contained. Sparky terrifies Victor's neighbors and they turn into an angry mob; Bernie and Frankie's creation, "King," dies when he removes Liberace's penis with a chain fall (exclaiming "Free at last, free at

Victor checks Sparky for signs of life in *Frankenweenie*.

last, thank God Almighty, I'm free at last!"), and Frankenhooker's unquench-able desire for paid sex results in mayhem and a trail of bodies. Gary and Wyatt's "perfect" girl wreaks havoc with their friends and families—bombarding the boys with "challenges" to build their confidence, freezing Wyatt's grandparents and hiding them in a cupboard, and turning his brother Chet into a talking pile of feces.

However, Victor, Jeffrey, and the rest are, in their attempts to create life from death, becoming actors, not only in a sort of divine horror-comedy spawned from the Frankenstein cinemyth, but in their own lives as well. These acts, misbegotten and fraught with peril as they are, represent the de-mocratization of reanimation. No longer is the fictional creation of life the domain of brilliant, elite medical scientists; it now rests in the hands of "ev-eryman"—from precocious children to inept adults—making the characters across these four films poster children for do-it-yourself undeath.

Still Needs a Few Adjustments

The understandings of the science of nature (and the nature of science) in these DIY adaptations of the Frankenstein tale bring us back to Shelley's era, when nature was viewed by many as one vast machine, automata were con-structed to simulate life, and the animation of a corpse seemed to be merely an electrical problem to solve.[30] It is small wonder then, that the themes of power and control, removed from elite, professionalized knowledge, would be tempered by comedy.

Individually, these films offer a different variation on the humor and horror of reanimation, from the dead being revived *in toto* (*Frankenweenie*'s Sparky), to an original augmented by new parts (*Frankenhooker*'s Elizabeth), to a whole cobbled together from unrelated parts (*Rock 'n' Roll Frankenstein*'s King), to physical and conceptual elements imagined and given form (*Weird Science*'s Lisa). The comedies range from light to pitch black and the social commentary from shallow to deep. On the surface, they seem to have little to say to each other, or to us. Taken as a cluster, however, these films bring the awkwardness, ineptitude, and chaos of everyday life to the disciplined, sterile, well-ordered world of science, denying audiences the ability to take death, or the making of life, seriously.

The introduction of humor—from affectionate sight gags, like Sparky's joyfully wagging tail refusing to remain attached to his behind, to cringe-worthy jokes about King's attraction to men's derrieres, thanks to the inclu-sion of Liberace's penis in his assembled parts—mediates both grief (in the case of *Frankenweenie*) and the grotesque (in *Rock 'n' Roll Frankenstein*). In some cases, black humor accomplishes both in one broad stroke, such as a scene from *Frankenhooker* in which Jeffrey has dinner with Elizabeth's severed head at an elegantly set table. After "discussing" all the possibilities for her new body ("honey pie, can't you picture yourself in this body, kneeling on ma's couch in the basement?"), he reads her a love poem, entitled "Warning: Contents under Pressure":

> My heart is packed so full of love for you,
> that I dreamed I exploded like aerosol cans sometimes do;
> I blew with such force, that my bones became shrapnel,
> and leveled the town except the small chapel;
> My teeth flew like bullets,
> I didn't know what was happenin';
> They killed everyone in sight,
> except for the chaplain;
> And then thanks to him, we were happily wed,
> even though at the time, I think we were both dead.

Similarly, ghoulish scenes of Iggy and his friends scavenging body parts from dead rock stars are mitigated by stoner humor reminiscent of Cheech and Chong. When their final task, stealing Jim Morrison's penis from a private collection of celebrity genitalia for Bernie and Frankie's new creation ("Wow . . . Jimmy Morrison's love tool!"), goes horribly wrong, hilarity ensues. The bungling thieves light a bong during the heist, setting off the building's fire alarm. In the chaos that ensues as they flee, Morrison's penis is dropped into a jar of acid, and the trio grabs another at random. The substitute, of course, belonged to Liberace, and becomes the source of constant humor as the patchwork rock star is plagued by his attraction to men ("My boneheaded boner wants to stick it in men's bung holes!"), as are those around him ("I think the King's a fuckin' poof!"), exacerbated by the fact that his member talks, taunting him at every turn. Even after King has caused his own death, ridding himself of the troublesome member, Liberace's penis lives on—an unanticipated side effect of the reanimation.

For Wyatt and Gary, the road to relieving their teenaged angst also turns out to be far more complicated than simply designing the ideal woman in order to gain popularity and the *real* girls of their dreams. Lisa's creation becomes an extended rite of passage for the pair of awkward adolescents, as her ability as a "Maker" exceeds their own. On one hand, she does, in fact, provide the two boys with the social capital they sought at the time of her creation: She conjures up flashy vehicles, sophisticated clothing, and social experiences beyond their imaginations—all superficial stepping stones to popularity. On the other hand, she provides the pair with comedy-infused lessons about confidence, independence, and agency that speak to a range of adolescent insecurities and fears—all lessons of substance softened by over-the-top humor. Once her purpose is fulfilled, she dematerializes (according to her own will) and vanishes, reappearing only at the end of the film, as an autonomous entity—another aspect of creation that Gary and Wyatt never saw coming.

None of our amateur "mad scientists," in fact, know quite what to expect from their experiments in creating life. Lacking a professional background, nothing in their histories—other than, perhaps, biology class and old movies—has prepared them for this. From King singing "Well, it's one for the moolah" in the shower and lusting after other men, to Frankenhooker's oversexed killing spree, to Lisa's freewheeling affronts to Gary and Wyatt's comfortable and conformist suburban life, the films' reanimated characters are full of surprises. They upend expectations; reject, intimidate, or discomfort their creators; suffer from self-loathing; and in strictest terms, are disappointing progeny. None, other than Sparky, acts predictably or provides the wish fulfillment that originally sparked their creators' imaginative efforts. Comedy, however, makes these unanticipated outcomes inconsequential, whether or not things are set right in the end. Jeffrey is, ironically, beheaded by Frankenhooker's pimp, and the Steins end up with a dead star, but Gary and Wyatt survive the roller coaster of Lisa's manipulations and end up both happier and more mature. Victor is not only permanently reunited with his beloved Sparky, but both ultimately gain the understanding and compassion of their neighbors and become part of the community. As a story specifically crafted for young audiences, both the short and feature-length versions are allowed a happy ending. Even when it appears that his reanimation is only temporary, Sparky returns to life in the end, and finds the acceptance that Frankenstein's monster was denied.

Conclusion

Is it all madness? Maybe. As he plans his reanimation of Elizabeth, Jeffrey confesses to his mother:

> Something's happening to me, I just don't understand. I can't think straight anymore, like my reasoning is all twisted and distorted, you know? I seem to be disassociating myself from reality more and more each day. I'm antisocial; I'm becoming dangerously amoral. I've lost the ability to distinguish between right from wrong, good from bad. I'm scared Ma, I feel like sometimes I'm plunging head first into some black void of sheer utter madness.

His mother, of course, asks him if he wants a sandwich.

What our collection of reanimators here suffer from may not be madness, but rather, something far more ordinary. They suffer from dreams—dreams of agency, of unlimited potential—and the desire to bend fate and nature to their will. Like Shelley's Frankenstein, they dream of power and control, but unlike their predecessor, their dreams are much smaller. They just want their own way, and all become "Makers" in order to get it. None of these characters desires to conquer death in the big picture—to know, as Victor Frankenstein wished, "what it is like to be God"—they simply wish to conquer *one* death. That wish alone would be enough to make them terrifying . . . if they weren't so funny.

And there, perhaps, is the overarching lesson of do-it-yourself reanimation—the open-sourcing of the specialist knowledge and access needed to cheat death—the democratization of creating life from dreams, desires, scavenged parts, duct tape, and maybe Liberace's penis: To be an average person is to be, with a range of frequency, inept; to use whatever is at hand, to substitute, to not quite hide the seams and hope for the best. In laughing at (or with) the characters here, we not only take comfort in their ineptitude—which perpetuates our illusion of safety as more and more democratization of knowledge and opportunity occurs in the world—we also laugh at ourselves, and at the awkward collisions between fantasy and reality that we recognize all too well.

Notes

1. Shelley, *Frankenstein*, 4, 42.
2. Butler, "Introduction," xv–xxxiii.
3. Joseph, quoted in Tropp, *Mary Shelley's Monster*, 52.
4. Mellor, "Frankenstein: A Feminist Critique of Science," 287.
5. In Cunningham and Jardine, *Romanticism and the Sciences*, 15.
6. In Mellor, "Frankenstein: A Feminist Critique of Science," 107.
7. In Keller, *Apocalypse Now and Then*, 165.
8. Ibid., 166.
9. Shelley, *Frankenstein*, 30–31.
10. Ibid., 36.
11. Graham, *Representations of the Post/human*, 77.
12. Ibid., 78.
13. Shelley, *Frankenstein*, 33.
14. Holmes, *The Age of Wonder*, xx.
15. Montillo, *The Lady and Her Monsters*, 66.
16. Ibid., 67.

17. Ibid.

18. Picart, *Remaking the Frankenstein Myth on Film*; Picart, Smoot, and Blodgett, *The Frankenstein Film Sourcebook*.

19. Picart, *Remaking the Frankenstein Myth on Film*, 201.

20. Tropp, *Mary Shelley's Monster*, 2.

21. Aristotle, *Metaphysics*.

22. Ibid.

23. Heidegger, *Being and Time*, 15, 98.

24. Hatch, *The Maker Movement Manifesto*, 1.

25. "Impact of the Maker Movement," Deloitte Center for the Edge and Maker Media. http://makermedia.com/wp-content/uploads/2014/10/impact-of-the-maker-movement.pdf.

26. Crawford, *Shop Class as Soulcraft*, 7.

27. Ibid., 69.

28. Florida, *The Rise of the Creative Class*, 6, 8.

29. "Impact of the Maker Movement," Dale Dougherty letter, June 2014, 10. makermedia.com/wp-content/uploads/2014/10/impact-of-the-maker-movement.pdf.

30. According to Tropp, Johann Ritter declared that "galvanic phenomena seemed to bridge the gap between living and non-living matter" (53).

Bibliography

Aristotle. *Metaphysics*. http://classics.mit.edu/Aristotle/metaphysics.1.i.html.

Butler, Marilyn. "Introduction." In Mary Shelley, *Frankenstein: Or: The Modern Prometheus*. Oxford: Oxford University Press, 1998.

Crawford, Matthew B. *Shop Class as Soulcraft: An Inquiry into the Value of Work*. New York: Penguin Press, 2009.

Cunningham, Andrew, and Nicholas Jardine, eds. *Romanticism and the Sciences*. Cambridge: Cambridge University Press, 1990.

Florida, Richard. *The Rise of the Creative Class and How It's Transforming Work, Leisure, Community and Everyday Life*. New York: Basic Books, 2002.

Graham, Elaine L. *Representations of the Post/human: Monsters, Aliens and Others in Popular Culture*. New Brunswick, NJ: Rutgers University Press, 2002.

Hatch, Mark. *The Maker Movement Manifesto: Rules for Innovation in the New World of Crafters, Hackers, and Tinkerers*. New York: McGraw-Hill Education, 2013.

Heidegger, Martin. *Being and Time*. 1927. Translated by J. Macquarrie and Edward Robinson. Oxford: Basil Blackwell, 1962.

Holmes, Richard. *The Age of Wonder: The Romantic Generation and the Discovery of Beauty and Terror in Science*. New York: Vintage, 2010.

Keller, Catherine. *Apocalypse Now and Then: A Feminist Guide to the End of the World*. Boston: Beacon Press, 1996.

Mellor, Anne K. "Frankenstein: A Feminist Critique of Science." In *One Culture: Essays in Science and Literature*, edited by George Levine and Alan Rauch, 287–312. Madison: University of Wisconsin Press, 1987.

Montillo, Roseanne. *The Lady and Her Monsters: A Tale of Dissections, Real-Life Dr. Frankensteins, and the Creation of Mary Shelley's Masterpiece.* New York: William Morrow, 2013.

Picart, Caroline Joan S. *Remaking the Frankenstein Myth on Film: Between Laughter and Horror.* Albany: State University of New York Press, 2003.

Picart, Caroline Joan S., Frank Smoot, and Jayne Blodgett. *The Frankenstein Film Sourcebook.* Westport, CT: Greenwood Press, 2001.

Shelley, Mary. *Frankenstein: Or, The Modern Prometheus.* Oxford: Oxford University Press, 1998.

Tropp, Martin. *Mary Shelley's Monster: The Story of Frankenstein.* Boston: Houghton Mifflin, 1976.

Index

About the Contributors

Deborah Carmichael is an assistant professor in the Writing, Rhetoric, and American Cultures Department at Michigan State University. Her publications include the edited volume *The Landscape of Hollywood Westerns: Ecocriticsm in an American Film Genre* (2006). She is currently the managing editor of *Journal of Popular Culture*. Deborah's research interests also encompass documentary and Depression-era films and local film exhibition history.

Lisa Cunningham is a PhD candidate at Georgia State University, focusing on psychoanalytic, gender, and film theories. Her current body of work is on violent little girls on film and can be found most recently in *Monstrous Children and Childish Monsters: Essays on Cinema's Holy Terrors* (2015). She lives with friends who will listen to her talk about theory and, as is expected, with too many cats.

Leila Estes is an instructor and a PhD student in the English Department at the University of Florida. She previously attended Wesleyan University for her BA and New York University for her MA in cinema studies. Her areas of interest focus on the study of film noir and classical Hollywood cinema. She is currently beginning preliminary research for her dissertation on post–World War II "passing" films, particularly focusing on narratives where characters are "passing" from black to white.

Mary Y. Hallab is professor emeritus of English at the University of Central Missouri. She is the author of *Vampire God: The Allure of the Undead in Western Culture* (2009) and has published literary criticism in *Southern Review*, *Henry James Review*, and other journals. Her paintings have appeared in juried art shows across the United States and have been featured in *River City* magazine and *Phoebe* and appeared on the covers of *Connecticut Review* and *Pleiades: A Journal of New Writing*.

Katherine Kelp-Stebbins is an assistant professor of English at Palomar College in San Marcos, California. She received her PhD in comparative literature in 2014 from University of California, Santa Barbara. Her work examines comics and visual media as tools for rethinking world literature and transnational flows of cultural objects. She tirelessly works to develop feminist and antiracist strategies in her teaching and scholarship. Her work has been published in the journals *Studies in Comics* and *Media Fields*, as well as *Horrors of War: The Undead on the Battlefield* (2015).

Christina M. Knopf is an associate professor in the Department of English and Communication at SUNY Potsdam, where she teaches communication theory, rhetoric, and political communication. She is the author of *The Comic Art of War: A Critical Study of Military Cartoons, 1805–2014, with a Guide to Artists* (2015). Her research also appears in several anthologies, including *Horrors of War: The Undead on the Battlefield* (2015) and *The Rhetoric of American Exceptionalism: Critical Essays* (2011), and in journals such as *NANO* and *Political and Military Sociology: An Annual Review*.

Murray Leeder has a PhD from Carleton University and teaches in the Film Studies program at the University of Calgary. He is the author of *Halloween* (2014) and editor of *Cinematic Ghosts: Haunting and Spectrality from Silent Cinema to the Digital Era* (2015). Forthcoming projects include *Horror Film: A Critical Introduction* and *The Modern Supernatural and the Beginnings of Cinema*. He has also published articles in *Horror Studies*, *Journal of Popular Film and Culture*, *Journal of Popular Culture*, *Canadian Journal of Film Studies*, *Clues: A Journal of Detection*, and *Popular Music and Society*.

Eric César Morales is a PhD candidate in the Department of Folklore and Ethnomusicology and an associate instructor for the Latino Studies program at Indiana University, Bloomington. His research engages with Latino and Polynesian populations at home and in the diaspora, focusing primarily on large-scale cultural productions. His key sites of interest are film, festival, and foodways, concentrating on issues of globalization, cultural transmission, appropriation, commodification, and the construction of ethnicity for outside audiences. In addition to his scholarly endeavors, he is heavily involved in the public sector, having worked with arts institutions across the country.

Martin F. Norden teaches courses in film history/theory/criticism and screenwriting as a professor in the Department of Communication at the University of Massachusetts Amherst. He has more than one hundred publications to his credit and has presented his film research at dozens of professional conferences across North America and Europe. He was the principal on-camera commentator for *Cinemability*, an award-winning documentary film produced by Gold Pictures in 2013.

Thomas Prasch is professor and chair of the Department of History at Washburn University. His recent publications include essays on Richard Lester's *Bed Sitting Room* (in Karen Ritzenhoff and Angela Krewani, eds., *The Apocalypse in Film*, 2016), Alfred Russel Wallace's spiritualism and evolutionary thought (in Alisa McIntyre and Julie Melnyk, eds., *"Perplext in Faith,"* 2015), Michael Winterbottom's *The Claim* (in Cynthia J. Miller and A. Bowdoin Van Riper, eds., *International Westerns*, 2014), and ethnicity in Henry Mayhew (in Marlene Tromp, Maria Bachman, and Heidi Kaufman, eds., *Fear, Loathing, and Victorian Xenophobia*, 2013).

Shelley S. Rees is an associate professor of English at the University of Science and Arts of Oklahoma. She earned her PhD in English from University of North Texas, specializing in nineteenth-century British literature, and continues to research her dissertation subject, poet and playwright Thomas Lovell Beddoes. Rees has published articles on Joss Whedon's *Dollhouse*, AMC's *The Walking Dead*, and *The Lord of the Rings*, and edited a collection titled *Reading Mystery Science Theater 3000: Critical Approaches*. She lives in Oklahoma with her husband, son, and rescued Yorkshire terriers Dash and Dobby.

Michael C. Reiff teaches English at Ithaca High School and is a community lecturer at Cayuga Community College (CCC) in Auburn, New York. In Ithaca he teaches the senior courses Film Studies and Digital Media Production. He is currently a curriculum leader in integrating cinema and technology into a range of grades. At CCC he teaches the Auburn Film Seminar, which covers a range of historical films. Reiff has been published in a number of anthologies, including *Horrors of War* and *International Westerns*. He has published reviews in *Film & History*, and his work is forthcoming in *Science Fiction Film & Television*. He lives in Auburn with his wife, Anna, and Maine coon cat Phineas.

Gary D. Rhodes currently serves as postgraduate director for film studies at The Queen's University in Belfast, Northern Ireland. He is the author of *Lugosi* (1997), *White Zombie: Anatomy of a Horror Film* (2002), and *The Perils of Moviegoing in America* (2012), as well as the editor of such anthologies as *Edgar G. Ulmer: Detour on Poverty Row* (2008) and *The Films of Joseph H. Lewis* (2012). Rhodes is also the writer-director of such documentary films as *Lugosi: Hollywood's Dracula* (1997) and *Banned in Oklahoma* (2004). Currently he is at work on a history of the American horror film to 1915 and a biography of William Fox.

Steven Webley is a lecturer and researcher at Staffordshire University in the United Kingdom. He currently runs MINISTRY—the military and civil simulation research and enterprise institute—in the Games Technology Department of the Faculty of Creative Arts and Technologies. His research has three interlinked spheres: psychoanalysis, Clausewitzian war studies, and our enjoyment of the products of the military-industrial sector. Along with war and game studies, he specializes in consultancy for war game and simulation design and interactive narratology.

Chris Yogerst is assistant professor of communication for the University of Wisconsin Colleges, where he teaches classes in film, mass communication, and popular culture. Chris is the author of *From the Headlines to Hollywood: The Birth and Boom of Warner Bros.* (2016). His work has also been published in *Journal of Religion & Film*, *Senses of Cinema*, *Journal of Film and Video*, the *Milwaukee Journal Sentinel*, and the *Atlantic Monthly*. Additionally, he is the "Hollywood Studio System" area chair for the *Film & History* national conference.

~

About the Editors

Cynthia J. Miller is a cultural anthropologist, specializing in popular culture and visual media. Her writing has appeared in a wide range of journals and anthologies across the disciplines. She is the editor of *Too Bold for the Box Office: The Mockumentary, From Big Screen to Small* (2012) and coeditor of *Undead in the West: Vampires, Zombies, Mummies, and Ghosts on the Cinematic Frontier* and *Undead in the West II: They Just Keep Coming* (both with A. Bowdoin Van Riper, 2012, 2013), *1950s "Rocketman" TV Series and Their Fans: Cadets, Rangers, and Junior Space Men* (with A. Bowdoin Van Riper, 2012), *Steaming into a Victorian Future* (with Julie Anne Taddeo, 2012), *Border Visions: Identity and Diaspora in Film* (with Jakub Kazecki and Karen A. Ritzenhoff, 2013), *International Westerns: Re-Locating the Frontier* (with A. Bowdoin Van Riper, 2013), and *Horrors of War: The Undead on the Battlefield* (with A. Bowdoin Van Riper, 2015). She is also film review editor for the journal *Film & History* and series editor for Rowman & Littlefield's *Film and History* book series.

A. Bowdoin Van Riper is a historian who specializes in depictions of science and technology in popular culture. His publications include *Science in Popular Culture: A Reference Guide* (2002), *Imagining Flight: Aviation and the Popular Culture* (2003), *Rockets and Missiles: The Life Story of a Technology* (2004; reprinted 2007), and *A Biographical Encyclopedia of Scientists and Inventors in American Film and Television* (2011). He was guest editor, with Cynthia J. Miller, of a special two-issue themed volume (Spring/Fall 2010) of

Film & History ("Images of Science and Technology in Film") and the editor of *Learning from Mickey, Donald, and Walt: Essays on Disney's Edutainment Films* (2011). He is also coeditor, with Cynthia J. Miller, of *Undead in the West: Vampires, Zombies, Mummies, and Ghosts on the Cinematic Frontier* and *Undead in the West II: They Just Keep Coming* (2012, 2013), *1950s "Rocketman" TV Series and Their Fans: Cadets, Rangers, and Junior Space Men* (2012), *International Westerns: Re-Locating the Frontier* (2013), and *Horrors of War: The Undead on the Battlefield* (2015).